WILL YOU
DIE
WITH ME?

...

WILL YOU
DIE
WITH ME?

• • •

My Life and the
Black Panther Party

• • •

FLORES A. FORBES

Foreword by Elaine Brown

ATRIA BOOKS

New York   London   Toronto   Sydney

ATRIA BOOKS
1230 Avenue of the Americas
New York, NY 10020

Grateful acknowledgment is made to the Dr. Huey P. Newton Foundation
for permission to use the photographs on insert pages 4, 5, 6, 7, 8, 9, 10,
11 top, 12–13, 14, and 15 top. Photographs on insert pages 1, 2, 3,
11 bottom, 15 bottom, and 16 are courtesy of the author.

Library of Congress Cataloging-in-Publication Data
Forbes, Flores A.
Will you die with me? : my life and the Black
Panther Party / Flores A. Forbes.
p. cm.
1. Forbes, Flores A. 2. African American political activists—
California—Biography. 3. Political activists—California—Biography.
4. Black Panther Party—Biography. 5. Black militant organizations—
United States—History—20th century. 6. Black power—United
States—History—20th century. 7. United States—Race relations. I. Title.
E185.97.F685A3 2006
322.4'20973—dc22   2006042716
ISBN-13: 978-0-7434-8266-0
ISBN-10:   0-7434-8266-2

First Atria Books hardcover edition July 2006

1 3 5 7 9 10 8 6 4 2

ATRIA BOOKS is a trademark of Simon & Schuster, Inc.

Manufactured in the United States of America

For information about special discounts for bulk purchases,
please contact Simon & Schuster Special Sales:
1-800-456-6798 or business@simonandschuster.com.

For my father, Fred R. Forbes, Sr.,
for raising me to be a man

Acknowledgments

• • • MANY PEOPLE played a significant role in the development, writing, and completion of my story, and I would like to thank everyone, even if I don't name you below.

A chance encounter in the art/clothing boutique of Sydney Kai Inis introduced me to my editor, Malaika Adero. I'm grateful to Malaika for believing that my story was important enough to our history to publish.

To Marie Dutton Brown, the mother of black literary agents, who helped me to develop my craft.

To my agent, the fabulous Faith Childs, a mover who pushed my work close to perfection.

Thanks to the late Calvin Hernton, who also thought my story was important enough for me to write. And to David Henderson, thanks for the master class.

To my sister, my friend, my comrade Elaine Brown, who lived through most of the story with me and who encouraged me early on to tell it. I will always watch your back.

To my family: my mother, Catherine; my brother, Fred; my sisters, Katherine and Helen; and everyone else—thanks for being there when I got back.

To the men and women who risked their lives and to those who gave them while part of the Black Panther Party, especially Huey and Masai. Power to the people!

And, finally, to my wife, Jill: thanks for your love, understanding, and patience while I put this manuscript together. Will you die with me?

Foreword

ELAINE BROWN

• • • CONFRONTED WITH the constancy of black oppression and other oppression here in the United States, reflected most recently and poignantly in the floodwaters that overwhelmed the streets of Evangeline, and throughout the African diaspora in the pounding of poverty, highest in the world in sub-Saharan Africa, one can only wonder whether there ever was an attempt for change, for freedom. For those of us who once dreamed of and fought for freedom under the banner of the Black Panther Party, this brutal continuum is made even more unbearable. For, even in the recognition of the millions of anonymous martyrs among our ancestors who shed their precious blood to make us free and of the price paid by all the beautiful heroes we know and honor, including Huey P. Newton, the full story of our glorious struggle goes wanting. Comes now the light of this writing.

With a kind of proverbial tug and pull of pain and joy, I again remember George, the living George Jackson, his idealism, his resolve, his powerful commitment to the freedom of black and other oppressed people, his whispered urgings that none of us leave this life as broken men who failed to fight for freedom, all snatched by the bullets of a state assassin. I remember Bunchy Carter, founder of the Party's Southern California chapter, where I joined the Party, "Mayor of the Ghetto," leader of the five-thousand-strong Slausons, gifting his street savvy and strength to the revolution until the government-sponsored murderers destroyed him, as, John Huggins, the soldier-scholar whom I always recall as my personal savior. And I see now Jonathan Jackson, the magnificent man-child, slain in his seventeenth year, as I recall the booming figure of Fred Hampton, wiser at twenty-one than the old men who praised him after the FBI murdered him in his bed, even as he called for the building of a *revolutionary* rainbow coalition. I remember the Sister Warriors, Ericka Huggins, my comrade and my captain. And the martyrs who spent lifetimes behind bars, including the tender Romaine "Chip" Fitzgerald, languishing still in a California prison cell, since 1969. And among the heroes who did not die, who are more numerous than one might think in this abyss of apathy, I remember Flores Forbes, friend, comrade, revolutionary guerrilla, freedom fighter.

Oh, I was so in love last year,
or, rather, the year before,
and if it wasn't death that claimed them,
it was the hard, cold prison door . . .

I was in love with many soldiers,
for they were a part of me,
a part of all I'd grown with,
though they'd somehow grown free.

They were all such young and fine men,
such well-defined men,
but if we remain reminded of them,
then no wall or grave can confine them.

Usually, the soldier dies or goes, silent, from the battlefield, leaving the history of struggle to be written by the generals or rewritten by the conquerors. Here, finally, is the soldier's story. It is more, though. This is our story, the story of an oppressed people, of our resistance to oppression, told by one of us, a revolutionary memoir, a memoir of a revolutionary, an unadulterated truth, told in a pure voice, recalling the purity of our effort. This is the story of the Panther.

Through tears, I am forced to see how tragically small the Black Panther Party was in relation to the forces mounted against us and our goal of freedom. Yet through these words, I am born again in the memory of how big were our heart and our commitment. My eyes blurred by the night of time see clearly now our young selves, resurrected, and I am astounded by the recollection of our willing surrender to "serve the People, body and soul," to be "twenty-four-hour Panthers" not "part-time revolutionaries," to "die for the People," and to "live for the People," as we published and distributed our news organ every week, cooked and served free breakfasts to our children every day, maintained free clinics for our people, distributed free groceries to the hungry, defended our lives and our communities with our lives against the thousand assaults, believing in freedom, fighting for freedom.

This is no nostalgic colorant. The memories are here validated. We lived, despite the efforts to erase us, then as now. The truth is here told. And that truth is that, in the pantheon of Africans struggling for freedom in America, there has been no greater, enlightened, organized effort than that of the Black Panther Party. This is a powerful telling of our story, of our history, which cannot now be unwritten, for which I am grateful, as shall be the next generation of freedom fighters.

E.B.
Brunswick, Georgia

WILL YOU
DIE
WITH ME?

• • •

Prologue

OST OF MY FRIENDS were living regular lives working and raising families in Southern California, and some
were dead from the violence on the street or from the
bullet of a Vietcong guerrilla. Many, I was to find out later, had chosen the street life and drugs and as a result were languishing in some
California prison. The Vietnam War was over, and black people in
America had reached many of the goals they had fought for in the civil
rights/black liberation struggles. But by the summer of 1977, I had
been with the Black Panther Party for close to ten years. I was twenty-
five years old, and like many of the members who were my age, the
Party was all we had known of adult life in the United States of America. I, for example, hadn't finished college but had accumulated sixty
units at Laney College in Oakland, California. I had only a GED to
my name, but I had traveled far in the profession of my choosing: a
revolutionary.

I was the youngest member of the Black Panther Party's central committee as well as a member of the de facto inner circle that included
Elaine Brown, chairman; the chief of staff, Comrade Bethune; and Big
Bob Heard. My rank and title was assistant chief of staff. I was in charge
of the "fold"—the slang term we used within the Party to describe the
military arm or the security cadre. Huey P. Newton's appellation for
those members of the Party who indulged in the covert operations

assigned to this cadre was the "Buddha Samurai." This name had no spiritual or religious meaning to him or to us. "Buddha" stood for the administrative or traditional work responsibilities within the Party that he believed we all should attend to on a daily basis. And the "Samurai" represented one's military position within the ranks of the BPP.

I was the Party's chief armorer and, along with Texas, my assistant, was responsible for the maintenance and, when needed, the distribution of weapons to Party members performing any and all military tasks. I was in charge of the Party's field operations (fund-raising for our various programs via street solicitation), transportation, and anything else that was not on our organizational chart. Also, Elaine had appointed me to the Party's disciplinary arm, the Board of Methods and Corrections. In this capacity, along with Ericka Huggins, I was responsible for adjudicating all infractions of the rules and regulations in the BPP and, predicated on our decisions, meting out Panther justice. This process was one of the most controversial aspects of the BPP history, more so than the military component from which it derives its beginnings and existence.

I grew up in the Southern California chapter of the BPP. The discipline was fierce and often brutal because we were trained to believe that we were at war and that, during wartime, soldiers get shot for, say, falling asleep on guard duty. The discipline could be mild; a minor infraction was punishable with a few lashes on your bare back from a bullwhip. If you really fucked up, like falling asleep on guard duty, you would be mud-holed. This was the most severe form of corporal punishment in the Party. No one—and I mean no one—wanted this to happen to them. A person who got mud-holed usually left the Party very soon after. This involved an individual being beaten to the ground and stomped by some of the toughest men in the BPP. Many were trained from years of fighting on the streets of America, and many were trained to kill by America. So either way, it was unhealthy to fall asleep in the "Red Zone," Los Angeles. Across the board, the discipline varied from chapter to chapter and branch to branch. But once the Party was consolidated in Oakland, things had to change. The board was created in the early '70s and usually consisted of two Panthers (male and female) who served on a rotating basis. But that stopped, and ultimately Ericka and I would hear and decide on all cases. We cut back on the brutal methods and started some real mild shit like placing people on drinking restrictions and stuff like that. But things stayed the same for the Buddha Samurai, because technically we were still at war.

I shared a comfortable apartment on Fairmont Avenue, near Lake Merritt, with Minister of Culture Emory Douglass and my girlfriend, Frances Moore. I was in pretty good physical shape at the time, standing about six-two and weighing around 180 pounds. I'm not sure if it was due to the pressures of my hectic life, but I had developed some terrible vices. I smoked about a pack of Kool Filter Kings cigarettes a day. I drank maybe a pint of cognac with club soda back and I smoked four or five joints of Buddha Thai every single day. I never read the daily newspapers or watched the news. Most of my information came from street informants, general conversations with people who had the "inside scoop," and reading books. During the summer of 1977, I was reading Livy's *The War with Hannibal*, Gay Talese's *Honor Thy Father*, and Nietzsche's *The Will to Power*.

I never wrote anything down, or at least that's what I told people. In fact, I did. Behind a picture on a wall in my apartment was the Black Panther Party's complete armory inventory list. It included the type of technical equipment (TE): guns, ammo, and accessories; and a code to indicate the various locations throughout the San Francisco–Oakland Bay Area where we stored the TE. My job was one of the most secretive in the Party, and to this day most of the people who were in the Party over the years had not a clue as to what I really did on a day-to-day basis. I had been carrying a gun every day since the spring of 1972. My personal weapon of choice in 1977 was a 9mm Browning automatic pistol, which I carried in an inside belt holster on the right side of my body at the forward rake position. I also had a riot shotgun in my closet and a Colt .45 Gold Cup in the drawer next to my bed.

I always wore a jacket, usually leather but not black, because in an effort to change our image, we had stopped wearing black leather jackets, especially when armed. I had in my wardrobe several suits and sport coats that I had purchased from "Ruby the Booster" and her pimp. In 1977 I was considered a natty dresser or, as we put it, "clean as a broke-dick dog." My fun came from running the streets, chasing women in and outside of the BPP, watching ball games and situation comedies on television, and going to R&B and jazz concerts at the Circle Star Theater in San Carlos or clubs in San Francisco. I also went to the movies, usually alone and during the day.

I worked twelve- to twenty-four-hour days. I could receive a phone call anytime between midnight and 6:00 A.M. and be expected to quickly respond to situations that were urgent and deadly. My mission was clear. I was willing and able to do anything that would further the cause of my people and the BPP. I was not bothered by criticism or the fact that I could lose my young life. Foremost on my agenda was securing the safety of my prince: Huey P. Newton, the leader and founder of the Black Panther Party.

Most Buddha Samurai street operations had been successful, but some were failures. We were willing to live with that, though I understand now that my behavior in 1977 challenged the "arrogance of our success." We in the Buddha Samurai of the BPP did not realize that we were "throwbacks" to anachronistic gunmen who believed, as Mao did, that "political power grows from the barrel of a gun."

• • • Huey P. Newton and Bobby G. Seale founded the Black Panther Party in Oakland, California, in October 1966. The Party's foundation was a ten-point platform and program that Huey and Bobby developed as a result of a far-reaching survey they conducted throughout the black communities of the Bay Area. Beginning with the words "what we want and what we believe," respondents told the two Merritt College students that people needed jobs, clothing, justice, and peace. But most of all, they wanted an end to police brutality and the senseless murders of black people by local policemen. Drawing on this overwhelming response, Huey and Bobby began the Party's first community service program by arming themselves and their first recruits with weapons and law books and patrolling the Oakland police, interdicting when they perceived that a local black citizen's rights were being violated. Harassed and repressed for this action, the Party as a whole came under attack from the local police. The first BPP victim was Huey P. Newton himself. Huey was wounded and charged with the murder of a white policeman. The demand for his release became a clarion call taken up by many young black men and women throughout the country. "Free Huey" became a chant heard from coast to coast. It was such a powerful calling that, at the age of sixteen, I decided to dedicate my life and every ounce of energy to the struggle.

From 1966 to 1969 the BPP expanded exponentially, taking its fierce brand of the black liberation struggle in America across the land, swelling to more than forty chapters and branches with approximately five thousand members. The Party's political organ, *The Black Panther* newspaper, enjoyed a circulation of more than a hundred thousand each week. Beginning in Oakland, the BPP instituted several community service programs, most notably a "free breakfast for schoolchildren" program that would feed thousands of hungry kids every school morning. These programs were developed in Party chapters all over America. A 1969 Lou Harris poll of black males between the ages of eighteen to forty-two gave the BPP an 80 percent approval rating.

In 1969, Director of the Federal Bureau of Investigation J. Edgar Hoover declared the BPP the most serious threat to the internal security of the United States. While city after city was erupting in civil disobedience, the FBI and local police agencies targeted the BPP for death and extermination. Under the auspices of their Counter Intelligence Program (COINTELPRO), the FBI coordinated a national police effort to destroy the BPP. This action resulted in numerous police-versus-Panther gun battles, along with a more subtle disinformation campaign targeted to create internecine warfare with other black groups and dirty-trick schemes that caused several dozen Panther fatalities, show trials, political prisoners, and forced exiles. When you entered our national headquarters in Oakland, the first thing you noticed was a wall of honor covered with the pictures of Panthers slain in battle.

In response to this government-led onslaught, the BPP devised a plan à la Mao's Long March to repel the attacks and take the struggle to a higher level. The first phase of the plan was to create its own disinformation scheme announcing the retrenchment and near demise of the BPP. Next, the BPP began closing down one chapter after another, relocating the most trusted and talented members to the original base of operations: Oakland. The third part of the plan was to organize and mobilize followers to take over the city of Oakland and its lucrative containerized port. The final phase, once Oakland was taken, was to relaunch the revolution and replicate the Oakland success in other major U.S. cities.

In 1972, Huey P. Newton—who had been released from prison in 1970—created an elite group within the BPP called the Buddha Samurai, to assist with this political and urban military plan. His tenure as our leader on the ground was short-lived, though. In 1974 he was charged with several felonies and fled to Cuba, where he remained in exile for three years. Under the leadership of the Party's new chairman, Elaine Brown, the organization flourished, almost completing the Oakland phase of the plan with the election of Lionel Wilson as the city's first black mayor. It was through the actions of this rejuvenated and thoroughly modern BPP that Huey P. Newton's return to the United States from Cuba was negotiated during the summer of 1977.

BOOK ONE

1

I WAS TWELVE YEARS OLD that day in 1964, riding my brand-new Sting-Ray bicycle up the hill from my parents' home on Forty-seventh Street in Southeast San Diego. When I reached the intersection of Forty-seventh and Market, I could hear the tires of a car slowly following behind me on the gravel of the parking lot. I stopped at the light and heard a man with a distinctly Southern drawl call out, "Boy, come over here."

I was pretty scared by the time I turned around and saw two white policemen just getting out of their cruiser. The officers came over to me and said, "Would you come with us?" I started looking around for help. I wanted to shout, but nothing came out of my mouth. I was terrified. The policemen took my bike and put it in the trunk of their car, opened the back door, and told me to get in. People in their cars were looking at this scene, but they just passed on by. Like a frightened fool and the innocent I was, I hopped in. There was some degree of positive excitement: I was getting a ride in a police car. They drove me up the hill on Market Street toward downtown San Diego.

After a ten- or fifteen-minute ride, they pulled into a residential area just short of downtown and drove up to several other police officers and a white couple. The car stopped and the cop on the passenger side got out and walked over to the group of people and pointed back toward me while explaining something. The couple walked over to my side of the car and peered in. They looked at me, then at each other, before the white man shook his head. He took the woman by her hand and walked back toward the policemen, who returned to the car, then drove me back to Forty-seventh Street and pulled into the parking lot I was kidnapped from. There was this huge crowd of people, and standing in the center was my mother. The policemen stopped, got out, and went around to open the trunk and get my bike. My mother, with the crowd of neighbors in tow, approached the cops, asking, "What are you doing with Flores? Did he do anything?" The cop got my bike and told my mother to "back off, bitch. This is official police business." My mother stopped in her tracks. This was the first time I ever saw my mother kill someone with a look. They let me out of the car. I ran to grab my bike and get near my mother. No sooner did this happen than the police car pulled off, spinning its tires in the gravel and kicking up rocks and dirt as it dipped into the street and drove away. For me, this was strike number one against the police.

The second strike came just two years later. It was nighttime and I was jogging around the track up at Lincoln High School, about two long blocks from my house. I was playing Pop Warner football, and I was two or three pounds overweight. So I wrapped my body from the waist up in cleaner's plastic underneath my workout clothes so that I could sweat the pounds away. I ran hard to the top of the hill where Lincoln High School sat. Tomorrow was Saturday and also game day, and I really wanted to play. On one corner, where the old Hudson store used to be, was a dance hall for young people. This was Friday night and it was packed. I could just barely hear the Temptations' latest record, "It's Growing," over the outside speaker. I turned left at the intersection and carefully crossed the street and headed toward the track. I crawled under the fence surrounding the track and began sprinting. I had been running for about fifteen minutes when I saw dozens of police cars racing past the track, headed for the dance hall. The young blacks at the dance were restless or something, or maybe it was the first signs of rebellion in San Diego, but they started throwing rocks, bottles, and what have you at the policemen, who had taken up positions behind their cars. The police made a push and everyone outside of the dance started to break for it, scattering down Forty-seventh Street and Ocean View Boulevard. Many were heading toward the campus. I continued my workout. Then this spotlight started following me as I ran around the track. Innocent and unsuspecting, I continued to run, thinking only about losing the weight and showing Coach Wallace that I was not the "lazy slob" he had called me at our last practice. All of a sudden I could see cop cars lining up along the fence just above the depressed field I was running on. As San Diego cops in beige uniforms began climbing the fence, I heard one of them say, "Here's one running down the track." I kept going, and as I made the turn, this one cop who was near me hit my legs with his club. The blow knocked me off my pace and I tumbled to the ground. I was then hit again with a club and kicked several times. Several cops with clubs, flashlights, and scowling faces surrounded me. One black cop interceded. It was Mr. Cunningham, the first black policeman I knew of in San Diego and the father of Marty, a friend. He walked over quickly and pulled me up and toward him with one hand while he pulled my sweatshirt hood off my head with the other. He flashed his light in my face.

"What are you doing up here running from us?" he said.

"I'm trying to make my weight for tomorrow, Mr. Cunningham," I said, almost crying.

The other cops pulled at me and jostled me before Mr. Cunningham said, "My God, this is the Forbes boy; he goes to school with my kid." They calmed down then. One of them said, "Get out of here and run home as fast as you can."

I broke the grip they had on me, ran to the fence, scaled it, and headed home. My heart was still pounding into the next day at the game. Two years later, when it finally dawned on me that there was something wrong with how the police had treated me, I got mad and wanted revenge.

This was actually an unusual occurrence for my quiet neighborhood and me. In the black community of Southeast San Diego, it had always been relatively quiet and safe. There was a time when you could leave your front doors open and unlocked. The community was populated with stable families. Everybody on my block and most of the people I knew had two parents. The single-parent households could be counted on one hand. However, we weren't without our problems. After saving every penny he could, plus his GI Bill voucher for housing, my father had attempted to purchase a home outside of Southeast San Diego in an area called Allied Gardens/Princess View Manor. This location was just east of the area called Hotel Circle, where Jack Murphy Stadium was located. His contract to purchase the home was blocked as the broker tried to steer him to another area that was predominately black.

Welcome to sunny San Diego.

It wasn't just mistreatment by police and the housing discrimination against my parents that motivated me to want to fight to change things and eventually join the BPP. Much of it had to do with the example my parents set, always trying to help people in general and our homeboys in particular. Both Fred and Catherine Forbes were extremely active in the black community of Southeast San Diego. They worked with and led the Horton Elementary School PTA. My mother was the president. My father was a scoutmaster with the Boy Scouts, and my mother was a den mother with the Cub Scouts. My father was a Little League coach, and both of my parents were very active in the church. Watching them working to help many of my friends made a lasting positive impression on me.

2

S AN DIEGO in general and Southeast San Diego in particular was an interesting community for a young black male to grow up in during the '60s. I worked in almost every part of town. I sold kitchenware door-to-door in Cottage Grove and magazine subscriptions in Chula Vista; I was a pot washer at the King's Inn in Hotel Circle (my brother Fred was a dishwasher across the freeway at the Town and Country club and golf course). I was a dishwasher at the May Company, in Mission Valley Center, and a piano tuner's assistant, traveling all over Southern California tuning pianos. But the best job I held during this period was as a laundry worker at the Naval Training Center (NTC) near Shelter Island.

At the NTC, I washed and pressed the training blues and dress whites for the new sailors being trained at the base. I remember these huge ships sailing into the harbor, with all of these colorful flags that my father had told me were used by the ships to communicate. The image of this would trigger a flashback to when my father was in the navy and then returning from a tour of duty overseas. My work experience at the NTC led me to feel that something was terribly wrong with life because of the color of my skin. I was fifteen years old and my supervisor, in his unintelligible Southern drawl, would call me "boy" or "niggra" without missing a beat. Coupled with my treatment by the police when I was twelve and fourteen years old, and seeing how this man could say just about whatever he wanted to me, I began to realize something about life. I was a boy or a nigger, niggra, what have you, in a racist country and didn't even know it because sunny San Diego had lulled damn near every black person there to sleep.

The Watts rebellion in 1965 sent a shock wave throughout this sunny Southern California community and made it clear to those of us who were unconscious that what was happening in "La La Land" was unacceptable to black folks who were conscious.

San Diego was a navy town, and most of the people there were navy people. Everyone knew someone with the nickname of "Chief" or "Sarge." My father, Fred Roosevelt Forbes, Sr., was a navy man of twenty years. We were a navy family—my mother, his wife, Catherine Seymore; my brother, Fred Roosevelt Forbes, Jr.; my sister, Katherine L. Forbes; and me—as were most of our friends. My father and mother were from Bertha and Currituck counties in North Carolina, respectively. After my father retired, we settled at 411 North Forty-seventh Street in Southeast San Diego. My parents struggled to make ends meet once my father retired from the navy. At one point my father had three jobs. He worked as a waiter at the Kona Kai Club on Shelter Island, which may have been easy for him because in the navy, he was a steward/servant for an Admiral Barnesmith. (Admiral Barnesmith used to send a Christmas card with a picture of his family and a $20 bill every year.) President Eisenhower used to frequent the Kona Kai Club, and after a round of golf, my father was one of the waiters who served him and his party drinks and stuff. One of the other jobs my father held was as a janitor cleaning up a huge factory in National City. At least once a week he would take the entire family with him and assign each of us a task, so that he could hurry up and finish in order to get to his next job. My mother was a domestic for several years, working for this rich old white woman in La Jolla named Ms. Martin. Both of my parents got tired of the shit work and got out of the business of being servants when my father landed his dream job at General Dynamics in Torrey Pines and my mother became a nurse at the Balboa

Navy Hospital. These were the jobs both of my parents would hold for the rest of their lives.

San Diego was not the urban center in the '60s that it is today. It was the stepsister to that big city up north: Los Angeles. The population was around five hundred thousand during this period. Most of the people here were white, with smaller percentages of blacks, Chicanos, Asians, and Pacific Islanders.

Compared to LA, which was a big-time city with major league professional sports teams, San Diego was a small-time city with minor league professional sports teams. There was minor league baseball, with the San Diego Padres of the Pacific Coast League, and the San Diego Chargers of the new American Football League. Basketball never caught on; I wonder why. The mayor I remember was named Frank Curren. He dressed like a gangster. He stands out in my mind because he used to throw out the first pitch on opening day at the Southeast San Diego Little League. After his black chauffeur drove his limo onto the field, Curren would walk to the flat pitching mound, throw the pitch, take a bow, and then walk to each team that was lined up and shake every one of our little black hands before speeding off in his big black limo.

For miles and miles all you could see was this fledgling urban center. There were freeway complexes—depressed and elevated—that consumed an enormous amount of land. There were long, wide streets with interior malls lined with palm trees, and thousands of cars and pickup trucks. Along the coast were white sand beaches with sunbathers and surfers and sailors and marines hanging out at the foot of Broadway. With the increased U.S. involvement in Vietnam, you would see more navy ships sailing in and out of port. Almost every day, the sky would shake from a sonic boom caused by a low-flying navy fighter jet zooming over the city. But regardless of this emerging boomtown, navy-town, what have you, my town was Southeast San Diego. That's where the black folks lived.

The black community was small in the '60s compared to that of South Central Los Angeles. But I thought it was the center of everything. It was comprised of several smaller neighborhoods such as Logan Heights, Little Africa, Emerald Hills, Michel Manor, and Ocean View. Most of the housing was single-family detached with a yard and garage. Two-story public housing developments were built in certain parts of Southeast San Diego. Even though Southeast was the black community, it was not as segregated as my boss at the NTC would have wanted. Most of the schools I attended were integrated and you could ride in the back, front, or middle of the bus. Based on my best memory then, I never knew of any public accommodations being segregated, as they were in the Deep South.

Church was the center of life for my family, just as it was for most of the black people in Southeast San Diego. Everyone went to church, and my family would stay all day on Sunday, except when my Little League team had a matinee game. In fact, church was a three- or four-day happening with choir practice, usher board meetings, Bible study classes, and just hanging out. For a teenager interested in girls, church was the place, because that's where the girls hung out. My mother took us kids to Mount Erie Baptist Church on Forty-seventh Street and Ocean View Boulevard. My father, who said he didn't trust those "jackleg preachers," attended a Methodist church named Chollas View, which was also located on Forty-seventh Street. Black folks in Southeast from all walks of life attended the various black churches in the community. These were folks who worked on the local marine and navy bases; doctors like Andrew Lucky and Harold Burke; the Ragesdales, who owned the largest funeral home in Southeast San Diego; Mr. Cunningham, the first black policeman I saw in San Diego and the man who probably saved my ass from a serious beating at the hands of San Diego's finest; and all of our neighbors on Forty-seventh Street.

On Forty-seventh Street, the family makeup was typical for black families during the '60s in Southeast San Diego. All of my childhood neighbors had two parents who worked. I can recall only two young women during this period who had babies before they left high school. The parents, or at least the fathers, were all ex-navy or -marines. All of the kids were involved with Little League baseball, Pop Warner football, Boy Scouts, Girl Scouts, Cub Scouts, and the Boys Club and went to church. But as we got older and many of us began to mature and get with the changing times, we—or should I say *I*—started to backslide and drift away from the church and other extracurricular activities.

When I was fourteen or fifteen, I began sniffing glue, drinking Colt 45 and Olde English malt liquor, and smoking cigarettes while hanging out late at night looking for a house party to drop in on. My father, who was definitely not down with the hanging out late at night, used to bust my ass, and I mean literally. I became a zip-damn fool and used to lie about going to decent events, but instead I would sneak off with my homies to sniff glue, drink, and hang out. I got pretty good at lying to my parents about this kind of stuff. The only requirement was I had to be tough enough to take an ass whooping from my dad. He didn't believe in restriction and shit like that; he would just kick my ass and tell me not to do it anymore. Anyway, things really started to change in Southeast San Diego. Lowrider cars began to appear, and the place to be was Ocean View Park, which was the hangout for young blacks on Sunday, instead of church or organized sports. On weekends, the center of the nightlife was attending the Friday-night football games of my older brother's school, Abraham Lincoln High School, where there was a fight almost without fail. Most of the time it was black on black, sometimes it was blacks against surfers/white boys, or on other occasions it was blacks against Chicanos or blacks against Samoans.

There weren't many gangs and there were no drive-bys. But I could sense that the times were seriously changing. Every now and then I heard people talking about weed, but there was no evidence of any other type of drug until the late '60s. And then the change stepped up for me. I started smelling weed outside of school. Especially when I met this guy named Jackie Lewis. He told me that what he had rolled up in his hand was hipper than anything I could learn in one of them dumb-ass books. I believed him and started ditching school every day to get high with Jackie and my new friends. With this new crowd, I started seeing my young friends sitting in the park, nodding. Sometimes they would walk by me and not even speak, their eyes all glazed over.

Violence began to rear its ugly head. Kenny Globe, just sixteen years old, was gunned down by accident. The story I heard was that Kenny and some friends were sniffing glue and started playing around with a shotgun that went off. If you've ever sniffed glue, you understand there's no way anyone present could have known what actually happened. I stopped sniffing glue. James "Pops" Tanner, this diminutive brother who used to terrorize us other brothers at Gompers Junior High School, was gunned down with three other young brothers by the San Diego Police in an attempted liquor store robbery. Can't say I was going to miss the little terror, but when anyone gets killed at that young an age, it makes you take notice of your world. Young black males were being busted on a regular basis during this period and being sent to gladiator schools up north like Tracy, Preston, Norwalk, and other youth authority prisons.

By the time I was sixteen years old, I had dropped out of high school. Education was extremely important to my parents, but so was having a job. As long as I had a job, my folks didn't trip with me about school. Besides, I promised both of them that I would go back and finish. Anyway, I had been designated an incorrigible in the San Diego school system. From the first grade to the sixth grade, everything was fine. I worked as hard as I wanted to, which was enough to pass each year. But when I got to junior high school, I was distracted by the girls and all of the new people from different parts of Southeast San Diego. Actually, the downward spiral of my brief career in school began with an insult that I could have let slide.

I was in English class, and this Chicano guy who was really one of my best friends was talking shit about my girlfriend, Eniweta Teart, and then I said something about his mother. He told me to take it back and I said no. He jumped up in class and took this fighting position. I responded and we went a few rounds until the teacher and the vice principal broke up the fight. We were told that we would both be suspended for three days, and after that, we had to come in with our parents. However, the vice principal warned us that if we fought after school, we would be expelled. Now, why did he say that?

There was no way Eddie or I was going to back down. We were going to finish the fight after school. Well, the fight went down and was broken up by my father driving his pickup truck into the crowd, which made everyone scatter. I got expelled and was on my way. From Gompers, I went to two other junior high schools, with each trip ending in expulsion. My high school years were uneventful. I went to three high schools in about a year and a half. I finally dropped out and just went to work every day.

My brother, Fred, a brilliant student who got A's in every level of school, was attending college at UCLA. He used to come home on weekends and holidays and would leave his books stacked up on the table in his room. I began leafing through them and discovered a new world. Some of the books were *The Autobiography of Malcolm X*, Frantz Fanon's *The Wretched of the Earth* and *Black Skin, White Masks*. But most important, there was this newspaper published in Oakland, California, by the group we all had heard about on the news because they took guns to the state capitol at Sacramento, protesting some bill that was put forth to stop them from carrying guns while they patrolled the police. This paper, *The Black Panther: Black Community News Service*, spoke huge volumes to my lost little soul. I must have read Fred's two or three issues ten or twenty times.

I stayed up all night talking to Fred, asking him questions: Who are they? Are these guys for real? Have you met any of them? Fred said they were at UCLA and all over Los Angeles on Central Avenue at the Black Congress. Damn, I was obsessed with something for the first time in my life besides girls and getting high.

The times were really changing. The war in Vietnam was on the news every night, and many of our older friends and cousins had all been over there. Their message was confusing, especially coming from guys whose families had served for years in the navy, marines, or army: Don't go, because it's not our war. They told me stories of the racism in the "war" and that the white soldiers had told the Vietnamese people that black people grow tails after they turn twenty-one and other crazy stuff like that.

I thought I was achieving clarity. I thought I understood the war, police oppression firsthand, and other forms of discrimination from books and some of the other experiences I had had while working and traveling the streets of San Diego. I was a dropout, but I was growing aware of the current political strife in this country. Rebellions were taking place all over the United States, and then there was Ahmed Evans in Cleveland, who staged a ruse in the Glenville section, luring three policemen into a deadly ambush. My political consciousness was expanding, and I felt I was becoming more militant by the day. I was absolutely sure now that something was wrong in this country and that I had to do something to make it safe for myself and for my people. I wanted to help make this change. The transformation I was going through reminded me of the time I joined Mount Erie Baptist Church at thirteen. It was during that period of the service when the pastor asks people who've been touched by the Holy Ghost to come forward and dedicate their life to the Lord. Well, I felt something move me after his sermon, and I walked up front and told the congregation that I was ready to serve the Lord. People started shouting "Amen!" and "Go ahead, little brother." I was moved, inspired, and just about full of myself because it was a lot like getting an orgasm. You can't explain it, but you know you're right about the decision you've made.

Well, that's how I was feeling about my next move. By my brother, I was introduced to the brothers and sisters in the leather and powder blue up north, and they had captured my soul, forever.

3

S AN DIEGO POLICEMEN began kicking my ass from the time I was twelve years old. By sixteen I had decided that I would do something about it. I wanted to get back at them and do something to help my people overcome the oppression we all experienced living in America. So, on one warm summer day in 1968 I hooked a U-turn on Imperial Avenue and pulled my parents' 1960 Mercury in front of what appeared to be the local office of the Black Panther Party.

One man was sitting at the only desk I saw in the one-room office. Papering the wall were posters celebrating the BPP. Among them was the famous poster of Huey P. Newton seated in a wicker chair holding the shotgun and spear in his hands. Others depicted revolutionary slogans like "All Power to the People" and "Off the Pigs." Stacked neatly on a table were new issues of *The Black Panther*. Wow! I thought, as a chill went down my back. The guy at the desk greeted me with a clenched fist and said, "Power to the people, little brother." I didn't respond right away because I wasn't sure what I wanted to say. I just said hello and walked over to the table to pick up a paper to purchase. I asked him a few questions about how long they had been here and what I had to do in order to join. His name was Walter Wallace. The branch, he said, was founded by this brother Kenny Denman, who had been in prison with Eldridge Cleaver. If I wanted to join, he said, I needed to start coming to political education classes, which were held every Wednesday here at the office. "Great," I said, bubbling with youthful enthusiasm. I paid for the papers and left the office feeling satisfied. I was convinced that my calling was to be a Black Panther.

As I then read every single article in the newspapers, I couldn't imagine what my future role would be in this organization. I couldn't have imagined the hard work a person would have to do as a member of this organization. While I had read about the Panthers who had been killed by the police and knew that Huey P. Newton was in prison charged with the murder of a policeman, what I really had on my mind was the black leather jacket and how I would look in one with my black beret cocked to the side and my afro sticking out. I thought about which buttons I was going to place on my lapel. I thought about this organization like it was going to be a passing fad. Like a circus coming to town and leaving at some point. Never did I think about long-term consequences.

I returned the following Wednesday with my brother for the political education class, bright-eyed and ready to go. There were about twenty to thirty young black males in the room with about two or three black women. The founder of the branch, Kenny Denman, was at the head of the class. He was a short, light-skinned, kind of husky brother. He held a little red book in his hand.

"This is our Bible," he said. "You should read this cover to cover and get to know and understand what Chairman Mao is trying to teach us." The group of people all said "Right on" in unison. Each person in the room was given a free copy of the Little Red Book. He then told us to open to a certain page and asked for volunteers to read certain sections out loud and explain what we thought it meant. No hands went up. I was seated next to my brother and looked over at him. He just sat there and thumbed through the pages of the book. Finally, one brother stood up and began to read from the passage that Kenny had us turn to. He stumbled over every word, and these were simple words. It never dawned on me that most of the guys in the room could barely read. In hindsight I can see that these were the lumpen proletariat, the guys

Huey and Eldridge wrote about and the people Huey had recruited as the vanguard of the struggle in the first place. Fighting had occurred to me as a way to wage revolution, but not reading. This stuff included using your brain and having functional skills that would make the organization work smoothly. Well, the brother struggled through the passage, as did several others. I got up and read a passage, but when it came time for me to explain what I had read, I didn't have a clue. I froze. Denman pushed me to try and comprehend, but I didn't get it, and I wasn't willing to even guess.

After the class, Denman said that all of the people interested in joining the Party should step forward and let themselves be recognized. I stepped up and introduced myself to Denman. Walter Wallace told Denman that I had come by the office earlier in the week.

"Young brother, you have a long ways to go. You need to be down with Mao and get that together. This is hard work and a dangerous thing we are doing, you know. People are getting killed, and you need to know what this is about, because you're still pretty young."

"Right on," I said in response.

Fred and I joined the Black Panther Party. He was off from school for the summer, and I was working the graveyard shift at the NTC, so after work I pretty much committed my time to the organization. This was the BPP before the survival programs, constitutional convention, and a host of other major initiatives. At this stage of the organization, we had to create a lot of activities to occupy our time. Most of the Free Huey activity was confined to the Bay Area. We sold papers erratically but should have sold papers every single day. Our main focus was the seventh point in the Party's Ten Point Platform and Program: we want an immediate end to police brutality and the murder of black people. Huey and the brothers up north employed a strategy including armed patrols of the police. The idea was to keep an eye on the police and to demonstrate to people their right to bear arms in self-defense. We had no such strategy in place, so we spent a lot of our time talking rhetoric and wolfing about what we would do when the "pigs" showed up.

Sometime in mid-August, at one of our PE classes, Kenny Denman

said that we were to come to Oakland and participate in the largest Free
Huey rally to date. Man! I was finally going to the place where all of the
real action was: Oakland, California, the birthplace of the BPP. We
organized our vehicles, confirmed how many would make the trip, and
left in late August. Fred, Trenell Price, and this brother named Jerry
Hawkins rode to Oakland with me in my parents' car.

We had been instructed to drive to a house at Thirty-fourth and
Chestnut in West Oakland. This was the house of the BPP's chief of
staff, David Hilliard. When we got to the house, this short, very
slight brother with a kind smile and comradely handshake met us. I
guess I expected a ferocious nigger talking loud and high-stepping,
but this was not the case. David was all business. He asked us how
our trip was and did we have any problems when we got to town. We
told him that everything was fine, but I confessed I was a little nervous. David said, "You should be nervous, because we're serious
about seeing Huey P. Newton free, and you should be, too." Man,
the way he said that—with real conviction—I wanted to run then,
but I didn't. I would learn later that being scared and nervous was
part of the program. It was okay, you just had to control it.

David told us that he would take us to a place where we could rest
before going to PE class later that day. He took us to the house of one
of the BPP's top captains, a brother named Tommy Jones, Jr. His nickname was "Dip." We hung out at this place for a few hours. Among the
unforgettable people I met were Glen Stafford, Captain Wendell
Wade, Orleando Harrison, Randy Williams (aka Cold Steel), Robert
Bay—who later was my direct contact with Huey P. Newton—and Landon Williams, another captain I would work with years later, when he
was an underground operative. There were dozens of other Panthers
who came through.

Later that day we left with Dip and went to Father Earl Neal's
church at Twenty-seventh and West Grand Boulevard for PE class.
Everyone was there. Bunchy Carter and John Huggins (his wife would
become one of my best friends) from LA; Emory Douglass, the minister of culture, was over from San Francisco. (He was to be my future

roommate.) Elbert "Big Man" Howard, June Hilliard, and John Seale. I would work very closely with all of them. The exposure was good for me, but I was walking into what was always the most uncomfortable situation in the BPP for me: political education class.

There were about 150 Panthers gathered in the church meeting hall. Landon Williams taught the class. He whipped out his little red book of quotations from Chairman Mao, gave out the page number, and picked someone to read. Oh shit, I thought, and I can't hide here because these niggers don't ask for volunteers, they pick you and you better be prepared. This sister stood up and started reading. She was really breaking it down, turning to the Panthers seated, waving her arms, and expounding on the text. I was impressed. I had met this sister on one of our visits to the LA chapter, and I remembered her because she was so nice and fine. Her name was Ericka Huggins. Landon continued to select people to read as he walked around the room. He spotted me and nodded but picked Trenell Price, the brother seated next to me. Trenell got up and he got down. Damn, Landon, I said to myself, don't pick me. I ain't ready. He didn't. When class ended, I was relieved. We just mingled and introduced ourselves to everyone. I tried to remain inconspicuous, but you know, if you try and do that, a big fish always finds you. People were walking by and shaking hands and exchanging pleasantries when Ericka waved me over to her and her husband, John. They were standing with Bunchy Carter and Franco Diggs. Bunchy had a reputation that was preceded only by the one Huey P. Newton had. He was the founder and leader of the Slauson street gang in LA. They numbered five thousand strong. After a stint in prison and a chance meeting with Huey P. Newton, he founded the Southern California chapter of the BPP. I had seen him in LA before, but he was so unapproachable, I just avoided him. I walked over and Ericka started to introduce me, and Bunchy said, "I've seen this young nigger around. Yeah, Denman told me about you. Keep up the good work, comrade."

"Right on," I said with a jumbled voice. Man, was I nervous and glad as hell when he walked away to speak with someone else. Ericka and John were a great Black Panther couple who loved each other and the revolution with the same zeal and fervor; they just smiled and walked away with Bunchy. Later that night we hung out at Tommy's place and then drove around town visiting other Panther pads. The next day was the big rally at Bobby Hutton Memorial Park.

Li'l Bobby Hutton was the first member of the Black Panther Party. He was recruited by Huey and Bobby at the age of sixteen and also earned the dubious distinction of being the first Panther killed in combat at the age of eighteen. I saw grown men cry as they described the courage of this first Panther soldier, shotgun under his arm as he led a delegation of armed Panthers down the aisle of the California legislature, protesting the Milford Act, a bill created to disarm the Party in 1967. Bobby Hutton was the standard for the Panther at any age.

In response to the Party's legal armed patrols of the Oakland Police Department, the OPD lobbied local assemblyman Donald Milford to introduce a bill that would amend state and local fish and game regulations allowing California residents to carry loaded firearms in public. Huey had discovered this loophole in the California statutes while attending San Francisco Law School in the mid-1960s. His professor was Edwin Meese, the future U.S. attorney general during the Reagan administration. Once Milford's bill became law, it was illegal to carry loaded firearms in the state of California, thus ending the BPP's armed patrols.

There were thousands of people and hundreds of Panthers all decked out in their black leather jackets and berets. Most of the day we were being placed in formation and marching from one place to another. We would get a break, and then we were placed back in formation or on the security line, which stretched around a flatbed truck that functioned as the speaker's platform. The speakers, a who's who of the BPP, were Chairman Bobby Seale, Chief of Staff David Hilliard, Kathleen Cleaver, Stokely Carmichael, and the keynote speaker, Minister of Information Eldridge Cleaver. I had read Cleaver's book *Soul on Ice*. He was the Panther who had the most public exposure. I just loved the way he would say, "We need to get our shit together." I think every Panther tried to talk like him. Our captain, Kenny Denman, stayed close to Cleaver; they were tight partners. They had bonded from being in the penitentiary together.

Each speech was powerful and sent chills down my spine. Every last one of the speakers said that the "sky was the limit," which I believed to mean that if Huey was convicted, we were going down with our leader.

We had another chance to hang out and let our hair down the evening following the big Free Huey rally. I drank too much and smoked too much weed and stayed up most of the night. The next day we'd have to get back down to business. We staged a huge demonstration in front of the Alameda County courthouse to show our support for our leader, Huey P. Newton. His trial for the murder of an Oakland policeman was beginning in the next few weeks, and we had publicly proclaimed that if Huey went down, we were going down with him. Huey was accused of fatally shooting Oakland police officer John Frey and wounding another policeman in an early-morning gun battle on October 28, 1967. The policeman was wounded five times.

That night and the next morning were the most embarrassing events of my life in the BPP. When I woke up the next afternoon, the demonstration was over. I had missed the entire event. I should have been disciplined. But I didn't say anything and neither did the other Panthers who knew. Maybe they thought I was just jiving and wasn't worth an ass kicking. This was the reason we were here, and until this day it is the lone black mark in my BPP career. I let it go and never brought it up again. Even years later, after I got very close to Huey P. Newton, I would feel this shame every time I saw him.

Major faux pas aside, I returned with the San Diego Panther contingent on cloud nine. Oakland had been a breathtaking experience. Even as a member of the Party, I felt a certain mystique about the brothers and the organization they had built. To be that close made me realize how much further I had to go to understand more fully what the revolution was about. At this point I knew more about show than about substance. I did not understand the philosophy or the ideology. I read more and tried to study the concepts, which were the most difficult for me because it doesn't make sense to die for something you can't at least clearly articulate.

Understanding the revolution was not my biggest problem—my parents were. Ever since I had joined the Party, they'd been on my ass. They were from the Jim Crow South and had some very strong ideas about this country and what it meant to be a young black man. I had bought my first gun, and my father told me that if I wanted to live in his house, I would have to take the gun elsewhere. So I did. My mother was saying, "Them niggers in the Party ain't shit. They ain't putting no food or a roof over your head." My father would say, "Boy, you still smell your pee. How do you think you can change things when you're just a pissy-ass boy? You need to get yourself a real education and stop reading that bullshit in them crazy Panther books. That shit ain't gonna help you in the future." I would counter with "This is my life. This is all I'm going to do for the rest of my life, so I need to know this stuff."

This kind of conversation between parent and child was going down in the black communities all across the country. It was a generation gap, but I knew it only as a problem I was having with my folks.

Well, one night we were at the Panther pad across the street from the Party office, and there was a lot of police activity outside. The police were surrounding the office. I never found out why they were surrounding the office, but things were pretty hot. There were Panthers on the roof with guns, and I thought this could be deadly for a lot of us. Was this the showdown? There was someone ringing our bell. Kenny answered the door downstairs. He was talking to someone for a while and then he called me downstairs. My father was at the door. When I got downstairs, Kenny told me that I should go with my father until I worked things out because "we have rules and you need your parents' permission to be here." The rule requiring that sixteen-year-olds have their parents' written permission was created at the inception of the Party because the very first member, Bobby Hutton, was sixteen when he joined. Man, was I hurt and embarrassed as hell. I looked at my dad and he just nodded toward the car out front. My mother was in the front seat. It was like being told I couldn't stay out and play with my friends.

But these weren't my friends, this was the BPP, and I could get killed. Whether I understood that then wasn't important, but my parents sure as hell understood. I didn't argue. I just walked out with my head down, got into my parents' car, and left.

I went to work and dragged around the house for months on end. I was devastated. I stopped talking to both of my parents. For them life went on; I'm sure they felt that they had saved their son from a foolish mistake. They didn't bother Fred because he was of legal age. But when he caught a concealed-weapon possession case later on, he left the Party and continued his college studies at UCLA. I, on the other hand, just bided my time. I would return to my calling.

4

THE PARTY HAD RULES that were enforced. So my running away to join the Party while underage was no good. I went to my dad and said, "Can we talk about this?"
And he said, "Sure, why not."

I said, "Daddy, this is what I want to do. I want to be a Black Panther so that I can help my people. I see how things are in this country, and you always told me those stories about growing up in North Carolina and having to sit in the back of the bus. And then you and your brother refused to sit back there and you fought back and had that fight where you knocked the white boy out and stuff. You know what I mean? I'm tired of being pushed around and I want to fight back."

"Who can you help?" my father said. "You're just a boy who barely has a job that pays for your cigarettes. Flores, you're a high school dropout. I want you to get a high school degree and go to college like Junior. Then, if you get your high school degree, you can join them Black Panthers, and I won't say anything because then you'll be grown."

I heard what he said, but that still didn't reduce the pain that I was in. "Get your high school degree and go to college and be like Fred." I heard that, and that wasn't so bad, but I wasn't thinking about what seemed like a far-in-the-future stage of life. My fear was that I would miss out on the revolution. That was a big deal at the time. I thought I was old enough to make my own decisions, and I wanted to risk my life for the cause whether I completely understood it or not. It was something I felt, not something I thought. I was afraid that the feeling would go away before I understood what it was all about. But I could see I was going to have time to think about it. I thought I understood the times and current events. Revolutions were under way across the world, and they were dealing with imperialism, colonialism, police brutality, Jim Crow, race, culture, economics, politics, clothes, sex, and lifestyle. This was very exciting to me—people were fighting and dying for causes and beliefs, and that's what I believed I wanted.

I continued to work at the NTC and gave my supervisor hell. I talked so much shit that he said if I didn't stop, he was going to fire me. I said, "Fuck you." He said, "You're fired." I cleared out my locker and went home. All the while I was thinking about what my father had said: "Get your high school degree." My parents were pissed off. Not because I lost my job, but because they had rules. If you stay in my house, you either will go to school or get a job. So I went job hunting again.

I went to downtown San Diego to a youth employment facility that had various job training, employment, and educational resources. I filled out the application and waited to see a counselor. I met with a brother who told me that there was a great program that would allow me to get my general equivalency diploma, earn a salary, and possibly obtain some job skills or a trade. He said it was called Job Corps. It took me about thirty seconds to make up my mind. "Sign me up," I demanded. "Don't you need to talk with your parents and get their permission?" he asked. "I already have it. No problem; they'll sign, believe me."

It was 1969 and I had just turned seventeen when I boarded the Greyhound bus that would take me to the Wolf Creek Job Corps Center in Roseburg, Oregon. I had a plan. I would go to this program, get my GED, and, while I was there, hit the books so that I would better understand the philosophy and ideology of the BPP. I packed all of my books: Mao's Little Red Book, Fanon's *The Wretched of the Earth,* and an assortment of other books that would keep my mind together. I also had my folks forward my subscription to *The Black Panther* to me in Oregon.

The bus ride was eighteen hours. The bus moved up the coast and picked up other young men, most of them black. When we got to Roseburg, all of us got off at the depot and gathered around the Job Corps worker who was waiting to take us to the camp.

Oregon is a beautiful place. The camp was surrounded by plenty of trees, mountains, babbling brooks, and lots of open space. The environment was serene and breathtaking and I'd never seen anything like it. The camp was about fifteen long log cabins lining a single blacktop street. There was a basketball court near the largest building, which was the dining hall. All of the counselors were white men, and the majority of the academic instructors were white women. Most of the Job Corps youth were black males, but there were a number of white males and some Chicano males. These young men were from San Diego, Los Angeles, San Francisco, Oakland, Georgia, and Tennessee. And there was a large contingent of brothers from North Carolina. These were some large dark-skinned black males who referred to themselves as "Geechee Men." They would talk shit all day long, capping on other people's mothers and the like. If you responded, they would threaten to cut you but not before pulling a train on you. Most of the brothers never took them seriously because these niggers talked a bunch of shit. But they didn't last long. After they attacked a white boy, just about all of them got shipped out.

The Job Corps did not fool around. We were tested, analyzed, and placed in various programming modules that would put us on the road to graduation from six months to two years. In addition, you were assigned to a trade based on your test scores. For example, if your Adult Basic Education (ABE) reading level was below 6, you could train to be a maintenance engineer. If it was from 6 to 8, you could train to be a commercial painter or a carpenter. And finally, if your ABE was 10 or

WILL YOU DIE WITH ME?

above, you could train to become a heavy equipment operator. I had no interest in any of those trades. I just wanted to get my GED and get back to the business at hand.

The school program was difficult. I tried to complete the GED course as fast as possible. The course consisted of 124 lesson plans that should take a person with an ABE level of 10 to 12 at least one year and no more than two. I settled in and began to attack the 124 lesson plans while staying abreast of my revolutionary studies and the current news with regard to the BPP, which got worse by the day. I had been at the camp for only a few weeks when I got a letter from Fred telling me that Bunchy and John had been assassinated on the campus of UCLA. In addition, the papers my folks were sending me reported raids on Party offices and police confrontations that resulted in dozens of Panther fatalities. I read about close friends who were being killed by agents provocateurs from the United Slaves organization. Two brothers I worked closely with in San Diego, Sylvester Bell and John Savage, were gunned down by members of this group who had suspected connections to the authorities that were trying to destroy the BPP. Shit, the irony in what happened to Sylvester and John Savage is that the guys charged with their murders were niggers I knew in San Diego, either from school or from organized sports. It looked like we were fighting one another instead of focusing on the real enemy. Go figure!

What my father had said was starting to make sense. He thought I couldn't make a difference, being so marginal and not really understanding what was going on. I needed to be able to contribute something to the struggle and not just be deadweight. I needed to make an impact. As I reflected on the tragedies and the difficult road ahead, I made a commitment to myself to make a significant contribution when I returned to the Party

I had to stay focused. I was midway through the GED course of study when my instructor suggested that I take the next GED examination that was scheduled in Roseburg. She told me that, based on the progress I was making, she thought I would benefit from taking the exam because the time pressure of the test would prepare me to ace the final once I had completed the balance of the lesson plans. I agreed. So I went to town on the next Job Corps bus. To my surprise and hers, I passed the exam and was awarded my GED. I called my folks and told them what had happened and that in a couple of months I would be on my way home.

5

I WALKED UP TO THE screen door of the Black Panther Party office at 2090 Imperial Avenue in Southeast San Diego, just as I had done in the summer of 1968. I didn't immediately walk in because I was somewhat apprehensive about my first encounter and embarrassed about having been pulled out of the Party by my dad. I opened the screen door and walked in. I recognized the brother behind the desk from around town. He moved slowly from behind the desk and extended his hand. "Can I help you, brother?" he asked.

"Yes, I'm looking for the defense captain, Kenny Denman. My name is Flores Forbes, and I wanted to rejoin the struggle."

He smiled and looked at me suspiciously. Clearing his throat and moving back around behind the desk, he said, "Kenny Denman was expelled sometime ago." I stood there thinking about what I should say next, because this brother wasn't very open, but I had come a long ways and I was not going to be denied now.

"Well, can I speak with someone about joining the BPP?"

"No, because membership is closed in San Diego. The only way you can obtain membership is get it cleared from the chapter head-quarters in LA. Or just give me your name and number and I will have someone contact you. You know things are—" And then he cut it short. He handed me a piece of paper and I wrote down my name and number and left. Damn, I thought, Kenny Denman expelled. I started to go back and ask about some of the other people but decided against it.

One week later I got a call from Zeke Taylor. He was around when I first joined and he cautioned me about joining again. He said that after I left, things really changed. He said that national headquarters had cracked down and sent a goon squad down after John and Sylvester were killed. They expelled the entire group of people who had been originally here and instituted a lot of radical changes that made it almost impossible to join. Which is what he thought they wanted. Then he said if I was really serious, he would arrange for me to meet with the brother who was running things now, named Shabazz. I told him I was, and the next day I met Zeke and Shabazz at Ocean View Park. I was curious as to why we didn't meet at the office. I soon found out. Shabazz was a tall brother who spoke like he was from the South. He wore a big straw hat and overalls. Wearing dark glasses, he approached me and extended his hand, saying, "Power to the people, my brother. What can we do for you?"

"I had joined the Party back in 1968 when I was underage, and now I'm back and I'm ready to get down again."

He just laughed and said, "You're ready to get down again? Did you get down before, when you were here last time?" This brother was making fun of me. Or was he?

"No, I didn't get down before, but I'm serious, I—"

He cut me off with a wave of his hand and said, "Come on, brother, get in the car. Let's take a ride."

Shabazz began by explaining to me what had taken place in San Diego. "These niggers was jiving, man. They barely had any programs, and you had to drag them niggers out at gunpoint in order to get them to sell papers. Elmer 'Geronimo' Pratt sent a goon squad down here to clean the shit up, and now we're getting ready to close down the branch and move the people who are left to Riverside. Now, if you're serious, and you check out, you'll have to leave with us."

"When would that be?" I asked. Shabazz got quiet as he gunned the Volvo we were riding in.

Zeke cut in. "Look, Forbes, don't ask too many questions, you know. Shit, you might be the police."

They were silent and then both of them busted out laughing as Shabazz said in a loud voice, "Look, Forbes, we know you ain't the police, but if you come with us to Riverside and then LA, you'll have to learn not to ask the wrong kind of shit, right on?"

I said, "Right on."

This was an extremely awkward situation and not just a little stressful, but I was down with the program. I spoke to Zeke later and he filled me in on a few things. "Look, Forbes," he said, "I vouched for you with Shabazz, so don't front me off. Anyway, when we first started out, we were paper [not serious] Panthers, man. This shit is real serious, man. People are getting killed and the discipline in the Party right now is real harsh. You know you can get mud-holed and rushed to the dirt for a minor infraction and then kicked out like that. And that's no shit. So if you ain't serious, stay home, man." I never forgot what Zeke said, but it did not deter me. I was serious.

Every single day I was involved in some activity with Shabazz and Zeke or just Shabazz. Shabazz was someone I was going to know well, and I think he took to me, too. He talked a lot about the Party and how it had changed, with the various purges and upheavals that had transformed the organization. He spoke about the discipline, the rules, and the fact that because of all the so-called agents, people in the Party were very paranoid. "We're at war, and you should never forget that, young brother." He told me he had a feeling about me in his gut. A feeling that made him believe I was for real and serious.

As soon as I turned eighteen, I informed my parents that I was going to be leaving and moving to Riverside and possibly LA and that I was again dedicating my life to the Black Panther Party and the struggle. Someone else was watching my birthday besides me. I'm not sure when the FBI or the San Diego police started paying attention to me, but they were. I was surprised, because I was nobody in the book of people they could have been watching. But I was seen all over town with Shabazz and Zeke, and while I was running around with them, they were stopped several times by local police who called them by name.

A week or so after my birthday, the FBI came to my parents' home asking questions about my brother, who had caught a gun beef at school more than a year ago. I was the only person home at the time. They were polite and shit—you know how they do it—but I started talking shit, and as I talked, they kept asking questions and I kept on acting dumber by the second. I remember saying I had just turned eighteen and one of them wrote that down. That's the answer that brought them back, the one regarding my age. And then they asked about the war and the draft, and I said something to the effect of "Fuck you and your god-damn war, which I'm not fighting for you motherfuckers." And then I slammed the door.

A few days later they came for my ass. I was pulling my parents' 1960 Mercury into the driveway when I saw a car pull in behind, blocking me from the rear. About four white men in suits appeared with guns drawn. They told me to put my hands up and that I was under arrest for not registering for the draft. I didn't know you could be arrested for this. One of them pushed me against the car and patted me down. He pulled my hands behind my back and cuffed me. My mother came running out of the house, shouting, "What are you arresting him for?" One of the agents asked her to calm down and explained to her why. After hearing that, Mother asked, "Does he need a sweater?"

The agents stopped and looked at one another. One of them said, "No, Mrs. Forbes, he won't need one where he's going." And with that they pushed me into the car and drove me to the federal lockup in downtown San Diego. My father, who was pissed as hell, hired a lawyer who instructed me to say I would register as a conscientious objector and then they would release me. I did, and two days later Shabazz, Zeke, and I left for Riverside, California.

• • • The Riverside branch was a fully functional BPP branch with about ten Panthers; a single location for a Free Breakfast Program for Children; a Black Panther newspaper distribution of close to five thousand weekly; a separate office on a tree-lined street in the black community; and across the street, a Panther pad where many of us slept. This branch had one shotgun that belonged to Shabazz. About four or five of the Panthers here were from San Diego. This may have been a small operation relative to LA, but I was in seventh heaven because I was doing my thing every day now. I worked on the breakfast program in the morning: cooking, serving the kids, and cleaning up. For the rest of the day I sold newspapers in the downtown area, along several of the commercial strips and at one of the local malls. The work was hard, but I wanted to do it. Shabazz held PE class in the evening.

I was a little more confident, and my comprehension of the material was better. I was ready now. The numbers in the collective were almost evenly divided between women and men. In fact, two of the women, Cheryl Curtis and Primo, were friends of mine from my earlier days in San Diego.

Shabazz spent most of his time traveling to LA and developing other underground resources in the area. One day he told me he needed me to go somewhere with him. I would not be going into the field to sell papers. We met these two brothers dressed in marine battle fatigues in the backyard of one of Shabazz's friends. These brothers walked around to the alley. We followed them to their car. They popped the trunk, and man, my eyes spread and my nerves rattled a bit. The trunk was full of government-issue M16s, two M79 grenade launchers, and hundreds of rounds of ammo. Shabazz and the two marines haggled over a price. He told the brothers that he wanted the entire cache. He pulled out a roll of bills and paid them. We unloaded the weapons and they drove off. Shabazz told me that the brothers in LA had sent him to make and close this deal. They were coming to pick up the guns tonight. They needed to replenish their stock after a big shoot-out and raids in which they lost a great deal of their shit. I felt a rush. Then a sense of calm. This was what some guys did full-time. I knew someone in the Party did this kind of work. If you weren't involved, whether you were part of the general membership or not, you wouldn't know about it. Even with this brief exposure to the secretive side of the BPP, I never thought I'd be involved beyond this.

Three Panther veterans, all from Los Angeles, came to town. One of the brothers, Robert Bryant, was called "Dramatic Bob." He looked real mean with his mustache and small goatee, all decked out in his hip late-'60s outfit: Big Apple hat, bell-bottom pants, and semi-platform shoes. He was slim but muscular and had a strong pimp walk. The second brother was named Albert Armour. Al had this long, loping gait and was dressed similarly to Rob. He had a happy-go-lucky countenance that would fool you into thinking he was something other than a really dangerous nigger. The guy calling the shots was James Thomas Johnson; everyone called him Jimmy. If you knew him well enough, though, you could call him by his nickname: the Black Dog. Jimmy was the defense captain of the Southern California chapter of the Black Panther Party. He was Geronimo Pratt's deputy. Elmer "Geronimo" Pratt had succeeded Bunchy Carter as the deputy minister of defense for the Southern California chapter. This was the guy who led the goon squad down in San Diego. He was dark-skinned and a little heavy but seemed to be light on his feet. He had a big smile, also deceiving. He was dressed stylishly like the others but wore a Big Apple cap cocked ace deuce. They pulled up in a big red ride, with one of them carrying a grocery bag with two bottles of dark port wine and lemon juice so that they could make a traditional Panther drink called Bitter Dog, aka Panther Piss. All three of these guys were damn near legends in the BPP. Two of them were involved with the December 8, 1969, shoot-out in LA when the LAPD rolled out their crack SWAT team for the first time. Jimmy was known for other shit far and wide.

We all thought it was a grand time, with BPP notables dropping by like this. After we were drinking for a while, it seemed as if by some sleight of hand they had all eleven of us lined up against the wall telling each of us shit about the other that was not true. They were making all kinds of charges, throwing out words like "shirking one's responsibility," "practicing liberalism," and every other kind of counterrevolutionary act that a Panther could be charged with. Conspicuously absent were Shabazz and Zeke. I wasn't acting as afraid as I should have been. Maybe that's why Jimmy zeroed in on me. Jimmy looked at me and said, "How in the fuck did I miss you in San Diego? I know you wouldn't be here now if I had spotted yo ass down there, nigga. You know you don't belong here. Do you?"

I didn't say a word. "Answer me, muthafucka!" he screamed. I still didn't say anything. "How come you ain't saying nothing, nigga?"

"Because I haven't done anything, comrade brother," I said in a low voice.

"Oh," he said, looking at his two backups, "you're a tough guy, huh?"

"No, I just didn't do what you said I did." He ultimately got tired of fucking with me, and they moved to a few other people. Some of them got their asses whipped. This shit went on for hours. When they were done, they packed up their shit and left. But before he left, Jimmy looked at me and said, "I still don't like you, so you better watch it." I kept my mouth shut.

This was my first encounter with a goon squad. Their purpose was to whip people into shape and to get them to perform their jobs better. Now I don't believe it was effective, but then I didn't know what to think. I always believed I was a person you didn't need to scream at or threaten in order for me to do my job. I realized from this incident, once again, that I had a long ways to go to be the effective kind of Panther I thought I had to be. Once the goon squad left, Shabazz miraculously reappeared. I didn't ask him if he was in on the move that had just gone down. Years later, though, I learned that he probably got jacked, too.

One major part of the education process I was to master was security. Security was 50 to 75 percent of a member's focus in the BPP. You trained in the field while selling papers to be vigilant, always watching for the police and, to a greater degree, those enemies of the BPP who could not be identified by uniform. This type of security consciousness can also make a person extremely paranoid: no detail is overlooked because your guiding principles allow you no time to rest your mind. When you're trained to walk down the street against the traffic so that you see all the cars coming toward you, you know to look over your shoulder in order to pick up traffic coming in the other direction. Vigilance was the key for all matters.

But no detail was paid more attention than the security of the office, especially at night and in the early morning. The latter was when most of the raids had taken place. Every raid against the BPP in every chapter or branch had become a case study of sorts. Many times we would sit around the office at night or at our pads and listen to Shabazz regale us with the stories of the many raids and shoot-outs, from the murder of Fred Hampton to the December 8 shoot-out in LA and even Huey's confrontation with the OPD in 1967. But out of all of these stories there was always a moral, and it usually had something to do with a breakdown in security.

The biggest breakdown in security that could ever occur in a BPP office at night or in the early-morning hours was for the person who was on guard duty to fall asleep. There were rumors that many of the raids by local police forces were facilitated because the Panther on watch fell asleep and was unable to wake people up to defend the office. If a raid took place in Riverside, we weren't prepared either technically, with the weapons and defense, or skill-wise, with the training. The LAPD launched their newly innovated SWAT team at the Panthers in LA, and they got down like we were supposed to.

One evening, after a long day in the field selling papers and tending to other tasks, I was assigned the last shift in the watch detail. There were usually two people on duty for a couple of hours. Here in Riverside, I was to learn that what we called security was a joke compared to LA or national headquarters in Oakland. We had two people on each detail—one person outside and the other inside. We would rotate every hour. The office was not fortified, and we had only one 12-gauge pump shotgun. I was outside first. The time was maybe three or four in the morning. When we changed, daylight was breaking and the sister who was outside stayed there for a short moment. When she came back inside, we were relieved by a single brother, and I lay down on the couch. The Browning automatic shotgun was on the floor next to the couch. As I dozed off to the lingering sounds of Smokey Robinson, which played over and over, I heard a *boom!* And then another *boom!* I rolled over and saw lights and men in black with ski masks. It was the police. I rolled off the couch, covered my head, and landed on the shotgun. I heard one of them say, "This one has a gun over here." I felt a gun pressed against the back of my head. I froze and stayed that way until one of the cops rolled me over and placed my hands in plastic handcuffs. Everything had happened so fast I didn't even have time to be afraid. They lined all of us up and kept us in a little circle for the entire time they were there. They searched the house from top to bottom and found nothing outside of a legal shotgun. Through the entire ordeal, the Smokey Robinson album played over and over again, without interruption.

This was my first serious bust as a Panther. We were taken to the Riverside jail and fingerprinted but not booked. Shabazz came and picked me up after we had been locked up for two or three days. I asked him what we'd been busted for and he just said, "This is how things are, little brother. They wanted inside the office and to get the lowdown on the local branch. It's over now. Geronimo's closing us up and transferring everyone to LA."

We were never charged for any crime. They were merely on a search mission. They were probably looking for the weapons that Shabazz had gotten from the marines.

This was a major incident in the chapter. One false move and I could have been shot. But that didn't happen. Naïve I was, but not afraid. I believed in what I was doing. Shabazz said this was good experience for my next move. I was being transferred to the main chapter in Southern California: Los Angeles.

6

Los Angeles was known in Panther lore as the Red Zone. There were constant shoot-outs with the police, and eleven Panthers—one fourth of all Panther fatalities from 1966 to 1977—died here.

PANTHERS from all over the country were amazed at the behavior of the LAPD. With the exception of the Chicago police, there was no more hostile police department toward the BPP than the LAPD. And they let you know they were the enemy. They were formidable, nasty, racist, and always trying to start some shit. And many times it was the little things they would do. Sometimes they would approach me wanting to buy a paper. I would refuse to sell them one, as they knew I would, and that's usually when the shit would start. But it was when they drove by the office and shouted, "Know your enemy and know yourself" over the loudspeaker that I realized these fast-drawing motherfuckers weren't playing around. By quoting Sun-tzu and Mao, they let me know they were really studying us, and that couldn't be good. They would jam us on the street while selling papers, shoving and pushing would start, and on two or three occasions I got my young ass jumped on in the Red Zone.

———

• • • Shabazz pulled his 1964 Volvo slowly up to the Southern California chapter headquarters on Stockwell Avenue in Compton. He sped up again and drove down the block, passing the office, making a U-turn at the nearest intersection. As he pulled the car around toward the office, he gunned his engine, racing back down Stockwell while searching for a parking space. When he spotted a space, he shut off his lights and, with great skill, turned sharply into it. In a serious tone of voice, he said, "Flores, when we get out, walk quickly toward the office, but don't run. They will cut the floodlights off to cover your entrance. Okay?"

"Right on," I replied.

We did as he said, and as we approached the office, the floodlights went out. It was then that I saw what Shabazz was concerned about: barreling down Stockwell Avenue with its lights off was the silhouette of a Los Angeles County Sheriff's car heading directly for us. They were waiting to jam anyone they saw entering the office that night. We continued walking across the front lawn and down the driveway to the back door, where a Panther sentry was waiting to let us in the office.

Once inside, we exchanged the greeting "Power to the people" with several people inside. One brother, short, light-skinned, and buff, wearing a safari jacket and a small black seaman's cap, made a fist and said, "Death to the fascist pigs." This was Elmer "Geronimo" Pratt, deputy minister of defense for the Southern California chapter. G, as he was called, was the closest a person could come to the prototypical Panther. He was not known just locally in the Party but also nationally. He was an ex-paratrooper and war hero. G was the architect of the chapter's defense against the infamous LAPD and the LA County Sheriff's Department. He appeared to be unafraid of the lurking danger outside of these fortified walls. Seated near him was Jimmy Johnson, the defense captain, and Gwen Goodloe, one of the leading members in the chapter. I was very nervous but tried not to show it. My head was spinning with the same type of jittery feelings I had in 1968 when I was around all of the seasoned Panthers in Oakland.

This was 1970, and these people were very serious warriors in the struggle for liberation. These were the Panthers who had stopped time when they fought toe-to-toe against the LAPD's SWAT team for six hours. This was the Red Zone, and my soul could feel it. The reputation of the Black Panther Party's Southern California chapter could be surpassed by none, not even national headquarters in Oakland. Founded by Alprentice "Bunchy" Carter, the leader of the five-thousand-strong Slauson gang in South Central Los Angeles, the LA chapter's history was well known to all. Since its inception, eleven Panthers had been killed in clashes with the LAPD and other government-sponsored agents provocateurs. Bunchy Carter himself was killed in one of these encounters. There were three others whom I knew: John Huggins, Sylvester Bell, and John Savage. There had been shoot-outs on the street, Mexican standoffs, and early-morning special operations against these Panthers that had resulted in a one-of-a-kind urban firefight in December 1969. The chapter persevered through it all. As a result, the LAPD and the LA County Sheriff vamped and harassed the surviving members like no other chapter had seen before. The intensity of the harassment was nerve-shattering. My first experience with this at the Stockwell office should have caused me to reconsider my calling. It did not. It would be only the beginning of my education and development into a Panther who could live and thrive in the Red Zone.

• • • The Red Zone was my station for the next two years. I worked out of every branch office in LA, participated in every survival program they had instituted. Shabazz told me that I would first be posted to the Watts office located at 113th and Croesus, across the street from the Imperial Court Projects. Shabazz was reassigned to the chapter headquarters on Stockwell Avenue.

The Panthers assigned to the Watts office were all tried-and-true operatives. The coordinator, Craig Williams, was one year older than me. He was one of the eighteen Panthers involved in the three raids conducted by the LAPD in December 1969. Craig was from the west side of LA and was one of the top military/security personnel in the

BPP. Whenever anything serious was happening in Oakland, or in other parts of the Party's world, and called for serious men and women to be involved, Craig and several other Panthers in LA would be called in to secure the matter. Randell Jefferson was the officer of the day (OD) for the Watts office. The OD reported to the office coordinator and was responsible for running that office and all of its day-to-day activities. Randell was from the Slauson area of LA and had been in the LA chapter from the beginning. His brother, John Jefferson, was a major underground operative. Randell early on took me under his wing and showed me the ropes in Watts and other parts of LA. We sold papers together for years; he gave me his best routes and locations and took me through many of the neighborhoods that he used to hang in while growing up. On a rotating basis, other Panthers were assigned to the office to perform fieldwork and other activities, but normally there was a cadre of four or five who maintained the Watts office.

The Watts office was not one of the offices that had been fortified. It had no sandboxes or sandbags, gun ports, steel plating over the windows, or tunnels. Because it was too dangerous to stay in the office at night, we retired to a safe house. Only the office staff and the defense captain knew of its location. But there were times when we didn't leave the office until early in the morning, and those were the times that my young ass got an eyeful of the LAPD in action. They would surround the office and shout over a bullhorn, "This is a raid." Nothing would happen, but I could see them outside through the windows. Sometimes a dozen tow trucks would ride around the office, circling the block for several minutes. Craig and Randell assured me that these were police maneuvers being staged as they were planning their next move against the Party. It didn't matter if what I saw was not what they said it was; just seeing this kind of activity convinced me that they were telling the truth. At eighteen years of age I was untested, but I had placed myself in harm's way. Each time our office was surrounded by the LAPD and they threatened to attack, I was there, not ready at first, but each succeeding incident would steel my heart and build my confidence.

• • • When I was a teenager growing up in San Diego, the numerous jobs I held all over the city afforded me the opportunity to travel and explore San Diego County. Now the numerous Black Panther newspaper routes gave me the same kind of opportunity to see the City of Angels.

Lugging from 100 to 125 papers apiece, Randell and I would depart the Watts office at about 9:00 A.M. We would usually walk down Wilmington Boulevard, heading toward downtown LA, selling papers to the people along the street and to the patrons and owners of retail businesses along the way. Our route took us throughout Watts and the many two-story projects like Jordon Downs and the Haciendas and by the Watts Towers—which, in my opinion, is one of the best examples of urban architecture in LA. When we got to Will Rogers Park at 103rd and Central Avenue, we would head down Central Avenue to Adams Boulevard. As we moved through many of these areas, Randell would point out significant locations in the LA chapter's history. "Flores, you see over there, that's where Tommy Lewis, Robert, and Steve were killed by the pigs in the shoot-out at that gas station on Adams and Montclair."

My favorite route was the trail we blazed down Manchester Boulevard, one of the main surface streets in South Central LA. We would hump down Manchester, making a right at Western Avenue, finishing at the shopping center at Western and Jefferson avenues. Hundreds of small businesses lined these streets. Some were black-owned, but I was sure that they were in the minority. Business owners got used to seeing me every week at the same time. I wouldn't just pop into their store and disrupt the business; I would wait patiently until they had completed a transaction and politely ask if they wanted the latest issue of *The Black Panther.* Most of the time I would strike up a conversation with the person purchasing the paper. I would answer his or her questions about what was going on with the Party and how we would deliver what we said we would. We also discussed other matters in LA politics. The biggest concern of the young black people who purchased papers was police harassment from the LAPD and other law enforcement agencies. Their questions about that were always difficult to answer because we had not figured out how to solve that problem for ourselves as an organization.

Robert Beck, aka Iceberg Slim—now famous for best-selling novels of street life in the 1960s, patterned after his adventures as a big-time pimp—was one of the most memorable business owners on my paper route. His boutique sold men's clothing. I had never heard of his books. He said he liked the Party because we stood up and demanded what we believed. He respected us for having a ten-point platform and program. He and I talked about the image of black manhood that the Party projected to the black community. He believed there was a strong relationship to our image of the black man defending his community and the lonely image of the pimp standing up for his manhood by refusing to play the game that society tricks all of us into. Pimp though he had been, Iceberg Slim's attitude was similar to many of the black small-business owners I encountered who had more lawful backgrounds: they supported the Party by selling and buying our papers. Many made financial donations and even provided certain goods for our programs.

The most papers were sold on the first and the fifteenth of each month, on Fridays, and on weekends at major downtown intersections, large shopping malls, and on college campuses like UCLA, USC, Cal State LA, and Long Beach State University. For security reasons we sold papers in pairs, usually a brother-and-sister team. We were instructed to call in to the office every hour and report to the officer of the day our progress, location, and if we were having any problems. For example, if the police were hassling us, we would be ordered to vacate the area and, based on the location of other teams in the field, reassigned. On several occasions things got dicey. We had confrontations with a local group, United Slaves, or the US Organization. This group of cultural nationalists was responsible for the murders of four Panthers and seemed to be agents provocateurs for local law enforcement agen-

FLORES A. FORBES

cies. So when we did run into them, fights would break out, and a few times we had to call for some serious backup to quell the matter.

Founded in the mid-'60s by Maulana Ron Karenga, the Los Angeles–based group was the direct opposite of the Black Panther Party. According to William L. Van Deburg in his *New Day in Babylon,* US believed that black people could obtain freedom and liberation only by throwing off so-called white cultural domination of the mind by embracing another language like Swahili, celebrating black art, wearing a natural, taking a traditional African name, and getting rid of their English surname (which was referred to as one's slave name). Karenga believed these acts were the first steps toward a greater future for black people.

• • • The work I most enjoyed was with the various community programs that the Party had created. The Free Breakfast Program for Children was the strongest program and the one with the most public appeal. I organized four Free Breakfast Programs for Children in the four major public housing projects in Watts: Jordan Downs, Imperial Court, Nickerson Gardens, and the Haciendas from 1970 to 1971. We fed hundreds of kids a day and approximately 1,200 per week. The organizing effort began with us going door-to-door in the projects, passing out free papers with leaflets advertising the program. We talked to parents, kids, and store owners near the projects. We explained why we had started the program: to help the kids grow and intellectually develop, because children can't learn on an empty stomach. The breakfast program was an excellent organizing tool, helping us make friends and comrades in the projects. While we might not need their direct assistance in waging armed revolution, we were hedging our bets that if we did, they would respond more favorably to a group of people looking out for their children's welfare. The response was overwhelming. All types of parents agreed to host and serve our efforts. We held the program in the homes of junkies, drug dealers, regular public assistance recipients, gamblers, and gangbangers. (The Bloods began to appear during this period.) Store owners donated bread, eggs, bacon, sausage, milk, and paper products. In addition to our organizing activities, we cooked, served the food, knocked on doors to let the kids know which apartment the food was being served in, and on many an occasion made last-minute pickups of donations from stores.

In addition to the breakfast program, the Party sponsored the Free Health Clinic, the Busing to Prison Program, and our internal day care center. After working in the Watts office for some time, Craig told me that Elaine Brown had wanted me assigned to the Party's ministry of information in Southern California. She had liked one of the articles I wrote for our newsletter and thought I would be helpful in expanding the operation. This was not the information organ of the LA chapter but the ministry of information for the BPP. Elaine, who had started out as a rank-and-file member, had recently been promoted to the central committee and was handling that portfolio, spending an equal amount of time in Oakland and Los Angeles.

If there was anything in the BPP that could be compared to getting a big break, this was it for me. Elaine Brown was one of the best things that happened to me in the BPP. She liked and trusted me from the first day we met. She used to come by the Watts office when she was in town, and I'd see her at our safe house in the evenings. Gorgeous and smart, she was dating Craig, was tight with the Servant, and would bring the news to us about him and all of the major happenings in the BPP. (Over the years, Huey P. Newton had several titles, including minister of defense and Servant of the People—Servant for short.) She worked directly with two people who served as the information staff in LA. The other was this fine high-yellow sister named Joan who had gone to UCLA with my brother and me. A directive came down from up north to place the information ministry underground in the LA area. So we established a special house dedicated to this work. It also was the place that some of the major players from Oakland came to when they were in town. I was getting close to the brain trust in the BPP. I didn't go in the field anymore. Every morning, after we finished with the breakfast program, I would go to this safe house near Central Avenue in the fifties.

The assignments varied. Most of the time I would help Joan and Elaine by doing research for articles Elaine was writing for the paper or for other documents the Servant had her working on. But I spent a great deal of time researching the BPP. Elaine, at the direction of the Servant, was developing a book about the BPP, so I was compiling all the sources that would help her tell our story. Elaine has a great gift of gab and was never at a loss for words about the Party and the Servant. And I was all ears. Every major policy decision, new area of focus, or creation of a major initiative I heard from Elaine. I was taking it in with a spoon. This exposure gave me a much greater appreciation for what our struggle was all about.

Another central committee member who played a pivotal role in my ascension in the BPP was Ray "Masai" Hewitt, minister of education. Masai, who was originally from LA, would stay at the safe house when he was in town. He was a tall, imposing figure—maybe six feet four—slim, and dark-skinned, with a deep bass voice. His nickname was "Bright Eyes" from when he was a member of the Slauson street gang. A former marine with a black belt in karate, Masai was a self-taught, dyed-in-the-wool Marxist Leninist. While Elaine spoke about the Servant and many of the events and initiatives the Party was involved with, Masai talked more about the Party's military apparatus. He once asked me if I ever talked to anyone about the conversations we had. I told him no, and he said, "You know, 'rade [Masai used this abbreviation for the word *comrade*], I imagine if you said something to Geronimo, Jimmy, or any of the other brothers here, they probably wouldn't get upset because they wouldn't believe that I would talk to you about these sensitive matters." He was probably right. But to my delight, he kept on talking and showing me stuff. He talked about weapons and the types we had. He talked about the need for training in combat handgun shooting and the need to diminish our reliance on long weapons like automatic rifles and shotguns. He said we were the first real urban guerrillas in this country. We understood, he said, the need to organize people around specific issues like our survival programs, because we would need their support when it was time to really get down for the revolution. He used my organizing in the projects as an example.

"The people in the projects trust you, Randell, and the others," he said. "If you knock on their door at any time of the night, not only will they let you in, they will probably help you. You may not understand that now, but if you stay around here long enough, you will."

7

PEOPLE STARTED DISAPPEARING. One by one or sometimes in twos and threes, the comrades under indictment following the December 8 shoot-out were going underground. I wondered if I would ever become a fugitive and join that mysterious and wonderful group of people who had disappeared. Many of us believed that this kind of life was the destiny of a true revolutionary: to be Wanted Dead or Alive. Their trial was nearing, and when it began, many of them would not be there to stand. The only comrades out of the eighteen involved with the shoot-out who weren't going underground were Craig, Dramatic Bob, Tommye Williams, and Albert Armour.

• • • The last time we were all together was at this big retreat called by Geronimo. There were maybe fifty Panthers at the gathering held in the backyard of a private residence on the west side of LA. We ate big plates of barbeque and sat around talking shit about the pigs and what individuals would do when confronted by one. I mostly ate and listened. I was not tried and tested, like most of the people here, so I just kept quiet and wondered, when I was really confronted, would I show up like they had? G talked about paper sales and the possibility of consolidating our numbers by reducing the number of offices. He said we were going to "hunker down," so he wanted more people together as opposed to the isolation so many offices offered. He talked about some of the new directives coming down from "central" and how the Servant was easing into things, even after being out of prison for a couple of years. After the shop talk, we broke the semicircle we were seated in and milled around talking among ourselves. I still didn't know many of the people that well. Most of them were older than me. They were fierce and cocksure of every move they made and every word they spoke. Even if they weren't, I sure thought they were.

I stole a glance at G. He stood out as more confident and more knowledgeable than everyone present. He had already been through a war and his poise showed it, you know, that verve that a cold, calculating guerrilla has when he knows what it's really like to get down. And then there was Cotton. Who would have thought that this nigger—the one who was firing the Thompson submachine gun at the pigs on December 8, who taught all of us about building defenses and how to use weapons—would take the stand against his comrades and be the traitor. (Melvin "Cotton" Smith turned state's evidence at the trial for the LA Eighteen in 1971.) But at this time, he was a mean muthafucka, legendary in the BPP for his stealth and guile under extreme pressure. After them were Jimmy Johnson and dozens of others who had proved themselves. They could stand around and talk shit about the things they would do. No one ever talked about what they had done. That was against the BPP's standard operating procedure except as pillow talk. I heard Will Safford tell Mims that aiming his gun at a pig made his dick hard. Several people overheard him, and they "dapped" and laughed like gunfighters or pirates retelling old but not tall tales. After that retreat, most of the eighteen Panthers involved with the December 8 shoot-out would disappear. Most I wouldn't see again, at least not for a while.

• • • The office on Seventy-eighth Street between Stanford and McKinley was just three blocks away from the LAPD's notorious

Seventy-seventh Street Precinct when I was transferred there. The ideological split between Huey and Eldridge scared me more than the police ever could. I thought my world was coming apart before I even got started. Elaine left LA and was permanently assigned to central headquarters. The ministry of information was closed down, and I remember Masai saying as he also left LA for good, "You know, 'rade, we just might have to close this chapter down and put some of you underground to save you niggers' lives." The shit was hitting the fan. The media portrayed the split as an argument between two crazy niggers: Huey and Eldridge.

I was not very clear on the specific ideological or philosophical reasons for the split. I don't know if my fellow Panthers were either. Huey wanted the Party to return to its original vision and focus on organizing the community around our various survival programs, like the breakfast program, pending any other extralegal moves. On the other hand, Eldridge Cleaver wanted to get it on with the "Pig Power Structure" and start offing pigs via urban guerrilla warfare in the streets right now. I told myself that Huey was right. I didn't read anything to convince me or get persuaded by someone; I knew in my gut that the Servant was right. Shit, were we ready to do that? Hell, fucking no. To me, as one of the brothers in the trenches, what Huey wanted to do made a hell of a lot of sense; it made sense to stop fighting the police toe-to-toe. After thirty-plus dead Panthers in two years, shit, I'm glad somebody up north realized that we could never win a shooting "War of Liberation" at this time. Based on the literature I was reading, like Mao's *Military Writings* and *The Minimanual of the Urban Guerrilla* by Carlos Marighella, I knew revolutions took a good twenty or thirty years in less-developed countries. What was wrong with Eldridge? These were actions and words worth fighting against.

The Black Panther called them jackanapes, and we called them "napes" for short. And then people started to die. Sam Napier, the distribution manager of *The Black Panther*, was murdered in New York City. One of the napes, Robert Webb, was gunned down on the streets of New York a short while after.

Anyway, many of the brothers and sisters from G to Cotton involved in the December 8 gunfight began to go underground. Other people who were underground for other reasons left the safe houses that the Party had provided for them. Almost all of them supported Eldridge Cleaver. I remember one evening this hard-core Panther named Paul Cross from the real old school was standing on the porch of Seventy-eighth Street, staring out into the night. I asked him if he was okay and he started this crazy, confusing conversation about what he thought Bunchy would do if he were here. "You know, young nigger, Bunchy would go with his homey Eldridge and take us with him." Paul disappeared the next day. Not long after this, Randell was looking real sad and moping around. When I asked him what was wrong, he replied, "Jimmy Johnson just told me that my brother Long John had left his safe house. He's gone over to them niggas, Flores." Many of the Panthers I knew sided with Cleaver. Our internal war was on.

Masai came back to chair a special meeting to brief us on the state of affairs and to put everyone on point. He said combat handgun training would be instituted for the officers of the day so we could properly defend the office against G and his band, who were very well trained and had made a direct threat to move on us. He said we needed to revert to our old training to defend our offices and personnel. So we began fortifying each office, tunneling at each site in order to build the sandboxes and subsurface gun emplacements from which to fire. He also left a photo lineup of the various napes from the East and West coasts, many faces unfamiliar to us. We studied and drilled their faces into our memories because they had attacked us, and that meant we would get down if we saw them near us or our offices.

In the meantime, the military training continued along with the tunneling. But as the months went by, desertions began to mount. Some people were going over to the Cleaver faction and other people were frightened away, as were most people, by the constant harassment of the Los Angeles Police Department. The LAPD experience was frightening on a day-to-day basis. I remember one night I was on watch at the office in the backyard. At Seventy-eighth Street we had two people on watch, one inside securing the front and one outside in the backyard, hidden behind the barricades.

I heard a car screeching down the street followed by five to ten rapid bursts from a weapon, and then I heard more shots coming from the front yard. I ran around the front and coming toward me was Cheryl Curtis, the sister on watch in the front. She told me that a black-and-white had just committed a drive-by on our office. The other shots I heard were her returning fire.

• • • The office was full of comrades returning from the field late on a Saturday afternoon. The officer of the day, Shelton Jones, had left his desk and walked out into the front yard, part of his daily routine to assess the conditions outside. Our office was typical of the homes in this section of LA: single-family, one story with three or four bedrooms, living room, kitchen, bathroom, and dining area. Earlier in 1971 we had moved our offices into residential neighborhoods because it was safer and less isolated than the storefront offices we had in the past, which were more vulnerable to police assaults. The front yard was expansive, and the main house was set back about forty to fifty feet from the sidewalk and the street. Prominently displayed in the front yard was a powder blue sign with black lettering and a Panther logo designating this site as a BPP office. The entire front yard was bordered by a wire fence that stood approximately four feet high.

Without the sign, this would have been a normal house—from the outside. But when you walked inside, the place took on a totally different character. We had been tunneling for about two months. We dug straight down through the floor of a closet in the bedroom for about ten feet and then created a subsurface vestibule that served as the exit for two different tunnels. Each of the tunnels terminated under the homes of our neighbors on either side of the office. Large plantlike boxes had been constructed in the living room, bedrooms, and dining area. The boxes were rectangles, made out of two-by-four frames that were built out from the interior walls. The frames were then covered with plywood on all sides, with a hinged plywood top. They were filled with the dirt from the tunnels, so the police would not see us transporting dirt. The boxes were either painted to match the office or decorated with wallpaper. These boxes extended out from the wall for about eighteen inches, and our resident engineer, Randell Jefferson, assured us that no police bullet or nape bullet could penetrate that distance. Randell was one of the Panthers who had fortified Forty-first and Central, the scene of the December 8 shoot-out. His effectiveness was proved.

In the attic, Simba, Jimmy Johnson's deputy and one of the many Vietnam veterans in the Party, constructed an "eagle's nest." This location was sandbagged and would be used as an elevated firing position. Under the house was a trench system that bordered the house and facilitated seven reinforced gun ports. In the bedroom, just off the dining room, in a locked closet was the gun rack, lined with twenty-inch pump shotguns, one AR-180, and an assortment of handguns.

Anyway, Shelton was outside by himself in the front yard packing a .45 automatic, as was customary for the OD. The OD, at designated intervals, walked down the sidewalk to the front gate to survey the streets in front of the office, checking for any unusual police activity that could signal a raid. And then this sister named Cheryl Curtis, who was standing on the porch, shouted, "The pigs have Shelton," and pointed to the front gate. Everyone looked outside and noticed Shelton standing just inside the gate with his hands in the air, surrounded by six to eight policemen with their guns all trained on him. They disarmed him and pulled him over the gate, but they didn't attempt to enter the yard. We all could hear the pounding of feet and the jingling of LAPD Batman utility belts from the side of the office. The police were taking up positions on all sides, including the back. Our office was so close to the back alley that we could hear the souped-up engines from the Metro Squad cars roaring through the alley. It didn't take us long to ascertain that we were surrounded and the pigs were armed with shotguns and pistols. It was time to act and to act fast. I collected myself and thought deeply. I guess we must have looked hilarious to the police. We all just stood around watching them surround the office and not making a move to counter their positioning. We were dazzled by the speed at which everything had unfolded. At age nineteen I thought this could be it for me.

We responded. Jimmy came quickly from the back of the office, keying the gun locker, and started handing out the technical equipment as we lined up to get our shit. A brother slammed the large reinforced door and locked it, sliding a two-by-four to secure the door between two metal L-shaped braces as Jimmy reminded each Panther of his or her assignment. When I got my riot shotgun, he said, "What's your position?"

I shouted back at him, "I'm in the trench, northeast corner."

"Right on," he said, adding, "keep your head down."

"Right on," I shouted back. I could sense from Jimmy's body language, his entire demeanor, in fact, that this was not just another drill.

I took the weapon and ammo pouch filled with 00 buckshot rounds and moved quickly (remembering to walk fast and not run) through the dining area into the hall and around the corner to the closet that was the entrance to the tunnel/trench system. There was a short line, so I waited my turn to climb down the ladder. I went down and followed the trench to my position in the corner of the house. It was dirty, and with all of these bodies moving around, dust was flying, which made breathing difficult. It was also hot and I started to sweat. I pressed my release button near the trigger guard, which slid the pump toward me. I inserted a 2¾-inch shell into the chamber and slid the pump forward, placing a live round in the barrel. I then loaded the tubular magazine to the max and checked to see if the safety was on. I set my ammo pouch next to me in the dirt and waited, sweating profusely. From my vantage point I could see our front yard, grass level. I removed the screen from my gun port, exposing the wire mesh that remained to protect me from teargas canisters. I put the barrel of my weapon near but not completely outside the gun port. It was now quiet in the office, which led me to believe we were all in position and ready to get down.

There was this long period of silence during which we did not move and they did not move. Upstairs, Gwen Goodloe called the local press, our lawyers, and the Seventy-seventh Precinct watch commander to ascertain the situation. We stayed in our positions for about thirty minutes, sweating, breathing in dirt-laced air, and glancing from time to time at one another, side by side. We did not smile or joke as we did during drills. This was for real. The silence broke with some movement outside. When the police started pulling back, we remained in our ready positions until they had moved beyond our sights. The message came from upstairs and was passed along to each person, "Stand down, stand down." I waited my turn and moved slowly down the trench and up the ladder to floor level. No one said a word as we lined up to return our TE to Simba. Not even the normally talkative Jimmy Johnson said anything. He just clenched his fist as each one of us walked by him. This sort of thing happened on a regular basis for the rest of my time in LA. We called it a "Mexican standoff" or "almost a shoot-out." Over the next week, of the ten Panthers stationed at Seventy-eighth Street, four deserted. One of them was the brother next to me in the trench. Eventually, central headquarters gave us three months to shut down the Southern California chapter, pack all of our shit, and move half the contingent to Oakland. The balance would remain under the direction of Jimmy Johnson to set up the Party's underground apparatus. I guess Masai was right after all.

8

THIS TIME WE WERE THE PEOPLE who would disappear. For the next three months we spent the bulk of our time preparing to shut down the chapter. Though the harassment and surveillance by the LAPD and other agencies continued, we set about evacuating the Red Zone. I felt some degree of satisfaction that what I had set out to do had actually happened. For the first part of my tenure in LA, things were always hazy, and my understanding of the events internally and externally was marginal at best. But as we prepared to move up north, my confidence was at a level that made me feel comfortable with the organization, its policies, and the prospect of what could happen to me: death, prison, or exile. I didn't think about them in that order, but the stark fear and persistent paranoia I used to feel every time I stepped out of the office or was confronted by the LAPD had subsided. Fear was not totally out of the equation. I had just learned how to control it. I saw how it affected people in the Party. I saw fear in the eyes of men and women who were in the Party just prior to deserting. I imagined them returning to what they thought was a comfortable prior life before the Party. Since I had been in LA, I saw the structure and personnel of the Party change drastically. The split caused hundreds to change allegiances and banished many household names from the BPP. I guess it was a purge of sorts, but I never imagined the people I had met over the years would leave the struggle for any reason other than the three major consequences I had dreaded for so long: death, prison, and exile.

Many of the people I met when I first visited Oakland were gone and not dead, in prison, or in exile. Tommy Jones, Jr., Glen Stafford, and a dozen more were expelled and labeled renegades for various infractions detrimental to the Party, like armed robbery. Landon Williams was underground and would remain so for years. His brother Randy was in prison and wouldn't be released until I was twenty-five years old and the assistant chief of staff of the Black Panther Party. I remember reading in our paper that Robert Bay had been expelled for some desperado actions. He was reinstated and was now the OD of national headquarters. I was afraid of this large, almost Buddha-like man. But in approximately six to seven months, he would befriend me as I was being groomed to join the Party's elite. Chief of Staff David Hilliard was in prison. The next time I saw him was at his father's funeral. The California Department of Corrections had given him a furlough so that he could attend. I would attend the funeral with his brother June, the current BPP chief of staff. And my close friend from San Diego and Riverside, Shabazz, well, he was gone too. He had been expelled several months earlier, after being implicated with some crazy girl shit that happen to involve an old girlfriend of mine from San Diego. Of the fourteen brothers and sisters who had gone underground because of their involvement with the December 8 shoot-out, all but one had been captured. Cotton turned state's evidence on the others, while Geronimo was convicted on an unrelated charge and was now serving life in prison. The only person who was not arrested was a big, fine sister named Sharon Williams. To this day she's never been captured or heard from.

My brother, Fred, was married and living with his family in Los Angeles and working as a librarian. My sister was finishing college at UC San Diego but would move to LA to attend USC's School of Dentistry. And my folks were doing just fine. The last time I saw them before I left LA for Oakland was around Christmastime, at my brother's place on the west side. We never really talked about the Party when I was with them during these early years. It seemed as if everything was kept below the family radar. I had gotten my GED and was now doing the type of work I wanted to do. They knew about the paper and the survival programs.

• • • I spent the bulk of my last days in LA working with Randell. Together, we deconstructed his handiwork at Seventy-eighth Street. We tore down every bulletproof box and barricade that was filled with the dirt from the tunnels we had dug. We took the same dirt and filled in the tunnels and trench system. We took the wood from the boxes and placed it in the tunnels' foyer, closed the trapdoor, dusted off our clothes, and reported to Jimmy that the work at Seventy-eighth Street was complete. Craig Williams came to the now deserted office and packed up all of the weapons and left in the night to secure them in the armory. I never saw Craig again.

Just days before we slipped out of town, we all got together to hang out and say our farewells to the comrades who were not leaving. This group, led by Jimmy Johnson, was to remain and establish an underground operation in Southern California. I would see many of them again in the future, but with one very basic change: they would be working for me.

The group of Panthers ordered to Oakland, including me, packed our belongings and supplies and drove to Oakland, California, on February 28, 1972.

9

THERE WERE MAYBE 250 or 300 Panthers milling around inside and outside of St. Augustine Church on Twenty-seventh Street and West Grand Boulevard in West Oakland. I had never seen this many Panthers in one place in my life. I had been in Oakland for about a week and was assigned to an office in the East Oakland branch. We were gathered here at the church for our first political education class at central headquarters. This was the same location of my first PE class in Oakland back in 1968. Many of the Panthers I had heard about who were from different chapters and branches were present because, like the LA chapter, they had been closed down and summoned to the base. They hailed from Chicago, New York City, Seattle, Detroit, Texas, Washington, D.C., Baltimore, Philadelphia, North Carolina, Boston, Dayton, and the greater San Francisco–Oakland Bay Area. They had all been ordered to Oakland because Huey had devised a new strategic plan.

Elaine had told me about the Servant's vision of the Long March; it was supposed to rejuvenate our Party, which had suffered so much from being under attack by the U.S. government and local police agencies. We were battered but not beaten. Elaine had said that Huey believed we needed to regroup and organize a real base of operation from which to relaunch our revolution. The first try, he said, was more educational, during which we made the masses aware of the right to revolution "by any means necessary." But the educational phase also became a mass organizing tool that attracted thousands of people to the ranks of the BPP. She said that Huey thought this was great, but it was also "ass backwards," because when the ranks swelled, many of the people joining were not known to the original organizers in Oakland, so what you got was a lot of little Black Panther fiefdoms. Huey said it was difficult for the Party's leadership to get its arms around this huge operation that had grown exponentially. It also made it easy for police agencies to plant informants and agents provocateurs. When Huey was released, the people who really ran the BPP—the Hilliards and the Seales—continued trying to manage this monster that they had created.

Huey believed that a major characteristic of any revolutionary organization was that its members should have face-to-face relationships. That was the key to the puzzle, Elaine said. She said Huey couldn't pin it down in the beginning, but he had finally figured it out. He believed we would never be effective until we knew one another and worked around one another implementing a common program and agenda. Elaine said that Huey had told her that Mao and his people didn't get it together until after the Long March, which was preceded by mass killings of members of his party by the Chinese Nationalists. So they retreated, trained, regrouped, and reeducated themselves for the long haul that was ahead. What came out of the Long March were a common program and agenda and a base of operations from which to sortie and wage revolution as one organization.

Anyway, we were all standing around when Robert Bay, the national headquarters OD, came in and told everyone to be seated. As we were being seated, someone from the back of the room shouted, "Attention." Each of us jumped to our feet, eyes front with arms to our sides. Seconds later, the double doors to the meeting hall burst open, and in a fast pace walked the chairman of the Black Panther Party, Bobby Seale, followed closely by his bodyguard Billy "Che" Brooks from Chicago. Chills ran up and down my body. I was on cloud nine. Man, was I thrilled. I tried to look at the people around me to see if they were as overwhelmed as I was at the theater of it all. If this was the moment and feeling I had been waiting for, it had definitely taken me by surprise. This must be the feeling a person gets when he believes he's in the right place at the right time. I knew I had to be.

Bobby Seale was in his middle thirties, slim and wiry-looking. He didn't really look as fierce as he had the first time I met him in 1968, but I guess after being persecuted by the police over the past years, he had kind of mellowed and was looking the role as the BPP's chairman, without the .45 strapped over his shoulder. He removed his jacket and said, "Power to the people, comrades." We all responded in unison, "Power to the people, Comrade Chairman."

He began by welcoming those of us who had just arrived and said that if we had any issues, we should take them up with the local coordinator who in turn would bring them up with Robert Bay. He paced a second or two and then launched into his monologue.

"Comrades, we are here to build the new revolution in Oakland, the 'base of operation.' Yes, this is the base of operation. We are going to learn what it is like to practice and implement 'the correct handling of the revolution.' The Servant and I brought you all here so that we can build an organization that has a common program and agenda—an organization that knows what it stands for. In the next several months I will declare my candidacy for the office of mayor of Oakland. And sister Elaine Brown is going to run for one of the nine city council seats. You know me and the Servant, we've been researching the government here, and we have determined that if we take over the city of Oakland and make it our base, we can wage a righteous revolution that will free the people of this city. And once we've done that, you comrades will be trained so that you can go back to your chapters and branches and do the same thing. You see, the Oakland government is what we call a weak-mayor government. The mayor has very little power. Most of the power rests with the nine-member city council. But the mayor makes appointments that the council must ratify. So we need to run a slate of candidates along with sister Elaine and take control of a majority to control the process. But the key to all of this is the port of Oakland." He pointed in the direction he believed the port was in. "The mayor makes the appointments to the Port Commission and the council approves. And comrades, that's were the loot is. The money we need to finance our revolution."

I sat breathless, as I'm sure everyone else was. The shit made sense to me and I didn't even know where the port of Oakland was. People were saying, "Right on, Chairman," and "Teach, Bobby." We were clapping and nodding, and all that was missing was for someone to jump up and get happy, you know. Just like in church, or should I say a Panther church.

And he was just getting warmed up. He was pacing from one side of the room to the other, pointing and talking all kinds of good shit. He went on, "Comrades, we are going to create the goddamnedest, sho 'nuff, highfalutin, best political organization this city and country have ever seen. We will register people to vote. Yes, we will train you to be voter registration experts. When we register people to vote, we will get them down to the Oakland Auditorium and give every person who signs up to vote for our program a free bag of groceries, a free pair of shoes, and a free sickle-cell anemia examination. That's right, we will organize the people with our survival programs, and at the same time we will bring them to the polls to get rid of Mayor Reading and those other right-wing racist motherfuckers that have been oppressing us here in Oakland for the last fifty years."

The room erupted. Panthers were on their feet, clapping and pumping their fists, stomping and grinning like they had all been delivered unto the promised land. I know I had.

When this PE class ended, I had this strange sensation, a kind of premonition, that I would play a big part in everything the chairman was talking about. The speech that Bobby made that evening signaled to me the beginning of the most effective period in the young existence of the BPP. He outlined a tangible and viable program that I could really go for, and judging from the other comrade's responses, they could, too. I had worked in a couple of chapters and branches before coming here, and most of the activities were marginal and bordered on just barely surviving, with maybe two or three basic survival programs. But now, with an effective force of almost three hundred Panthers, we were ready to make a real move against the system.

• • • Along with several other comrades from LA, I was assigned to work out of the BPP branch in East Oakland. This was indeed a drastic change for us after spending two years in the Red Zone. The office was an ordinary single-family home on a cul-de-sac across the street from a public housing project deep inside of East Oakland. The house was not fortified, and the night watch schedule was extremely lax compared to the rigid and paranoid system we left behind in LA. Masai spoke to all of the comrades who came up from LA and told us to lighten up and relax because the LAPD hadn't followed us all up here. I didn't think they had, but what Masai said was reassuring. There were five local Panthers also working out of this office whose average age was like mine, around twenty years old. The branch coordinator was a sister named Pam Lewis. Even before Elaine Brown installed a significant number of women in leading roles, there were sisters like Pam who were smart and taking on major responsibilities in the Party.

What Masai had told us was reassuring, but when we actually went into the field, it really hit home. In LA, when you went into the field to sell papers, you had to go with a partner who would watch your back. In Oakland, that was not the case. Oftentimes Pam would go into the field to sell papers by herself without ever having a problem with anyone.

The longer I was here, the more I could see that tension between individual Panthers in the field selling papers and the police was non-existent. In fact, I was in Oakland for two or three days before I saw a police car. But I could sense that the environment or the heightened contradiction between the Party and local law enforcement did exist. This was not the Red Zone, as in LA, but it was a completely different variation on the struggle that existed in this country during the 1960s and '70s. Seventh and Willow in West Oakland was viewed as hallowed ground in my world. That was the location of the shoot-out that had seriously wounded Huey P. Newton and killed Oakland policeman John

Frey, thus catapulting Huey in the international consciousness as the defender of the black community in America. The streets of Oakland are where armed Panthers used to patrol the police, confronting them with arms at every turn when it appeared that a black person was being harassed. Numerous other incidents that are legend in Panther lore can be cited, but it was the aftermath of these incidents that I could sense and feel as I walked and rode the streets of Oakland.

Once a week we all piled into one of the many Panther vehicles to attend PE class at St. Augustine Church, an event I now anticipated eagerly. Talking with other Panthers about why they were here and what they have been doing since they joined the Party was one of the greatest pastimes I could have had. This one brother, a former Vietnam combat veteran named Harold Bell, from Chicago, was a "surefire standout." He was one of the Panthers who had been in the house when the FBI murdered Fred Hampton. He was quiet and talked briefly about Chairman Fred, but not the incident, because the case was still pending. There was also this other brother from Chicago named Darren Perkins; he too was a former Vietnam combat veteran. He wore this huge fedora, broken down in the front and cocked ace deuce, and knee-high black boots tucked into his pants. He talked a lot of shit and came off as someone who was worldly-wise. Even though he was five-seven at the most and I was six-two, he called me his "little brother."

The classes and the current Party line were more along the lines of propagating what our strategy was in taking over the city of Oakland. I would find out later that this was the "genius of Huey P. Newton" at work. The traditional rhetoric from the classical Marxist and Maoist texts had been replaced by questions, answers, instructions, and directions about public policy, public administration, and the electoral process and how we could make them work to our advantage. In fact, the impression I gleaned from my early days in Oakland was that the Party could do just about what it wanted and was very much in control of its destiny. This BPP was not going to be run out of town in Oakland like we had been in LA. And I really dug that.

The Party's operation in the San Francisco–Oakland Bay Area was a vast and expansive enterprise worth millions of dollars. The Party owned enough housing to bed down several hundred Panthers and half as many children of Panthers. There were dozens of offices spread across the entire Bay Area, from San Francisco to Richmond. And there was a fleet of vehicles: large trucks, vans, and sedans.

When the free food giveaways and massive voter registration rallies were staged to promote Bobby's and Elaine's campaigns, large trailer trucks were leased and packed with thousands of frozen chickens, vegetables, bread, and other foodstuffs. We rented space at the local college across the street from the Oakland Auditorium to prepare for these colossal events. Nattily dressed Panther executive types armed with slide rules calculated the amount of space needed to place the ten thousand bags of groceries on the floor of the auditorium. Hundreds of Panthers dressed in short black leather jackets, berets, powder blue shirts, black slacks, or skirts were organized to fill the bags with food and distribute them to a thankful public of thousands. The program and food distribution had been organized by the Panther officials in charge so that your chicken wouldn't thaw until you got home. Bobby stood on the podium saying that if you voted for him, he would put a free chicken in every bag of groceries. There were Panthers roaming the rallies with large placards around their necks announcing that they could register anyone of age to vote. Tables were set up across the sides of the auditorium manned by doctors, nurses, and Panther free-clinic personnel, dressed in white coats, testing people for sickle-cell anemia next to rows and rows of free shoes being given away by Panthers fitting everyone who needed a pair.

• • • One of the first things I learned after being in Oakland for a couple of months was not to get too comfortable with my current work assignment and station. After a few months of soaking in the situation, I was transferred to the Party's central distribution center for the *Black Panther* newspaper in San Francisco's Fillmore district.

This was a key location in the vast enterprise. The office had a ten-thousand-square-foot floor and a mezzanine above the first floor. This is where the paper was packaged to be shipped to local Panther distribution outlets around the country, around the world, and to subscribers. At this time our newspapers circulation was over a hundred thousand weekly. Everyone in the BPP at one time or another has sold, talked about, fought for, and some even died for *The Black Panther*. It was our main propaganda and political organ and a primary source of revenue. This location in the Fillmore district had come under attack from police and napes and was heavily fortified with sandbags and twenty-four-hour armed Panther guards. They even had a soundproof indoor shooting range for the guards to practice. The Panthers stationed here were young, tough, and tested veterans. The coordinator, Carl Colar, was one of the more serious people in the Party. A crack shot and black belt in karate, Carl took no shit from his staff but was always fair. As the months went by, we got to be pretty good friends. Not long after my arrival, Carl was reassigned to the chairman's security detail.

I always felt cursed by my penchant to find myself in trouble. Because of the military posture of this organization, the BPP had embraced the street gang–style of discipline popularized by Bunchy Carter. Getting into a fix could get you ten lashes, or if the transgression was serious enough, a person would get mud-holed. The worst act in the BPP was falling asleep on watch in a high-security situation like in LA, central headquarters, or at central distribution. There were others, like hitting a comrade, especially a sister, or the one that got me into trouble: drinking on duty or just getting drunk. A couple of times I had too much to drink in LA and got disciplined. But this was the Bay Area. So I took my licking and thought I could just keep on working. Naw, that didn't happen. Because I was from LA, I had a rep to uphold, and that meant my fellow LA comrades were really down on me. All of them niggers were coming over to Frisco to check up on me and give me a long lecture about where I came from and who I was representing. Even Jimmy Johnson came up and chewed my ass out. It helped me, though. I never did anything stupid again. I got into trouble, but not for petty shit like drinking.

10

THE KIND OF ATTENTION that I was getting was making me paranoid among Party members. Every time I went to Oakland for PE class, I thought other comrades were looking at me like a troublemaker and one who had special privileges because I was from LA. The new OD, a brother named Bubba, told me he thought I got off light because Masai had intervened. That really made me think: why would the minister of education of the BPP get involved with a rank-and-file member who had been charged with several small violations? So when Masai showed up at one of our homes in San Francisco wanting to talk to me, I figured I was going to find out.

He was accompanied by a brother named Harold "Poison" Holmes, formerly of the New Orleans chapter. Masai told me that the Servant wanted to create a specific unit in the BPP that dealt only with security, street operations, and the "sterner stuff"—Huey's term for organized violence.

"You know, 'rade, of all of the people here," he said, "you are the one that we actually know the most about. I have been researching all of the qualified brothers and sisters, and every time I get back to you. You don't carry as much baggage as others. We trained you, so we know you have a sense of the type of street operation and evasion tactics we use. You participated in those sophisticated tunneling operations in LA, and you have had some weapons training and we know you can use them with proficiency. You have worked in almost every program the BPP has created, and you are one of the people who doesn't think you should be placed on the central committee because you consistently sell over a hundred papers when you go in the field." All three of us laughed at his last remark. No one, and I mean no one, had ever said this much good shit about me in my entire life. It sounded great.

"Flores, you grew up around us. I told the Servant that you were one of the people we should recruit because I can vouch for you as not being the police, a fool, or an agent provocateur."

"What about the stuff I just got into?" I said.

"That ain't shit compared to some of the shit these other niggers get into around here who are twice as old as you and act like they're younger than you are, 'rade. Listen, brother, you need to get your belongings and be ready to leave tomorrow. When the regular transportation leaves here in the morning, you be on it and tell them to drop you at Sixty-first Street in North Oakland. That's where the security cadre's dorm is. You got that?"

"Right on," I said. And then they left.

This was not what I had wanted or had in mind as far as my desire to serve and work for the betterment of my people. I saw myself working in the survival programs and just being another rank-and-file member of the BPP. I had heard jealous rumblings from brothers in the past who thought they'd been overlooked and should be in charge of this or in charge of that. They would criticize everything they saw going on, you know, like "I would do this that way, and so-and-so shouldn't be involved in that because of this and that." These were the would-be experts who didn't get a break. Now I was being chosen over many others who probably thought I was the wrong person on whom to bestow so much responsibility. I couldn't think of turning it down. I tossed and turned that night. My discussion with Masai had sealed my fate. I was committed now and there was no turning back. I was being chosen to serve in the most serious capacity in the BPP. I would be known for the rest of my life in the BPP as one of the people who dealt with military stuff. Masai was telling me, at this time in my life, the winter of 1972, that I was part of the Black Panther Party's best and brightest and that my services were needed, which meant that I would more than likely die as a Panther or go to jail for life or disappear as a fugitive never to be heard from again. I was young. I heard what he said but had no way of ever comprehending what the consequences of my decision would be. One way or another, I was doomed.

• • • I was transferred back across the bay. My new quarters doubled as a living and training facility. We had several bedrooms on the first floor, living room, bathroom, and kitchen. Masai had converted the basement into a soundproof indoor shooting range where we practiced every morning and on most evenings with primed practice ammo.

For the rest of my life in the BPP, this unit would be my only area of work and concern. Masai was taking me under his wing. Wherever he went, I went. When he had discussions with the top brass, they did not ask me to leave the room. I was privy to all of the heaviest stuff going on in the BPP. But first Masai made me hit the books.

He used to say that it was ridiculous for us to have guerrilla operatives who did not understand what we were trying to do. We needed to know the reason why we were fighting, not just how to fight. Everything we did, everything we read and studied, was geared toward some type of futuristic belief in an armed struggle that would be waged in secret while the Party continued to develop its political base of support through the electoral process and by other means. Some of the literature we read—Mao, for example—contained platitudes that were easily transferable to action-motivating phrases. Masai pointed out that we read this stuff to know the reason why and understand the ideology, and that we should not get too caught up with it because it was not our motivating factor. He said that to know for us meant only that we could explain why we squeezed the trigger and nothing else. Knowing why we needed to use force at any point was the most important lesson the books could teach us. Most of what we studied by Karl Marx, Vladimir ction with one foot in front of the other. He slowly squeezed the trigger, while tak-

I. Lenin, Mao Tse-tung, Che Guevara, Frantz Fanon, W. E. B. Du Bois, Malcolm X, and Marcus Garvey never really dealt with political violence the way we saw it. They were broad, worldly, and philosophical, to say the least, and on top of that, boring. But they were instructive. As Masai used to say, "Ours is the reason why, and we must also do and die."

Historically, the weapons of choice in the BPP had been the riot shotgun, automatic rifles, and various handguns. The training most of us received in the Party was in using these weapons. Because we needed to adapt to a more urban type of security operation that included protecting political candidates like Bobby and Elaine, the handgun was being emphasized more than ever.

During one of our early PE sessions, Masai handed out a beige hardcover book that was by some police-looking guy named Weaver. Masai told us to turn to certain pages and instructed us to read those sections pertaining to the "Weaver Stance." Masai said, "Now, 'rades, this may look like some police shit, which it is. But, as some of you may realize, the police are some of the best combat-handgun-shooting motherfuckers in the world. This is the same book they use, and it is the one you all will be taught from." He paused and walked away from us and dropped his book, reached into his open shirt, spun around, and drew his revolver in a lightning-fast motion while taking a shooting stance with one foot in front of the other. He slowly squeezed the trigger, while taking in a half breath. After he squeezed off the empty chamber, he quickly holstered his gun and looked at all of us through his octagon-shaped glasses and said, "Comrades, what you just saw was the proper use of the Weaver Stance." The Weaver Stance was for close-quarter combat handgun shooting, which meant that your intended target was ten to twenty-five feet away. It is a purely defensive move. This new technique was replacing some of the old-school belief in the sawed-off shotgun that Geronimo had said was for fighting in close quarters like phone booths and locker rooms.

We were all very excited as Masai worked with us individually on developing our personal technique in adapting this shooting stance. We learned the basics of drawing and what position gave us the best advantage, whether it was forward rake or backward rake. We spent hours working on the proper grip while pointing our weapons, always saying to ourselves "push and pull" and checking the placement of our hands, while at the same time taking in half a breath and letting it out. Many times, while practicing our stances, we would try to push each other over backward, a sure indication of a good firm stance or a shaky one. And then there was the draw. We used two types of holsters in the beginning: strapped to the belt or shoulder holsters. Masai had us practicing for hours in the morning and hours in the evening, sighting in with both eyes open so that we could see our entire field of fire. We would then go downstairs to the soundproof indoor range and practice dry firing before we loaded our weapons with simulated bullets that were plastic, with a small amount of gunpowder and a primed cap that made a sharp report but did little to simulate the recoil of the handgun. The plastic bullets did, however, land true to aim and technique.

After weeks of this instruction, we went to the live gun ranges to fine-tune our technique. Getting to the range would be difficult in the future, but we all continued to practice for hours every day of the week. As I practiced, I began to think about what was happening to me. My confidence was growing. I wasn't getting cocky; Masai wouldn't let that happen. But I was getting sure of myself in a quick-draw kind of way. I got better and better, and as that happened, Masai would let me lead class and discuss various points he had relayed to me in private. The little bit of fear that I used to always have began to dissipate, which caused me to view my new role with a serious attitude that I had never felt before.

Masai didn't just train us how to shoot, he also drilled weapon theory and safety into us. There were countless stories in the BPP of people accidentally shooting people or themselves because they didn't know jack shit about gun safety. We practiced gun safety to a fault, because as Masai constantly reminded us, "This is your job in the Party, so get good at it, because the central committee and the Servant have big plans for this new unit."

During one of the many informal discussion periods we had with Masai, when there was no book involved, he began to explain what this was all about and what the historical context was that we were operating in. He began by breaking down the Party's military history into three distinct periods: 1966 to 1969, 1970 to 1972, and a period that he called the dawning of the Buddha Samurai. Masai spoke in a deep bass voice with long pauses, during which he was putting together his next protracted statement. He said, "You know, 'rades, this is the first time that we have had you all organized into a cohesive unit that is responsible only to the minister of defense." I was a little shocked to hear Masai refer to Huey as the minister of defense because we had stopped using those military titles a few years back. (I surmised that in this branch of the BPP the title was appropriate.) "Flores, you are from LA; Perkins, you are from Chicago; Calvert, Phyllis, and Mojo are from Oakland; Philip and Brenda are from San Francisco; Poison and Betty are from New Orleans; and none of you comrades can recall an organized effort outside of the initial stuff the Servant was doing around 1966 to 1967."

He paused. "And that was theater, to attract people's attention and to organize them around point number seven of our program. From 1966 to 1969 could be called the years of education, with the armed patrols, Sacramento and Seventh, and Willow. The later years of that period resembled 'cow shit and gun smoke,' with big shoot-outs and heavy loss of life. And comrades, believe me—only a little bit of that shit was organized guns and stuff. You know, we had glorified niggers with titles like field marshal, defense captain, and all kinds of niggers who became jackanapes, fools, agents provocateurs, and what have you. But there was no organized central effort that trained people in the arts of war, organized people, and gave them a firm grasp of the Party's ideology and philosophy.

"Now, from 1970 to 1972, things began to open up and change because Huey got out of prison, which meant that the Chief didn't have to do all of this shit by his lonesome anymore. But as you all know, we retreated. We stopped talking about killing the pigs, and then the Hidden Traitor Renegade Scab showed his true colors and most of the so-called guerrilla types left the Party with him. Some of them were experienced weapons people, but they were not organized, and I place the emphasis on *organized* from here on out. The next period after 1972 is one of regrouping, or, as we put it on a mass level, 'returning to the original vision of the Party.' Between us, it's the beginning of the Buddha Samurai. Things got away from us, they got out of hand until 1972. Huey had said we don't know what we have as a Party, so let's find out who all of these niggers are. And that's when we started our long retreat, closing down chapters and branches, and bringing everybody here so that we could establish Oakland as the base of operations. Shit, before we did that, the Party was this national phenomenon, made up of twenty to forty chapters and branches of people who didn't know each other. That's not how this is supposed to be. How in the hell could we fight a war without knowing who we are and without having one centralized location to train people as a jumping-off point? As urban guerrillas, we must have a face-to-face relationship with each other, not some ridiculous long-distance relationship. We were doing this ass backwards, and now we got at least the first part right again. Now we have organized guns that can respond to one voice and not twenty or thirty individual bands under the guise of chapters and branches, half of which were probably organized by the police." Masai stopped and looked at each of us and said, "Don't forget this, because this is why you are here and why you have been asked to sacrifice so much."

11

THE MAJOR ASSIGNMENT of the unit officially named the security cadre was the protection of the Party's leaders running for political office and the protection of Huey P. Newton. However, Masai told me in private that we were being trained for a larger role in the Party's five-year plan to take over the city of Oakland. We were to be the shock troops that fired the first shots against the drug dealers whom Huey wanted to tax and regulate. But this would be only if they resisted the Servant's tax policy.

Anyway, the tactic we used to protect Chairman Bobby, Elaine, and Huey could be described as "shadow" or "stealth" security. This was around 1972. We began working on changing our image in the early 1970s and our individual appearances. We realized that we had alienated parts of the community with our rhetoric, bravado, and just outright bad behavior. So we stopped wearing the garb that was deemed the clothing of the revolutionary. We shed our black leather jackets, field jackets, jungle boots, buttons, and all things associated with the media's stereotypical picture of us. The brothers who had earrings had to stop wearing them, including me. And if you were one of those Panthers who wore a .50-caliber shell around your neck, well, that had to go. We began to dress like the masses so that we could blend in. The uniforms and other garish outfits may have been fine in the beginning, but we were settling down to business, so we had to get serious about the whole idea of fighting this revolution to win.

So this blending-in concept was the basic premise behind our shadow security. When Bobby and Elaine showed up at a candidate's night or event or at just another speaking engagement, the chairman was wearing a suit and tie and Elaine was suited and booted in a dress, heels, the whole nine yards. Their personal security people would also be dressed in suits, ties, et cetera. (BPP personal security personnel were often described by Huey P. Newton as decoys for lurking assassins. This was part of his sinister tactical mind that had to grow on you.) And the retinue of campaign workers would be dressed similarly while they distributed campaign literature and sold papers that offered campaign themes. But among the crowds or strategically seated in the auditorium would be the security cadre. We would usually be in couples. Sometimes several brothers and sisters would behave as if they were single, just enjoying a campaign night out on the town. We were inconspicuous until something happened. We then moved quickly to intervene. We wore suits, other casual wear, and dresses and carried cameras, but in their purses the sisters were packing their pistols. On hot days the sisters would hold all of the hardware in their purses so that we could discard our coats and not look out of place. Only the chairman, Elaine, the campaign manager, Herman Smith, and the Panthers who were campaign workers knew who we really were.

In several instances the chairman had received a credible threat against his life, so one of us was assigned as the designated shooter just in case we had to take someone out. If something went down, the person had an escape route and the number of Jimmy Johnson in LA. Once he got to the airport, he would call Jimmy, who would place him in the underground network he had set up down south. We had to use this system only once, but it didn't involve the chairman or the campaign. There were a few snags, but everything eventually worked out and the brother was able to return to the Bay Area about a year after the incident. As Masai would always say, "You can never plan too much." The planning part was important for us because living in America, with all of the surveillance and suspicion accorded black people with guns, we didn't have much of an opportunity to rehearse what we did.

Now, when it came to protecting the Servant, well, that was an entirely different set of circumstances from the average shadow security situation. We would shadow Huey in the speakeasies, nightclubs, and close-circuit boxing matches at local theaters, and sometimes in barbershops. One day I remember Masai getting a phone call from Huey's secretary, Gwen Fontaine, his future wife, notifying us that the Servant was going to this particular barbershop that was frequented by some of the drug dealers we were targeting. (Later on we thought that some of these same guys were behind the contract put out on the Servant.) Masai got the time and location and assigned the Duke to this detail. The Duke arrived at the barbershop before Robert Bay and Huey. Anyway, the Duke reported that he was strapped into the barber chair when the Servant and Rob made their usual grand entrance through the door.

• • • "Excuse me, but management wants you to leave," Masai said in a deep voice as he stood behind the brother during a role-playing session. He repeated the command and stepped away from the brother, favoring his gun hand. We were seated in a circle at our dorm, getting instructions from Masai about our next long assignment. The Party owned a restaurant lounge in a fashionable area of downtown Oakland on Telegraph Avenue.

"The Servant spends a great deal of time at the Lamp Post," Masai said. "It is also frequented by many of the drug dealers and other people in the life that we are leaning on. He wants us to secure the location. Technically, we will be the club's bouncers. Actually, we are being placed there to defend our turf should any one of them niggers think about attacking our establishment in retaliation for what we plan to do in North Oakland and South Berkeley. When you are placing someone under arrest and kicking them outside of the club, the phrase I just used with the brother is what you should begin with. If they do not respond, step back and away from them so that they will see your backup. If they still do not respond, you have a couple of options. You can take hold of them firmly if you're sure they are not armed. If they appear to be armed, you must disarm them. You can pull your weapon and make them spread-eagle for a search, or you have the option of taking immediate action by busting them upside the head with a sap, aka blackjack. Try not to use your pistol because it's for shooting, not hitting, people. Also, many of you carry buck knives. You can place the open end of the blade under their armpit and ever so gently push up, applying pressure. Or if you feel fit enough, as I know many of you do, you can apply some of the holds I taught you or just beat them down. Remember, try to move the instigator away from most of the patrons. Going outside is not good because we won't be on our property. Also the OPD watches the club on a regular basis." Masai paused and asked if there were any questions. No one said a word. We just looked at one another.

I raised my hand and asked, "What are the rules for engagement? I mean—"

Masai cut me off with a wave of his hand. "I know what you mean, Comrade Flores." He continued, "Every situation will probably be different. If someone reaches for your weapon, you have the authority to take them out. If someone is making a move on someone in the leadership, or, for that matter, a rank-and-file Panther, you can take them out. The standard operating procedure if that happens is for you to leave the post and go to the nearest safe house. Call the number you all have for JJ in LA and wait for us to move you out of the city. Everyone understand this?"

"Right on," we all said.

"Good. Now, there's two more things. First, if there's a robbery attempt, we always take the robbery, we'll find out who's responsible later on. Don't jeopardize any lives if you don't have to. And second, Flores is going to show us the hand signals we will use while we're in the Post. Everyone, including the Servant and Big Rob, will be briefed on these signals."

I got up and began explaining the hand signals when the Duke interrupted, "Where do these hand signals come from?"

"Church," I said. It got completely quiet. Masai snickered, and everyone else joined in, as did I. "Look," I said, "when I was growing up, I was in the usher board at church, and this is how we communicated during the services. I think they're effective, and this way we won't have to walk up to each other to say certain things. You see, when I touch the knotted area under my neck, that tells everyone to pay attention because I'm about to give you a signal. One finger means I need your help. Two fingers could mean the Servant's on the move toward the men's room, or if he's there and Big Rob's out of position, the Servant could give you the signal that he's heading to the men's room. And three fingers can mean something else, so on and so forth. Each day we can change the meaning so we don't develop a pattern if someone's casing us." All the brothers and sisters smiled in agreement.

The Lamp Post was like a Wild West saloon. We began working two shifts, morning and evening. And it didn't take long for me to see why we were there. Instead of crazy cowboys, cattle rustlers, and gunslingers passing through, there were pimps and players, drug dealers, professional gamblers, and stickup men, and just about every crazy motherfucker found his way into the club, apparently trying to show us that they were badass motherfuckers too. But this was our spot and we clamped down real hard. The shit was pure madness. Every nigger and his momma came to the Lamp Post acting crazy, and they all got the same treatment. I think I must have repeated the phrase "Management wants you to leave" a thousand times. And as Masai thought, this was an excellent training ground. We pistol-whipped niggers, undercover cops—it didn't matter. If you broke the law in the Lamp Post, your ass was grass. We had the place covered. There was a rover who circulated in the bar and restaurant areas on the first floor and mezzanine. In the kitchen, Mojo was a cook with his Colt .44 Magnum stashed in one of his pots, and some of the brothers bused tables as their cover. Sometimes we were there in couples or in full force for large Party functions.

But to me the best time was always had when the Servant showed up. I had seen him at a distance in 1971 during a large rally at the Oakland Auditorium and during several of the shadow security details. But when he came to the Post, I got one-on-one interaction with him. When he entered the club, whether you were facing the door or not, you knew it. He may not have liked speaking to large crowds from a podium, but the Lamp Post was his own personal stage. He knew many of the regulars from Oakland and the surrounding areas and often hosted his meetings at the club, talking loud and loving every moment. On several occasions he would meet with his allies from the street. Players like the Ward brothers, Frank and Buddy Bouisaire, Wilbert Latoure, and a professional gambler who also befriended me, named Cle Givens.

Masai and Poison were gone. Masai had some major differences with Huey, and they resulted in his demotion and transfer to the underground operation in LA. After a few weeks in LA, Masai left. I never knew the details of his falling-out with Huey and I never asked, but for the rest of my time in the BPP, I was indebted to his tutelage. And as for Poison, he was transferred and appointed the central headquarters OD. A few months after his reassignment, Poison had a mental breakdown and shot a one-legged man in front of central headquarters. He was subsequently convicted and sent to prison.

A few days after Masai and Poison were transferred in the fall of 1972, Robert Bay and John Seale came by to tell me that the Servant had appointed me the new head of security for the Black Panther Party. I was twenty years old.

12

I RECEIVED THE FIRST of what would become many phone calls from Huey's aide-de-camp/bodyguard Robert Bay. Rob said, "Fly, I'm on the car phone just down the street. Meet me out front in five minutes."

"Right on," I said. I was a little uneasy when I got into Rob's car because he had called me Fly. I didn't know what that meant. I got ready, strapping on my shoulder holster, which held my .45 automatic.

I liked Big Bay, especially because he remembered me from when we first met back in 1968. That was important, because most of the brothers in the Party were older than me and I'm sure most of them thought I was too young to be in such a prestigious position. That went double for the brothers in the security cadre. The BPP was a young person's haven and I was going to take advantage of every opportunity that came my way, especially an opportunity to work closely with Huey P. Newton. Elaine always said Huey knew only five or ten people in the Party by name. Well, I was one of them.

Rob looked like a big, light-skinned Buddha with a full beard. I asked him why he called me Fly. "That's what the Servant calls you, brother. He gets reports on you guys from all over the place, on operations, from niggers on the street, what have you. He likes your work, thinks you're what a real Panther should be like." He glanced at me when he said

WILL YOU DIE WITH ME?

that. "You got a lot of juice, young brother, and a lot of people think you're out of your league. But what matters is what the Servant thinks. Right on?"

"Right on," I said.

"Huey thinks you're a pretty cool customer, so he started calling you 'Fly' back when Masai was pushing you to be groomed for the top spot to replace Poison." I didn't respond but thought, That's why Poison used to treat me funny.

So while we're driving, Rob starts to tell me what the deal is. "There was an attempt on the Servant's life two days ago. He wasn't home, but [his wife] Gwen and Kathy, his niece, were there when they came in with ski masks, silencers on their pieces, and other stuff. Gwen faked like she was fainting and they kind of freaked and left. The Servant has a plan and he wants to talk it over with you. Besides, you're one of us now. Like me, John, and June, we're the guys who call all of the shots on the military side, and now you are the point man, Fly."

Man, was I flattered. To be ranked in the same category as the chief of staff, assistant chief of staff, and Big Rob. It made me feel uncomfortable, too, because there were dozens of brothers with serious experience from Vietnam in the Party. I'm sure they felt passed over. I needed to adjust because in the BPP, once you were headed for the top, you either accepted the praise and glory or you got dumped on for being ungrateful or just plain old yellow, a coward.

When we arrived at the Servant's housing complex at 1200 Lakeshore Drive, Rob pulled the car into the cavernous parking garage below the complex. We went up on the elevator, getting off on the twenty-fourth floor, and took the back stairs to the Servant's apartment on the twenty-fifth floor. Rob knocked on the door using some kind of code, and the Servant opened up with a huge smile on his face and a handgun in one hand.

"How are you, comrade?" he asked.

"I'm fine, Servant, just fine," I replied.

"Good, come in and take a seat."

Huey ushered us into his living room and offered us places at a long glass table in the dining room. This was a spacious penthouse that had received a great deal of publicity because it was costing the Party close to $650 a month to rent. The ceilings were high, and the living room was adorned with two large white leather couches and a matching pair of lounge chairs. The entire living room and dining room were bordered with a sliding glass door that led to a terrace overlooking Lake Merritt and the port of Oakland. Near the glass door facing the port of Oakland was a high-powered telescope. There were two bedrooms and a library.

He was in great shape, still cut from the weight training in prison. His hair was in cornrows, and he was sporting a five o'clock shadow. Huey sat opposite me while Robert Bay sat in a chair at the head of the table. Huey said, "Comrade, brother, do you know why you have been chosen for this dangerous assignment?" I thought he asked this not expecting me to really explain, so I just said, "No." I was kind of nervous because it did seem that my ascension had been fast. I still had my doubts about my own ability. But I tried not to show it.

"You have been chosen because you are part of the 'old guard,' one of the 'chosen ones.' " He paused to take a drag from his cigarette. "Years ago, in biblical times, a noted general was summoned by his king who told him, 'I want you to select the most dedicated soldiers from your ranks to perform a perilous and dangerous mission that they may not return from alive. The men selected will be given a place of honor and be called the chosen ones.' The general said to the king, 'My Lord, how shall I choose these men?' "

Huey stood up and walked, gesticulating and smoking a cigarette while glancing out his window. "The king told him to assemble all of his troops and to conduct a forced march to the River Jordan." He then stopped and adjusted a weird-looking picture of a Black Buddha Samurai before he continued. "So you see, Fly, the general assembles his troops and takes them on this forced march to the River Jordan, but he doesn't know that the enemy awaits their arrival on the opposite side of the river. When the troops arrive in three days' time, they are totally exhausted. When they see the river, they break ranks and run toward salvation and a cool drink of water. But some, as they reach the water, fall face-first into the river"—Huey made this gurgling sound like he was drinking water—"paying no attention to the enemy on the other side. But a small group approaches the river cautiously, kneeling on one knee, and, while keeping one eye on the enemy, they use the other to watch the water as they use one hand to scoop the water and drink vigilantly. The king tells the general, 'Those men who fell face-first into the water are just volunteers, while the soldiers who took a knee and scooped with one hand while watching the enemy are the 'chosen ones.' " Huey stopped, looked at me, and said, "Comrade, you are the 'chosen one.' "

Huey then said, "Now, comrade, this is the situation. OPD Chief Charles R. Gaines called Charles Garry [the Party's criminal lawyer] and told him the speakeasy owners, drug dealers, et al., have placed a ten-thousand-dollar contract on my head." He stopped and looked at Robert Bay, continuing in this whining theatrical voice, "They waited until we left and broke in on my wife, Gwen, and niece, Kathy, who passed out from the sight of men with masks, guns with silencers, and shiny white teeth glowing through the openings in their masks. Next time you will be here to greet them when they come. I believe the guy next door was involved, and the trap will be set with my best soldier as the cheese in the mousetrap. I think they plan to break into the house while I'm gone and intend to lay in wait for me to return. So every time I leave my house, you will be summoned to set the trap and lay in wait for them—the rats—to return."

We assessed the situation: we would come in the back so the guy next door couldn't see us entering. I would come in that way every time I came here, and Huey would leave out the front, making it appear that no one was home. Sounded real risky, but I thought I was ready. "Yes, Servant, I'm down with the mousetrap."

He said, "Good, I'm down too."

I would lay in wait for the next six months as the cheese in the mousetrap, armed with a riot eighteen-inch shotgun loaded with Magnum 3" 00 buck. The funny thing, though, was that half of the time, Huey never left. He would stay after I arrived and talk. We talked or I listened to him talk about the revolution, books, the Party, Bunchy Carter, Seventh and Willow, and almost every interesting subject under the sun. Sometimes when he did leave, he would return with all kinds of people and would always insist that I stay. He brought back newspaper reporters and others, including writer James Baldwin, movie producer Bert Schneider, and actors Candace Bergen, Marlon Brando, Warren Beatty, and a host of other celebrities who just happened to be hanging out with him. He also gave me access to his library, which stimulated my interest in reading Jean-Paul Sartre, Albert Camus, Plato, Baldwin, and a host of new writers I never would have known about otherwise. I was as close to the Servant as he would allow one of his soldiers to be. Anyway, the gunmen I was waiting for never came back.

• • • Most of the time spent at the Servant's house was not related to the mousetrap but rather to brainstorming some aspect of the Party agenda. The topics were often broad, but the most discussed was the plan to take over the city of Oakland, followed by how to regulate the illegitimate capitalists—the theme of an original essay by Huey in which he discussed organized crime in the black community—while at the same time coming as close to destroying them as possible without depleting their revenue stream. These strategy sessions were usually attended by the chief of staff, June Hilliard. He was a mild-mannered Manchurian-type administrator who was really nice to me but could unleash the wolves on one of these dope dealers and not bat an eye. John Seale, who was the assistant chief of staff, was also mild-mannered, but the 9mm he strapped to his side suggested that he saved niceties for his comrades, not his enemies. Robert Bay, the Servant's trusty bodyguard, was ever-present but quiet. He would sit like a silent Buddha during these sessions. And there were always others who were part of the Servant's extraordinary forces, like Big Booker, his bodyguard from the penal colony and now his scout and point man for all matters related to the street operations. The Bishop would also be present. He was from San Francisco and led a group of followers who worshiped musician John Coltrane.

The menu at these sessions was a steady diet of cocaine, cognac, and cigarettes. Huey didn't smoke weed, like most of us, because he said it made him paranoid. Anyway, most of the time he talked about the plan to take over the city of Oakland and other territories nearby, like the speakeasies and drug dens in South Berkeley. We would sit around while Huey roamed the house telling long, intricate stories that always led to a fascinating climax. Often the stories ended with some unsuspecting soul getting mud-holed or shock-a-boo-cooed.

There was this one time when the house manager of the Fox Theater was up at the house trying to cut some kind of a deal with Huey. This was the first time I saw the shock-a-boo-coo. This was during the period when the Party had a lease at the entertainment venue from which we showed movies and were planning to bring in live performances once we bought the place, which was the Servant's intention. I think this guy's name was Claude. He was short and dark and thought he was big shit. He was invited up to the Servant's house after running into him at the Lamp Post. He insisted that Huey had accepted him as a member of the Party. Huey said, "Well, comrade, we need to initiate you with the sacred ceremony so that you will be a trusted warrior incognito." When I heard that, I looked over at June, John, and Big Rob to gauge their reaction. They were stoned-faced but began to dress right (military style) behind Huey. They took out their weapons and crossed their arms with their handguns in their hands. Huey looked at me with those large deep eyes and motioned for me to take out my gun and walk over to Claude, who was kneeling in front of Huey, as he had been instructed to. Huey instructed me to place my gun at Claude's head. Then he began a long, unintelligible incantation about the street gods and black warrior trustees who looked over living Panthers and helped dead Panthers who were in purgatory because they were too tough for hell. At the end of this long spiel, Huey motioned his head at me and looked down at my .45 auto. I wasn't sure what he meant, but it appeared that he wanted me to cock my weapon. So that was what I did. He quickly moved my gun away from the man's head and pointed for me to go sit down. He lifted Claude, who was shaking from head to toe. He welcomed Claude as the newest member of the BPP and told Big Rob to give him a ride home.

Huey started laughing and looked at June and John, who were also cracking up. Huey came over to me and said, "What were you doing, comrade?"

I paused, then said, "I thought you were motioning for me to cock my gun."

"No," Huey said, waving his arms. "No, comrade brother, that's not what I wanted. Besides, what did you think of what just happened?"

"Well, I assume this guy will be working undercover for us or something because of the secret initiation." Man, let me tell you, that brought down the house. Huey turned around and started laughing again, as did June and John.

"This brother is okay. June, John, just what we thought, the brother's pure to the bone," he said to the now seated but hysterical pair of Panther officials. Huey said to me, "So, superfly, have you ever been through this ritual before?"

"No, I haven't."

He turned to June and John and asked them, and still laughing, they shook their heads. "Flores," Huey said, "the reason why you haven't been through this ritual is because you are a trusted member of the fold, the old guard, and a Buddha Samurai. We don't know what's-his-name, and the nigger won't be working for us besides working at the Fox. Look, Flores, rituals are for people we don't trust. The nigger wants in on the stern stuff, so why not do something to use him and make him think he's one of us. But remember, comrade, he will never be one of you." Three days later I got an assignment to publicly mud-hole old Claude at the theater because the nigger was running around town telling everyone who would listen that he was a secret member of the BPP. In addition, our negotiations to buy the theater went sour, so we burned the motherfucker down.

It was also during one of these sessions that I learned the real reason we were reading the novel *The Godfather*, by Mario Puzo. Huey thought it was important that we have an operational model for the Buddha Samurai that would protect the chain of command if we were infiltrated or an operation got botched. He didn't want the trail of evidence leading back to 1200 Lakeshore. He said we needed these buffers to protect our lines of communications in an urban setting. So he explained to me that when I got an assignment, it would never come directly from him. We discussed this so that I wouldn't believe it was mistrust on his part. I returned to the penthouse on a few more occasions. But as things on the street heated up, I was there less and less. This turned out to be a good thing in the long run. When the war on the street was at its highest level, I received all of my operational orders from June, John, or Big Rob. The Servant and I never talked about doing anything to anyone after this period.

13

T HE PARTY'S FORAY INTO electoral politics that began in 1972 started to pick up momentum. The polls showed that Bobby was a serious threat to the Republican incumbent, John Reading. Implementation of the five-year plan on the street side was kicking into high gear. Although the cadre probably numbered about a dozen trained Panthers at this time, only three of us—Mojo, Perkins, and me—were involved early on when it came to dealing with the Oakland underworld or the illegitimate capitalist on the streets. Our extraordinary forces or unofficial combatants comprised just one person: Big Booker.

Big Booker, once the Servant's bodyguard in prison, was a large, dark-skinned fifty-year-old man with huge hands. He reminded me of the dark-skinned Geechee Men in Job Corps, from North Carolina. He had been involved with the street life in the Bay Area for years and knew about most of the major drug operations in Oakland and Berkeley. Whenever I got an operation that involved this area they would always tell me to hook up with Booker because he had the details on the people, places, or things.

Maurice Powell, aka Mojo, was a longtime Panther military operative. He was now the Party armorer, which meant that he knew where all of the guns were stashed. When I needed to put together an operation, I had to work with Mojo to get the right TE for the job. He was a Vietnam combat veteran who was very tight with the Hilliards. He was short, rail-thin, and he used to wear this long black topcoat and a big floppy hat. He resembled a nineteenth-century gunman because under his coat, strapped to his hip, was a long .44 Magnum, single-action Colt revolver that he handled with the ease and skill of a professional gunslinger. At the firing range, while only using one hand, Mojo was constantly in the black and on target.

Darren Perkins, aka the Duke, was also a Vietnam combat veteran, who seemed not to have gotten enough of combat during his two tours. He was short, dark, and had little beady eyes and a big smile that flashed a set of perfect white teeth. He always wore sunglasses and was a very natty dresser who could recite Edgar Allan Poe's "Annabelle Lee" verbatim. This was the team set up to enforce our policy against the pimps, drug dealers, and any other motherfuckers who got in our way.

There was clearly a compartmentalization of the work with regard to our street activities. There were different people who dealt with the dealers and even dealt drugs. I knew them but never was involved with their activities unless they needed firepower and backup. And there were people involved with collecting the money the drug dealers were paying as part of a tax we levied. The going rate was constant, at 23 percent of their gross. Once after the Lamp Post was closed, Robert Bay had me meet him there to receive one of the big payments. This guy knocked on the Lamp Post's large wooden door around three in the morning. Rob had me stand at the ready with a riot shotgun as the guy passed a bundle of cash through the cracked door. I never asked any questions, nor did I want to get involved with other Party business related to our street operations. My job concerned enforcement.

When we began our crackdown, the calls from my messengers, June, John, and Robert Bay, came early in the morning and often. The drug dealers along Shattuck, Sacramento, Telegraph, and San Pablo avenues thought it was going to be business as usual once the message for them to pay tithes or taxes came down from 1200 Lakeshore. The team I normally went out with consisted of Mojo, Perkins, and Big Booker. Sometimes, though, the teams varied with the demands of the operation, special knowledge of the situation, or the whims of Huey P. Newton. I can remember only one large operation—when Huey wanted to send a specific message to the largest speakeasy on San Pablo, a placed called the Black Knight. We swarmed the place. Huey was inside with June, Big Rob, and about ten other Panthers. We stopped all business while the Servant read the owners, Cole and Larry, the riot act. Most of these niggers had never seen this many black men with guns carrying out a disciplined operation against them. They were defenseless against us. To whom could they go for support? As the Servant used to say, "They can't call the police."

There were some who took the position that they would rather go to war with the Black Panther Party than pay them. On Shattuck Avenue, just up the street from where the BPP used to have its national headquarters, was a big speakeasy with a mezzanine that was usually manned by about six or seven heavily armed gunmen who stood around with shotguns and other long weapons, gazing down at the patrons milling around on the first floor buying cocaine in little packets and sniffing their dope on the bottoms of large tissue boxes. These niggers said it would be a cold day in hell before they conceded to pay tithes to the Party.

Mojo, me, and three other brothers planned this operation as a team. We would use two rented cars. Mojo and a driver would pull up in front of the joint with an AK-47 and stitch a neat little pattern across the top floor, where the gunmen would be positioned. I would be in the second car for backup with an M16 and the other brothers with two riot shotguns.

We arrived at about three in the morning and the joint was jumping. I positioned my car on a street that was maybe a hundred feet from a street perpendicular to Shattuck. It was dark on this side street, so we were able to leave the car and crouch in the bushes nearby. We left our trunk open. Mojo and his driver pulled up in front of the club. Mojo stepped out of the car and walked to the middle of the street. His silhouette was eerie. Dressed in that long coat and large floppy hat, he was holding an automatic weapon in one hand and a cigarette in the other. He threw the cigarette in the street and stomped on it. He raised his weapon and the muzzle began flashing with a delayed report. We could see the impact as the bullets hit the club, shattering the silence outside. He was laying down tracks from one end of the club to the other. He stopped, flipped the banana clips, and continued shooting. The stampede began. Just as he jumped into his waiting car, people came bursting out of the front door running in these low crouches. Mojo's driver hit the gas and turned sharply onto the street where we were parked. We had moved to the corner, covering them as they drove up. Mojo jumped from his car and threw the AK-47 into the open trunk of our car. He jumped back into his car and sped off. We waited for a few more seconds as I surveyed the situation, taking careful note of the damage and the chaos. From this moment forward, they paid on time.

Some of the operations were more up close and personal. For example, I was assigned to harass, rob, and immobilize, if necessary, a specific drug dealer and his operation in South Berkeley. His house was a drug distribution center for a major cocaine dealer. This was not his primary base, so we didn't expect him to be there. We merely wanted to send him a message. If he failed to respond by making his payments, we would send a second message. If he ignored that, the third message would put them out of business and open the way for someone with more respect for the order of things. Big Booker knew the dealer and the location. I told him what we were meant to do so he could suggest an appropriate time to hit the location. Booker said he could get us in by just knocking on the door, but we needed to be nearby to get in. He also told me that this wasn't a heavily armed or fortified drug house. I decided I would take Big Booker and the Duke. I met with Big Rob to discuss the operation so I could get some perspective on our operating procedures for this one. How much latitude did the Duke and I have to deal with this guy if he disobeyed our orders to raise his hands, for example, or drop to the floor? In other words, what happens when the dude we're confronting challenges us or, as Masai used to say, takes those actions that "alter the scope of the operation"? Could we go beyond harassing and robbing the guy to blowing him away? Message still delivered. Once I got that issue cleared up we were good to go.

We got together the next morning, intent on hitting the pad sometime after noon. According to Booker, the guy who ran this location didn't open or even wake up until noon or 1:00 P.M. I met with Mojo to discuss our armament. I told Mojo the rules of engagement and he gave me two .45s, government-issue 1911s, and said, "Look, youngster, if you guys have to pop this guy, go to the marina—it's just a few blocks away—and deep-six the whole piece."

"Cool," I said. "I understand."

Booker carried a small snub-nosed .38, his personal weapon. If anything went down beyond the projected operation, Booker would not be doing the shooting, we would. That was our, job not his.

The Duke and I were wearing coveralls, and Booker was dressed in his street clothes. "Why you young brothers got them jumpsuits on?" Booker asked.

The Duke and I exchanged glances, and I said, "You know, Booker, just in case."

He made this funny face and said, "The Servant told me you guys were his main street people and that you all did the real dirty work. Don't get me in no mess I don't know about."

"Look, nigger, just get us inside and do what we expect and we will do our job. Got it, brother?"

"Yeah, but—"

Then the Duke cut in, "You heard him, nigger, just open the door and grab the drugs and the money and leave the rest to us." Booker kind of recoiled at that outburst from the Duke and didn't say another word until the operation started.

We parked the car about two blocks from the dope house and quickly walked to it. We weren't concerned with noise because it was a single-family home. Booker knocked on the door. The Duke and I stood on his side closest to the door, out of the view from the peephole. When the victim greeted Booker, Booker hesitated and made some funny body language moves that indicated to us that the nigger was a little nervous.

This alarmed the dealer. He tried to close the door on Booker. The Duke and I rushed the door, bowling over Booker and the drug dealer, who both tumbled to the floor. Once we were inside, the Duke slammed the door shut behind him and pointed his pistol at the hallway and scanned the room. While pointing my gun at the drug dealer, who was backpedaling on the floor, I leaned over to help Booker to his feet.

"Stay right there and don't move again," I said to the dealer, motioning with my gun. I nodded to him and moved my piece up and down for his acknowledgment. He nodded that he understood. I motioned to the Duke, who began to move through the house with his .45 raised in a shooting stance. I motioned for Booker to follow the Duke so that he could find the drugs and money. The dealer lay in front of me, motionless. I stepped back away from him toward the door but kept my gun trained on him. I could hear the Duke searching the rooms and Booker rummaging around looking for the loot. I heard the Duke say, "Fly, it's all clear," and then he shouted, "Fly, look out! She's coming your way!"

I saw a blur run to my right. It was a woman heading full speed to the front door or maybe the front window. The dealer started to get up and caught the heel of my shoe on his face and fell back down. I moved nearer to him in seconds and said, "If you move again, you're dead," pointing my .45 at his temple. He stopped cold. The woman was past me, and the Duke appeared from the hallway with his .45 leveled in a Weaver Stance that spelled death to the woman. I stepped quickly back and to my right, shifting my gun to my left hand while grabbing the woman and throwing her to the floor just near the front window in the living room. "Freeze, bitch," the Duke commanded, and she stopped moving. She pissed on herself right where she was crouching. I looked at the Duke, who had cocked his hammer with the thumb of his pull hand. He slowly lowered it and, in a fit of relief, raised his weapon to the ceiling, signaling to me that this operation would not go into the emergency phase. But as soon as he did that, he walked over to the woman and, with a swift kick, bounced her head off the floor while shouting, "Bitch, don't ever run from me again!" He then turned to the dealer and placed his foot square in his stomach, saying, "You need to show your woman how to act when shit is going down." He abruptly stepped back and trained his weapon on the woman, looking over at me as I shook my head, signifying, "No, Duke, we don't need to do that." He nodded that he understood. I started sweating then. Booker came rushing to the front with this shit-eating grin on his face and one bag full of drugs and another full of cash. The Duke and I agreed that these niggers needed an ass whipping after all of the trouble they had caused us. So we mud-holed them before we left.

As we walked out the door, I leaned down to the dealer and said, "Tell Larry this is just a warning. If he's late next time, he's out of business for good."

Larry paid on time after this.

From 1972 to 1974, I participated in and planned around thirty of these operations. With each one we became more and more efficient. But it was inevitable that something at some point would go wrong and come back to bite us in the ass. When it did, it was a doozy. Ultimately a victim did something that Huey had said they wouldn't do: they called the police. The Oakland Police Department jumped all over the opportunity.

The security cadre had expanded. We had relocated to larger quarters at one of the Party's residences, in East Oakland on Twenty-ninth Street near Fruitvale. This was a large two-story home with about eight bedrooms on the second floor. The first floor was spacious, with two large rooms that were used by the Bobby Seale–Elaine Brown campaign as a war room. We occupied the basement, which had been converted by its previous owner into a family entertainment area. In it we had several beds in rows to sleep on.

About two or three days earlier, a large truck arrived from the East Coast with a shipment of weapons. We unloaded them and Mojo began his inventory. As he completed each listing, we stored the weapons in a small room located in the stairwell next to the basement's entrance. The very next morning the police raided our facility. Mojo had planned to move the weapons the next day, but it was too late. They had identified one of us. I was asleep and I didn't hear the initial phase of the raid. One of the brothers in the cadre woke me up and in turn raised the rest of us. The majority of the cadre was out on the streets or had taken up lodging with their favorite female comrade. So there were only me and four other security personnel present. The majority of the folks in the house were campaign workers. This situation would have a terrible impact on the Party's new image.

The raid began upstairs. We could hear loud radio reports from the police radios outside and the commotion above us on the first floor and see the spiraling lights from police vehicles in the front of the house. Our first reaction was to scramble for our weapons. We didn't have much at this location, just our personal handguns and a few shotguns. But it occurred to me that we were to respond to the police differently, and I sent the message to the others. So we placed our weapons under our beds and hollered upstairs that there were people down here and that we were coming up to surrender. I was the last person upstairs, and when I reached the first floor, I was greeted by a policeman with a riot shotgun pointed at my head. I was searched and cuffed. After a few minutes I was led toward the rest, who were sitting in a circle in one of the large campaign war rooms. There were about fourteen of us, and from what I could determine we were all around the same age, except for two people who were well into their thirties. Everyone was calm. I made eye contact with Phyllis Jackson. Not only was she a member of the cadre but she was working on the campaign as one of the Party's most important coordinators. She was glaring at me, and I tried to avoid her penetrating and knowledgeable look. She knew, even though she spent 100 percent of her time on the campaign, that we had something to do with this raid on her political headquarters.

I hadn't thought of the consequences to the campaign right away. My first thoughts were what would the Servant and the chief say to me. I would be in trouble for the stupid operation that had led the police here, but that wasn't an issue with them or me. I was twenty-one years old and not afraid of the Party's discipline. The Servant, Chief of Staff June Hilliard, Assistant Chief of Staff John Seale, and Robert Bay had never said it directly, but I knew I had become one of the people in the

Party who was special. Or, to put it another way, my mistakes were the cost of our doing business on this scale. The person who was in trouble was the armorer, Mojo. I learned later that it was this type of sloppy work and bad judgment that got Mojo expelled from the Party.

We heard this loud roar from downstairs in the basement. I just dropped my head and said to myself, Damn, they found the shit. The cops were in the basement for what seemed like hours. We had also been seated in this circle for hours when they started coming upstairs with bundles of weapons in their arms. Phyllis looked at me and made this biting movement with her mouth. I think the sister was trying to tell me she wanted to bite my motherfucking head off. The Servant told me when I saw him days later, "Shit like this happens, Fly. Live with it."

Just before they hauled us off to jail, a short, dark-complexioned police officer with captain's bars on his lapel came over with a notepad and starting writing stuff down. He walked around our circle. When he got near me, he looked me in the eye and wrote something down. He was Captain Colletti, the officer in charge of the OPD's Special Response Team. I would see this man many more times in the future.

When we arrived at the jail downtown, we were placed alone in a large cell block. We were charged with possession of illegal weapons and stolen property (some of the weapons were stolen). Our stay was short; we were released in less than a week. The charges were dropped because of the illegal search and seizure of the weapons. The complaint filed due to the botched operation was also dropped. But this incident was not over.

Scrambling to defend the credibility that the Party was gaining due to Bobby's and Elaine's strong campaign runs, a press conference was called. Bobby Seale stepped to the microphone. He was flanked by two large poster boards that displayed identical enlarged pictures of weapons spread out on a table. Bobby pointed to one of the photos and said that that picture showed weapons that were confiscated from a Black Panther Party office in 1969. He then turned to the photo that the OPD had supplied to the press following the raid on Twenty-ninth Street. Bobby said, "If you look closely at this second photo, you will see that it is identical to the first one the police say represents the weapons taken in the raid last week. I contend that both photos represent arms confiscated in raids against the Black Panther Party in 1969. This is a setup to discredit the Black Panther Party's right to participate in a fair election to unseat a notorious and vicious government that has been oppressing black people in this city for decades. I'm telling you, the press, that there were no weapons at Twenty-ninth Street. Just think: the charges were dropped. Case closed." The chairman had made his point and the day was saved once again.

14

THEY SHOWED UP THE WAY they always did, usually in twos but never alone. This was done to keep you off guard so that you wouldn't know if the news was good or bad. This was how both promotions and bad news were handed out in the BPP. Two people would show up at your work assignment or living quarters to discuss something with you. The last time this happened to me, Robert Bay and John Seale showed up. Before that it was Masai and Poison. Robert Bay and John Seale came to Twenty-ninth Street to tell me I was doing a great job and that things were tight in the field and at the Lamp Post, but that I was being temporarily reassigned. They said the chairman was really exposed, with just one person with him all the time. John said, "Carl is a good man, but he's only one person, and because Bobby is in and out of the car at many of these stops, there are times when Carl can't really focus on just looking out for Bobby." The Servant thought the chairman needed more security on the campaign trail, on the street, and at home. I was being assigned to the chairman's security detail until the end of the election. So they told me to pack my shit because I was moving into the chairman's house on Santa Rosa Avenue, which housed Chief of Staff June Hilliard, John Seale, and their respective staffs, including Carl.

Oftentimes my experiences in the BPP felt like I was sleepwalking through a daydream. My mind was being blown and my emotions pulled in many directions. I chose but never expected to find myself in this kind of critical position. My beginnings in this organization were minuscule by comparison. I took a lot of bullshit as a young man in the BPP. Typically the youngest among any group of Panthers, I remember that not one of the sisters back in LA would give me any pussy. "Oh, he's so young," they'd say. Wow, I thought. I was risking my life just like the rest of the brothers, which was all that was required to get laid in the BPP. At least that's what I was led to believe. Man, the going in this organization was really tough if you were young, because you were out of the running for almost every little perk. Now that I'd put the time in, I was hooked up. Shit, now I had to fight the women off. I was head of security at twenty-one, organizing and planning the Servant's campaign against the illegitimate capitalist. I was also still coordinating the schedule for the brothers at the Lamp Post, even though things had cooled down at the club. Rob said the Servant wanted the amount of work I was doing on the street reduced, with the move to Santa Rosa. I felt a bit like I was being left out of a lot of the stuff that would be going down. I wasn't invited to the Servant's house anymore, and that was always a bad sign of your status in the BPP. But I would get over it with the shape of events to come.

Working with Bobby Seale was pure joy. He was extremely smart and funny and had a firm grasp of the Party's political-programmatic relationship and our current direction. With him as well as with Elaine, Masai, and Huey, my political education would be enhanced even more. Bobby's energy and ability to create program after program amazed me. He would get up in the morning and come downstairs with his yellow legal pad in his hands and sit down at the breakfast table, shoot the shit with Carl, his secretary, Frances Carter, June's secretary, Leslie, and me. Then he would begin these brainstorming sessions that would usually end with the creation of a brand-new survival program. Once that was over, we would hit a grueling campaign trail. It began in the morning, sometimes as early as 5:00 A.M., and could last as late as midnight or 1:00 A.M.

As we moved through this schedule, I began to understand what Rob and John Seale were talking about. Bobby's security needs were much more demanding than those of any leader in the BPP, even Huey. We were in TV and radio stations, the projects, and we also traveled into some of the toughest nightspots in town because Bobby and Elaine campaigned everywhere without restrictions. The only places we didn't go were the speakeasies. Bobby must have made four to five speaking engagements and other types of large public appearances a day. He was constantly in a crowd with people pushing and shoving and making all kinds of crazy demands on his candidacy. Sometimes there were niggers around who were from the "life," and they thought they could talk to Bobby about what was happening on the streets. I would always cut that shit short because Huey had told me that the chairman didn't need to know about the "stern stuff." Carl and I had to be on point 24/7 and stay on top of everything that might go down.

Bobby eventually forced a runoff with Mayor Reading but fell short in the special election.

I continued working with the chairman and Carl for a few months after the election, but things began to really change. Over the next several months, I was going to be involved in the most dramatic chain of events the Party would undergo since the split in 1970–71. From now until Huey set foot on Cuban soil in 1974, one calamitous situation after the next went down.

15

I GOT A PHONE CALL from Robert Bay. He instructed me and Comrade Bethune to meet Huey at the Lamp Post, in downtown Oakland, at 11:30. A.M. Bethune and I hustled down to the Lamp Post curious and anxious but eager to comply. We arrived promptly at 11:30. It was Saturday and the weekend lunch crowd was slowly trickling in. Bethune and I seated ourselves at the "captain's table" directly in front of an Emory Douglass portrait of Huey. We waited for hours. Sometime between 7:00 and 8:00 that evening, the Servant made a grand entrance through the double doors of the restaurant, closely followed by the BPP's general staff. This was unusual because the general staff normally did not travel together for reasons of security.

Huey sauntered down the aisle of tables, chairs, and bar stools, greeting various patrons. His entourage—Bobby Seale, June Hilliard, John Seale, and Robert Bay—stayed in the background and quickly seated themselves across the aisle from us with their backs to the wall at a table near the upstairs entrance.

Huey spotted and moved slowly toward us. He gave Bethune and me a big hug before requesting that we be seated facing him, our backs to the crowd. Huey sat down and said, "Don't worry, comrades, I got your back." He then sat back in his chair and ordered a cognac in a snifter. He leaned over the table, motioned us toward him, and said, "Look at them," nodding in the direction of the Seales, June Hilliard, and Big Bay. "They're old, getting lazy, and probably concerned about how long they will live." I was stunned and I bet Bethune was too. This was Huey P. Newton, founder and leader of the BPP, whom we respected to the hilt. The fat, old, and worried-about-life-expectancy people he was talking about were our heroes, too, not to mention the people I reported to on a daily basis.

"Comrades," he continued, "we are about to embark on a difficult journey that will take the leadership of men who practice the 'sterner stuff' of politics. I need soldiers that will fight, kill, and strive for excellence in every way. I need men who can also run this organization's administrative apparatus and within the same breath take shock troops out to shut down a dope operation. I need men who have skills in warfare and administration. I need men who can carry the mantle of the Buddha—as in administration—and the Samurai, as in being the soldier. I need Buddha Samurai like yourselves." He paused and looked each of us directly in the eye. "You guys are the future of this organization. It's brothers like you from the old guard who must take control of the Party at some point in the near future." Huey then sat back looking pleased with himself, cocking his head in the air, and waving his hand across his body in a dismissive motion, saying, "That's it. Now keep this among yourselves, but spread the Buddha Samurai message to the other brothers and sisters in the cadre. Make them understand so that when the change comes about, they will be ready."

This meeting and discussion changed my life forever because not only was I *in,* I was *in* from this point on to the end. Thousands of young black men and women had joined the BPP looking for acceptance in the movement as trusted members and leaders. This encounter with Huey was confirmation of my acceptance in the movement as a trusted member and leader. Huey got up and said, "Let's go." Bethune and I sprang to our feet, as did the others across from us. That night and the next morning we went out to the speakeasies to look over our territory, but before we left the Lamp Post, Huey closed by saying to us, "If you are true to the game, the game will always be true to you."

It was clear to me from this point on that Huey P. Newton was the person who controlled the BPP. Before we left, Bobby's personal body-guard showed up to pick up the chairman, June, and John Seale. Huey, Robert Bay, Bethune, and I piled into Huey's Marquis for the twenty- or thirty-minute ride to the Black Knight, a speakeasy located in South Berkeley at the corner of San Pablo and Ashby. While we rode to our destination, Huey launched into an explanation of why we were moving against the illegitimate capitalist operating in this segment of the community.

"Comrades, do you understand why we tax these guys and not close them down?" Huey asked. "Closing them down is the 'civil rights' solution. We are not 'Bible thumpers,' and I know what it is to be a thumper because my father is one. So because we are not that, then we must learn how to coexist with them. On the other hand, comrades, if they resist as some have tried, we will punish them severely. That's where the Buddha Samurai comes in, comrades. They will have to pay either us or the white boy across the bay, and I ain't having that. You see, we can't respect the laws of our oppressor or we would not be able to operate as men who are in a dangerous business. Yes, comrades, revolution is the most dangerous profession one can go into. We must understand and know the law of our oppressor, so that we can devise methods to get around it. We have our own laws and rules that govern us. So these guys can't call the police or shit like that because they are already breaking the law. And if they do call, they will be breaking our law, and then you and your people will ride down on them and place them under arrest, and then they will be tried under our jurisdiction."

It was dark outside and Robert took the surface street route instead of the freeway. We were cruising up Sacramento Avenue. As we passed different establishments, Huey pointed out the "joints," calling out the revenues and what percentage they were being assessed at and then taxed, their names, and how long he had known the specific proprietor. He said, "Comrades, you know we will use the money from these chumps to help pay for our 'survival programs,' any future political campaigns, and to underwrite our five-year plan to take over the city of Oakland." As he was finishing, Rob wheeled into a dirt parking lot behind what looked like a factory or warehouse. There were dozens of cars parked in the lot and on the street. There were Benzes, Cadillacs, Town Cars, you name it.

Big Rob leaned his 250 pounds back in his seat, causing it to press against my legs, as he said, "We are going in the back because Big Booker's waiting and holding down the back door for us so that people won't see us coming in." We had been here many times but never came in the back until this morning. We got out and went to the back door, and Rob knocked on the large door with the side of his balled-up fist. A little five-by-ten-inch door on hinges opened and a large black face with big eyes, a large nose, and big lips appeared; then the door closed. I could hear a wooden bar being removed and then the larger door opened. Big Booker stood aside, pointing toward the hallway. We walked through the door, which he then shut with great force. I could see a large revolver sticking out of his belt. As we walked down this dark wood-paneled hallway, I could hear music coming from a jukebox in the large bar and seating area just ahead. We stopped just short of going into the club area and turned left through an open door that led into a little office. As Frankie Beverly sang some sweet soul song, I could hear the chatter and hip banter of people in the "life." Before the door to the office shut, I took a peek up the hallway toward all of the people wearing bright-colored clothes, long coats, platform shoes, big floppy hats, and long conked hair. It looked like something out of the movie *The Mack*.

The place looked like a regular bar or club, with a bar and two bartenders, tables and chairs set up in rows in the large room, and a jukebox in the corner near the front door. In a room just off from the larger lounge area was a smaller room with a pool table where the brothers and sisters stood around shooting craps for cash. We went into the little room with a desk and chair, bar stools, and a row of about four chairs in front of the desk. It looked like this room wasn't used very much. Huey sat behind the desk, and Rob stood directly to his left and folded his arms, clutching the small .38 revolver that had been inside his soft black leather attaché case. Bethune and I were directed by Huey to sit on either side of the desk on some bar stools. Bethune was wearing a .45 auto government-issue, and I was packing my 9mm Browning. Huey motioned for Booker, who came over. Huey whispered something to him and then Booker left to collect the people for this morning's performance. Huey turned to Bethune and me and said, "Follow my lead, comrades. I will do all of the talking tonight and you guys will just sit and observe. You will get your chance to hold court later or after Big Rob and me have left this earth."

We both said, "Right on," and settled into our seats.

Booker ushered in a waitress, who took our orders. We all ordered cognac with a club soda back. And then, one by one, ushered in by Booker's large hands, these guys came through the door wearing big floppy hats, "Lord Jesus" hairstyles, platform shoes, and lots of gold around their necks and on their manicured fingers. They were coming in at intervals, three at a time. And they would occupy the chairs stationed by Huey, directly in front of his desk and chair. He was holding court on the streets. But as each guy came in, he put his hands in his pockets and leather bags. They each pulled out little paper packets, unfolded them, and neatly deposited cocaine on a mirror that was placed before Huey. I could smell the stuff from where I sat. Huey bent over with a hundred-dollar bill that was rolled up like a straw and started snorting.

They put so much cocaine down on the mirror that it looked like the little mountain of powder that Al Pacino's character snorted in the film *Scarface*. The pyramid ultimately stood about six to eight inches high. Huey was scooping and snorting something fierce. Next he used a straw. He built a little hill of the powder over to the side and took it down his nostril in several dips. These other guys were lining up to take their hits, too, leaning over and snorting with little spoons connected to gold chains around their necks. No one was talking. One of them motioned toward me, offering me the use of his little gold spoon. I shook my head no, thank you. "The brothers are on duty," Huey said. So they ignored us for the rest of the morning. The guys in the chairs were probably between thirty and fifty years old. They had names like Cole, Larry, Alameda Slim, Dog Slim, Howard Boyd, Billy Byrd, and Terrible Tom, who said he had dug a ten-foot-deep pit in his backyard that he used to throw his bad whores into and then fed them only raw meat. Afterward, Huey said we should not accept anything from them, because someday we would probably have to kill them for not paying. So it was better to distance ourselves from them.

Huey stood up and began to pace the floor while launching into one of his one-man performances. He spoke about Li'l Bobby Hutton and his courage as the first member of the Party and the first member of the Party to die in combat; Plato's Cave allegory; his shoot-out with the Oakland police in October 1967 in which he said the smoking gun was located in his hollowed-out law book; and what we would do when we took over the city of Oakland. Suddenly there was a knock on the door and Big Booker entered, moving quickly past everyone and then leaning over to whisper something in Huey's ear. Huey nodded his approval and then turned to Robert Bay, saying, "Big Man, call June and tell him the police are surrounding this place and that I may need his help."

Robert said, "Right on, Servant," and left to go use the phone in the lounge area. Huey then turned to Bethune and me and said with great emotion, "Will you die with me, comrade brothers?"

We responded in unison, "Right on, Servant."

He said, "Good, then we're not going to jail tonight."

Later that morning the police pulled back and we left without an incident.

16

IT ALWAYS SEEMED THAT THINGS in the BPP began with
a phone call announcing an emergency, and these emergencies
and events usually took place in the summer. I was in the living
room at Santa Rosa, listening to the chairman talk about a program
he was creating, when the phone rang. It was July 30, 1974. John
Seale came running downstairs and told me the Servant was in trouble and that he needed help. He asked where some of the brothers
were.

"They're at the Lamp Post," I answered while reaching for the
phone. John took the receiver and ordered the brother on the other end
to meet us at the Fox Lounge. John and I jumped into his car and sped
off for MacArthur Boulevard in North Oakland. We met four of the
brothers outside the club and then went inside, headed for the manager's office. Huey was inside. His bodyguard Big Bob Heard was
nowhere to be found. Huey was talking loudly about Big Bob, who had
been arrested only minutes before. Huey said the owner had set him up
and that the fix was in between him and the police. Huey calmed down
and looked to see who was in the room with him. He walked over to me,
smiled, and shook my hand while asking, "Are you armed, comrade?"

"Yes, Servant, I'm armed."

I was packing a .357 Magnum Smith & Wesson with a six-inch barrel. I wasn't sure who else was armed, but at that moment it didn't matter. Then there was a loud knock at the door. Huey looked around at the other brothers and then back at me. "Answer the door, Flores," Huey commanded. I went to the door with my hand on my piece, cracked the door, and saw two black men in plainclothes and then a lot of men in blue uniforms. It was the OPD. They rushed the door. I stepped back with one hand drawing my gun and the other steering the Servant behind me. My training had taken over my physical functions, and there wasn't a thought in my head that was unrelated to the moment at hand. All I remember was gripping my weapon as I was visualizing a shooting stance that was appropriate for the space available, and then everything went black. I had been knocked unconscious from a blow to the head, hit with a policeman's service revolver.

When I came back to consciousness, I was lying on the floor of a paddy wagon, on my back, looking up into five sets of eyes. "Fly, are you all right?" I heard a voice say. I waited a moment because I wasn't sure if I was lying dead in a box or just waking up from a dream. I shook off the cobwebs and said, "Yeah, I think I'm okay."

Looking down at me, John Seale said, "Brother, we thought you were dead from the way you went down."

Someone else said, "I thought they shot you, Fly, because you were over there by the Servant when the shit went down." They helped me to my feet.

When we arrived at the police station, they placed us in separate rooms. My door opened and in stepped the ubiquitous Captain Colletti and a Treasury agent from the Bureau of Alcohol, Tobacco, and Firearms named J. J. Newberry. They looked at me, said who I was to each other, and then closed the door. We were arraigned the next day. The Servant, Big Bob, and I were charged with possession of a firearm and assault on a police officer with the intent to commit great bodily harm. The other brothers were charged with lesser offenses. If convicted, I was facing five to life in the state penitentiary. We were bailed out several days later.

People began to disappear again a month after the Fox Lounge inci-

Above: My father overseas shortly after World War II.
Below: My mother, Catherine Seymore Forbes, and father, Fred Roosevelt
Forbes, Sr., together in a picture taken during the early 1950s, were married for
thirty-four years. My father died in 1978, during my first year as a fugitive.

I played Little League baseball in Southeast San Diego when I was twelve years old, the same year I was kidnapped by the San Diego police.

Me at fourteen in junior high school. During this period, in 1966, San Diego policemen beat me on the athletic track at Lincoln High School in Southeast San Diego.

From left to right: my sister Katherine, my brother, Fred, and me at home in Southeast San Diego around 1960.

My mentor and the person who trained most of the Buddha Samurai, Minister of Education Raymond "Masai" Hewitt (in trench coat). Above his right shoulder is Minister of Culture Emory Douglass. This picture was taken while Masai and Emory were on a visit to the People's Republic of China in 1971.

Doing my part in early 1972 at Bobby Hutton Memorial Park, Oakland, California. I'm at the far right with the sack of potatoes, assisting other comrades in packing bags of groceries for a free food giveaway. On the stage is James Mott and Clark Bailey (with clipboard), aka Santa Rita.

From left to right: Huey P. Newton, Robert Bay, and Huey's wife, Gwen. Robert Bay was my first line of contact after Masai resigned in 1972. We called him Guru.

Maurice Powell, aka Mojo, the Party's armorer, with Elaine Brown
in Oakland, around 1972.

Robert Bay, Huey's bodyguard and aide-de-camp
during the early 1970s.

While Elaine Brown talks to the press, I stand at the ready out of camera in the Swedish army coat. This was during the campaign in the fall of 1972, in Oakland.

From left to right: Bobby Seale, Elaine Brown, Huey P. Newton, and John Seale during the Oakland mayoral race in 1973.

From left to right, that's me (in the loud suit in the background) on duty watching the street with Huey P. Newton, Elaine Brown, and Bobby Seale during the campaign in 1973. During this period I was part of Chairman Bobby Seale's security detail.

Black Panther Party candidates Elaine Brown, candidate for councilman, and Bobby Seale, candidate for mayor, in 1973.

Darren Perkins, aka the Duke, a strong proponent of the Buddha Samurai, at the Lamp Post around 1973. He survived two tours of duty in Vietnam, as did many of the brothers in the fold.

The comrades who staffed the Party's bar and restaurant, the Lamp Post, in Oakland, around 1974.

Simba, one of my deputies, and I in 1975, on watch at a crowded event.

In 1976, my brother, Fred, visited me at the Lamp Post.
We are seated at the captain's table.

A family portrait: the Black Panther Party Central Committee when Elaine Brown was chairman (1974–77). Top row, left to right: Phyllis Jackson, Norma Armour, Ellis White, me, Michael Fultz, Emory Douglass, Joan Kelly. Bottom row, left to right: Ericka Huggins, "Comrade Bethune," Elaine Brown, "Big" Bob Heard.

Huey P. Newton, Gwen Newton, and Elaine Brown at a Party event
in Oakland in 1977, shortly after he returned from Cuba.

Buddha Samurai (left to right): Louis Talbert "Texas" Johnson,
Gerald Edwards, me, George Robinson.

I'm with my mother at my graduation from San Francisco State
University in 1986. I had been out of prison for less than a year.

When I received my master's degree in urban planning from
New York University in 1989, I was the Wagner Graduate School of
Public Service standard-bearer.

dent. Dozens of comrades who had been in the Party for years were either expelled or left of their own volition. I knew most of the expelled and personally showed some of them the door. This was what Huey had prepared us for. Chairman Bobby Seale, David Hilliard and his brother June, and John Seale were expelled or left voluntarily. Others, including Robert Bay, Gwen Goodloe, Elbert "Big Man" Howard, Bobby Rush, and scores more followed. The security cadre was not immune from this new purge. We lost about five or six good brothers for various reasons. Most of their expulsions occurred at the Servant's house and involved some incident where the Servant was concerned. The stories were always sketchy, but I figured most of them got up to his house and started tripping about their own self-importance in the Party. Hanging around Huey was like a high. I knew these brothers, and it wasn't unusual for them to be high-strung because they were involved in the stern stuff, and sometimes that shit would go to your head. Enormous egos are not willing to take any shit or back down. Those sessions at his house were like time bombs waiting to go off, as they did around August 1974. That's why when I wasn't invited up to his place like I was in the beginning, I didn't trip; I just let it go and continued doing my work. I guess that's how young guys see things.

17

AS THE NEWS BEGAN TO REVERBERATE across the San Francisco–Oakland Bay Area and then to the handful of remaining chapters and branches around the country, I just settled in and kept on working. I had known the leadership of the BPP, personally and professionally, better than anyone. So I should have at least mourned their demise, but I'm sure they would have told anyone, "We trained him not to crack and to be prepared for the uncertainty that is part of the life of a revolutionary." I didn't get misty-eyed when I saw John Seale or Robert Bay for the last time. Bobby Seale and June Hilliard just disappeared, as did many who were expelled or deserted. Many were what became known as Bobby Seale loyalists. They felt that they wouldn't get a square deal in the Party with Bobby gone. To me that was bullshit. I worked closer with the chairman and even protected his life with my own every single day. If anyone was a Bobby Seale loyalist or a June Hilliard loyalist or, for that matter, a David Hilliard loyalist, I was. I was because I was dedicated to the Party and to our cause and not dedicated to an individual. But if you were the group of people governing the Party, I would support you, as would the other Buddha Samurai.

The absence of the Seale and Hilliard brothers was of monumental

WILL YOU DIE WITH ME?

significance. Because up until the day they were no longer part of the organization, they ran the political administration of the BPP as well as the military and underground apparatus, from 1967 to 1974. People would argue that Huey was in control when he was released from prison in 1970. Well, he probably wanted people to think that, but no one ever received directives from him below the rank of chief of staff, A-chief, or any other central committee position. I was involved in the most dangerous aspects of the Party's business, and the few times I got a direct order from Huey I could count on my two hands. Most of the time I was given an assignment or directive by June, John, or Robert Bay, and believe me, I'm sure they often modified what Huey had told them to tell me. But those days were over now, and I had to adjust to the changes.

I was pretty much isolated in our quarters, work assignments, and activities on the streets from 1972 to 1974. So when Elaine, the new chairman, and Bethune, the new chief of staff, came to see me, I knew it had nothing to do with maintaining this isolation.

"Flores," Elaine said, "we will be asking you to do more." I nodded.

"Damn, Fly, you should be excited," Bethune said. "You've been here getting down for a long time, and now the other brothers and sisters will have to risk their lives doing some of this stuff."

"Right on," I said. "I'll do whatever I need to do to keep the Party moving ahead."

Both of them seemed disappointed that I had responded with so little passion. But at this time I couldn't worry about that. I knew the transition was going to be rough. I had nothing to be excited about because this wasn't a job or career for me. This was my life.

• • • I began spending a lot of time with Bethune, Big Bob Heard, and Mojo. (The Duke was underground at this time.) We talked about expanding the ranks of the Buddha Samurai and how we were going to maintain our foothold on the illegitimate capitalist.

Huey began to blow a gasket. He had been involved in a lot of extracurricular activity, pistol-whipping his tailor and a few other incidents that didn't get much or any press.

In any case, one Friday Bethune, Big Bob, Mojo, and I were over at Bethune's house hanging out, smoking weed, and getting ready to go to the Lamp Post to have dinner before heading to the speakeasies to check our traps. We were all in a great mood, except Big Bob, which led me to surmise that maybe something was wrong with Huey. Big Bob was a jovial six-eight, four-hundred-pound guy who was lighter on his feet than most middleweight boxers. He would usually smoke and drink and bust out laughing at Mojo's offbeat humor. But he wasn't doing that tonight. Anyway, we were at Bethune's place a little longer than we had anticipated because he was on the phone with Elaine trying to work out their new professional and personal relationship. Bethune was currently living with a woman and seeing about two or three others.

We didn't really sense anything, but Bob got nervous and demanded that we get out of the house. It was a good move. We turned off the porch light when we left but were startled once we got outside and noticed that all of the streetlamps on this particular block were out. It was odd but not alarming. Big Bob and Mojo rode in one car and Bethune and I rode in another. We caravanned down to Lakeshore Drive, passing the Servant's twenty-five-story apartment complex on the opposite side of the street. I saw police cars in the front of 1200 Lakeshore but didn't think anything of it at first. I told Bethune, who was driving, and he thought we should hurry to the Lamp Post and call to see if Huey was okay. When we pulled up to the light at Telegraph and West Grand Boulevard, our cars were side by side. Bethune rolled down his window and told Bob and Mojo what I had seen. They had seen it, too. I looked over to my right at the vehicle next to us and recognized the white man in the driver's seat. He was a plainclothes policeman. I told Bethune, who checked his rearview mirror to see that there were other police cars, marked and unmarked, behind us. The light changed and both cars raced for the Lamp Post parking lot. We thought if we could get inside, we could call our lawyer and avoid a messy scene that may involve our blood. Something was definitely afoot.

Now I know why we were all glad to be out of that house. We didn't sense it, but sometimes you just know. But I knew the nervous guy with us probably was right to insist we leave. Police raids on houses are just as close to death traps as any other kind of encounter with them, or maybe except for the one that was getting ready to happen. We pulled into the parking lot. Bethune drove closer to the building near the back of our club, and Big Bob parked opposite us near the street facing West Grand. The second we parked, it turned to daylight outside the car; there were spotlights and police lights twirling everywhere. Before I even opened the door I could hear shotgun rounds being jacked into their chambers. Bethune and I looked at each other before exiting the car. "No funny moves," I said to him.

"Right, Fly, no funny moves."

I opened the door and got out carefully. Over loudspeakers I heard voices shouting commands: "Run over here. Put your hands up. Lay down with your hands over your head." We ignored them and didn't move; we just put our hands up and stood still. I was blinded by the lights. We waited until they came to get us. At first I couldn't see them, and then they appeared through the lights, plainclothes and uniforms. They commanded me to lie down and I did as they searched me. For some reason we had broken our own rule: we were not packing.

These were the conditions and environment under which many a nigger was shot. But not us, we weren't going for it. With all of the confusion, shouting, lights flashing, and nervous tension, we calmed down and took the bust like we knew we should. They put us all in separate rooms again. At the police station I saw Captain Colletti and the ATF agent J. J. Newberry once more. I was fingerprinted but not charged. My release came several hours later, but as I was being led to the release point to sign some papers and meet Smokey, the BPP's legal affairs coordinator, I was astonished at what I heard as I waited in the hallway holding area.

"Comrade, I'm over here." It was Huey, in a holding cell.

I looked around and walked over to the cell. "Do you have any cigarettes?" he asked.

"Yeah," I said while reaching into my pocket and gesturing to the jailer that I was going to hand the pack to Huey. The jailer nodded that it was okay.

"Keep them, Servant, I'm getting out."

"Good, Flores, that's good. Sister Elaine will need you now more than ever."

I didn't realize what he meant then. However, the entire night started to come together for me. We had been arrested because they were looking for the Servant. We were released, uncharged, within hours. The Servant was released the next day on bail after being charged with the attempted murder of some prostitute on San Pablo Avenue.

The next time I saw Mojo, I was picking him up from the hospital and taking him to the Greyhound bus station in downtown Oakland. He had been expelled and mud-holed while at the Servant's house.

Huey P. Newton disappeared. Warrants were issued for his arrest.

The next time I met with Elaine and Bethune, they were not as vague as before. "Flores Forbes," Elaine said, "you have been appointed to the central committee of the Black Panther Party, and your title is assistant chief of staff. And you have also been appointed the armorer of the Black Panther Party. Congratulations!"

I still didn't say anything. I just shook their hands and went to be by myself. I had to be alone because it was at this moment that I realized I would never leave the Black Panther Party alive. I was twenty-two years old.

18

THE POSITION OF ARMORER in the BPP was one of the most important, most secretive assignments a member of the security cadre could receive. Aside from Huey, the chairman, the chief of staff, and the assistant chief of staff, or the existence of a field marshal, most BPP members would not know that it even existed. Members of the security cadre would know of the position because he was the guy who supplied them with their weapons and other logistical support for an operation. When I assumed the position, I had no one to talk to about how this thing called the armorer worked. I was given a quick tour and a sketchy inventory list by Comrade Bethune, but that was it. There was no institutional history or playbook.

I was the armorer for four years, and not once did J. J. Newberry of the ATF or Captain Colletti show up on any of the many gun runs I performed during this period. If they had, it would have meant that someone from the group of people above was a snitch.

The only armorer of the BPP I knew of was Mojo. I could probably guess who it had been before him, but until the retreat to establish a base of operations in Oakland, there might not have been a demand for one. What I did find out over the next several years was that, regardless of who the armorer was, he was an integral part in the entire structure of the Black Panther Party. The armorer probably traveled more than any other security personnel in the BPP. In a week's time I would visit every single property in the BPP's vast real estate holdings. I had a key to every private residence, office, educational facility, business, and dorm in the organization; the residences were where we stored our weapons. I met and developed a face-to-face relationship with almost every member of the BPP because of my visiting their homes to ascertain the security of our weapons caches. I began to understand why Mojo was so good at certain aspects of his job. He had developed many skills over the years that helped him do his job effectively. Most important were his people skills. He told jokes and would make rank-and-file members laugh, which in turn made it easy for him to visit and hang around without comrades feeling imposed upon or suspicious of his presence. He was a great cook and was known to whip up a meal while he was working on certain projects in comrades' homes. He had a good bedside manner. The children of Panthers loved to see Mojo coming up the stairs carrying some package that was more than likely a bundle of death. But he also had their candy.

I had to develop like skills, except cooking. I had one advantage that most past armorers didn't have, and that was rank. I was a member of the central committee and the assistant chief of staff. This helped to facilitate my visits and get people to cooperate, but I never abused my rank. I tried to be the same person I always was. Most of the people in the Party were older than me. I could play on my youth because many of the comrades were surprised I had so much responsibility. They would usually give me the benefit of the doubt if it looked like I was acting arrogant.

I had several duties as the armorer; paramount among them was maintaining the vast inventory of weapons and ammo. I made sure the weapons were functioning properly, by constant testing at the range, and that they were matched up with the right ammo. (I was surprised when people didn't know the difference between 7.62mm or 7.62X39. The former was for an American M14/M60 and the latter was for the AK-47.) I also serviced and cleaned the inventory and replenished it when necessary. Replenishing the inventory could be tricky. This meant I had to buy or trade with various sources like illegal arms dealers, gun shops, and gun shows. To assist me in these endeavors I needed a team. I had two assistants, both top-flight Panther security personnel: Clark Bailey and Louis T. Johnson. And I had one woman, a white woman. She was my girlfriend, and I also recruited her to assist me in my work. Roni was the only white person who was a member of the BPP. Until the feds caught on, she was my front person at the gun shops and gun shows. Elaine had encouraged me to move in with her because she lived with the Gladwins in the Oakland Hills, away from the flatlands. Tom and Flora Gladwin were major contributors to the Party. They welcomed me with open arms. They were two of the best white radicals I had ever known. Flora was the librarian at our award-winning school in East Oakland, and Tom, well, he was the most interesting of fellows. I never confirmed this, but I heard he had been a CIA analyst at one time. We got along famously and there were never any problems.

I used other people as well. For example, the Duke had a wealthy girlfriend and supporter who would go to the gun shows with us. Texas and I would walk several paces in front of them, pointing out the hardware we wanted to purchase, and the Duke and his woman would come along after us and purchase the weapons, usually semiautomatic handguns.

When I dealt with illegal arms traders, things usually were a little tense, but we would get what we wanted. We didn't look them up; they came knocking at our door. The trick was discerning which ones worked for J. J. Newberry at the ATF and which were legit illegal arms traders. I had learned from my experience with Shabazz and the marines in Riverside how to discern the real illegal arms dealers from those looking to entrap you. When a dealer approached us, I would make the deal right then and there. On the other hand, if they wanted to set a meeting, we would do it but wouldn't show up. The problem with this aspect of my job was that I had to be a great judge of the moment, because I would get only one chance. I had learned early on from Shabazz and the brothers in LA that the real dealers are ready to transact business at first contact, but the police, especially the ATF, always want a meeting to set you up and then they'll bust your ass while kicking back at some fancy rendezvous they handpicked.

The most important part of my job was arming the firing team/squads with the proper armament for their particular operation. At this point in my service, I was doing most of the planning, so how the teams were armed in the field had a lot to do with how they performed. It was difficult to control, but we figured it out. If you give people a bullshit weapon, they will perform like a group of bullshitters, but if you give them great leadership and state-of-the-art weapons, everyone makes it home in one piece. On the operational side, we created a model of what worked early on with the Duke, Mojo, and me. We developed three-man squads with a good mix of street experience and Vietnam combat experience. There were maybe a dozen brothers in the cadre with real serious Vietnam combat experience in elite U.S. Army units like the 82nd and 101st Airborne, the 173rd Airborne Brigade, and a half-dozen brothers with Ranger patches. We hooked them up with a group of street-smart brothers, making a great outfit. We had strong team leadership with veteran Panthers like Santa Rita, Texas, Aaron Dixon, Rollin Reid, George Robinson, and the Duke. We got even stronger when the brothers came up from LA for some joint operations. These brothers helped develop their individual units and prepare them for some of the stern stuff. We studied most of the so-called urban guerrilla texts, but none of them were written with a U.S. street in mind. So we had to develop our own operational standards. Our weakness was the inability to handle wounded comrades. Everything else we dealt well with.

• • • As the armorer, I had my job cut out for me in the beginning because the armory was a mess. That probably explained what happened to Mojo. I think he was a little lazy and let shit go to the dumps. I traveled the length of the Bay Area, surveying the inventory of weapons, and was shocked. The situation was beyond anything I could imagine. The weapons were in disarray and many were damaged and beyond repair. Half were no longer functional. They had been stored under houses in trunks, buried in the ground, and some submerged in water. The Servant must have flipped when he found out. We were in trouble. But there was plenty of stuff that was in excellent condition. We had dozens of every kind of automatic weapon: M16s, M14s, M60s, AK47s, Thompson submachine guns, 9mm grease guns, M79 grenade launchers, Boys Caliber .55 antitank weapons, AR-180s, and AR-7s with silencers. There were trunks of older weapons like M1 Garand Army rifles, M1 and M2 carbines, M59 Santa Fe Troopers, FN's, bolt-action high-powered rifles, Winchester repeating rifles, and about seventy-five riot shotguns of various makes. What needed to be upgraded were the handguns.

Masai was no longer with the Party, but his sage advice lingered. He used to tell me that all I would need to know about my job could be found in a book. My challenge was to find the right book. I found a small-arms encyclopedia called *Small Arms of the World*. This book cataloged every automatic weapon we had in our inventory. It gave me the proper nomenclature for each weapon and the function for each part, plus the type of ammo for each weapon.

For the first six months of Elaine's administration, I worked this out, with my two assistants Santa Rita and Texas. I spent hours cleaning and putting weapons together and reorganizing the armory into an efficient urban weapons system with a complete and thorough inventory of every barrel, receiver group, ammunition, scope, sling, flak jacket, piece of infrared equipment, and even cleaning materials. I even got into reloading. These experiences enhanced my confidence. I could name and find any part that was spread out over fifty locations without referring to my list, which I hid behind a picture on the wall of my apartment. My work with the armory became a labor of love. It wasn't so much that I liked guns, but rather that I would give it 100 percent of my effort, just as I had done with selling papers, organizing breakfast programs in the projects, or anything else. On the rare occasions we saw each other, Elaine would joke with me that I smelled like gun solvent. She was probably right. I spent hours under many of our homes and facilities, digging up weapons and drenching them with gun solvent in an attempt to save them. The salvageable weapons were moved by car, truck, or van to my workshop at a secret location. I usually traveled with a big load during rush-hour traffic in the morning or afternoon, when I believed I was less conspicuous, as opposed to traveling late at night. I would never travel with an assembled weapon. For example, when I was working on our M16 weapons group, I would move the barrel attachments at one time and then return and move the receivers separately to a different location. Each weapon group—whether M16, AK-47, AR-180, or M14—would be detached or broken down. I would organize their placement so that they could be assembled within fifteen to thirty minutes, depending on the traffic.

My inventory list consisted of twenty sheets of white lined paper. I used both sides. There would be an address in code, and under that address I would have a listing of weapons, accessories, and ammo located in that particular house or apartment. Once every weapon was assembled, broken down, and listed, I redesigned our armory storage system. We would no longer keep weapons in the ground or under houses but in closets, packed in clothing bags or matching suitcases and small trunks. I went to Norma Armour, our finance person, and explained what I wanted to do, and she gave me the money to go out and purchase all of the clothing bags, suitcases, and small trunks I would need. Using the clothing bags and other garment accessories made it easier for me to move around and not draw attention.

19

NOW THAT I WAS the new assistant chief of staff, my re-sponsibilities in the Party considerably expanded. Since I had a handle on the armory and the brothers and sisters in the cadre, Elaine thought I could do more. She and Bethune had told me that we needed to focus more on what the Party was doing in East Oakland with our most important base of operations: the Oakland Community School and the East Oakland complex at Sixty-first Street and East Fourteenth Street. Our central headquarters was relocated to Eighty-fifth Street, just up the block, and we had approximately thirty homes and apartments in East Oakland.

Based on the intelligence I was able to gather from the streets, the biggest issue facing us in this part of Oakland was the resurgence in youth gang activity and a rash of burglaries we suffered at several of our residences. I wasn't sure if there was a correlation, but I thought we would have a better handle on the area if we were working with the gangs instead of wondering what in the hell they were doing. When the burglaries took place, I was concerned that the police were responsible, or maybe the gangs, even though no property or weapons were taken. You never could be too sure. Anyway, I started working with our youth organizers to identify local gang leaders and meeting them one by one to see if we could reach some common ground.

Anyway, every Friday our youth programs sponsored dances for young people at our school complex. Bethune and I thought it was a good idea to invite some of these gangs to the local dance so that we could socialize with them. We had also decided that in order to show these young brothers some respect, we wouldn't conduct a search of all the people entering the complex for the dance—a bad move on our part. About a dozen brothers from the security cadre were in attendance, and so were about thirty to forty other Panthers who worked at the complex and were closing out their activities for the week. The sun was setting as the party hit its stride, in full swing at about 8:00 P.M. There were maybe five hundred young people inside boogying down to Frankie Beverly and Maze. I remember walking from the cafeteria to the courtyard, where twenty or thirty people were milling around smoking cigarettes and drinking punch. Near the front of the building, in the courtyard and just off from the hallway that led from the front entrance at East Fourteenth Street, a small disturbance was taking place between three young gang members—two on one.

I looked around and saw that three of our security personnel had peeped the situation. I waved them over to see what the trouble was. I kept a distance, thinking I would act as backup just in case. Shit, that doesn't make sense, I said to myself. In our attempt to avoid being heavy-handed with these young niggers, I had agreed with some of our concerned youth program personnel that we wouldn't pack with all of these young people in the complex—another terrible move on our part. Anyway, the three brothers—Aaron Dixon, Santa Rita, and House-man—moved over and intervened. As heated words were exchanged, the two young brothers who were talking started posturing and high-siding on Aaron and his folks. I heard one of them say in a loud and bois-terous tone, "What? I got my shit and I'm sure you got yours." And then one of the young gang members, with his back to the door, pulled out a pistol and pointed it in the direction of the three Panthers. As he did this, his partner pulled his piece, and Aaron, Santa Rita, and Houseman stepped back and crouched down as the gunmen started shooting. The people in the courtyard started screaming and running for cover, and the Panthers working in the offices along the courtyard turned out the lights and hit the deck.

Each trigger pull was jerked so each round was high and to the right and away from most people. The three Panthers moved left and low toward the gunmen, who apparently got nervous and broke and ran up the hallway toward the back parking lot. As they ran through the hallway, they were firing wildly; the shots echoed throughout the complex. The entire complex was now involved. I could hear the shouts from the Panthers in pursuit, alerting us to their whereabouts. I ran into the cafeteria, stepping on young people as I made my way to the side door that led to the parking lot. As I reached the door, the gunmen appeared and fired into the cafeteria, and I heard this unified scream come up from the floor of the cafeteria. And then they ran up the stairs into the parking lot. I shouted, "Is anyone hurt?" No one said anything, so I moved toward the hallway that led to the parking lot. The two desperados were finally corralled in the parking lot and disarmed by several unarmed Panther security people, but they broke loose and ran toward the street. Inside, Panther personnel were evacuating the building through the front entrance on East Fourteenth Street. The Duke, one of the people who disarmed the young thugs, took aim with one of the Saturday night specials, firing twice.

There was mass confusion in the parking lot as Bethune ran toward me saying, "Fly, what in the fuck happened?" I started to explain about the incident when Bruce "Deacon" Washington came hobbling toward us shouting, "Fly, I'm hit!" A chill went up my back. I told Steve Long and one of the Donald brothers to take Deacon to the hospital. Deacon, a dedicated Panther soldier from Philadelphia, died of his wounds the next morning.

We buried Deacon and decided that these young motherfuckers would not get away with this. Both of them were wounded and recovering in Highland Hospital in East Oakland, a hospital with a large police presence.

"Look," I told the team of volunteers assembled for this operation, "there is a big OPD substation at the hospital. So you just can't walk in and shoot these niggas. You gotta get up close, close enough to use a knife." They nodded that this was cool. "You all know this is not authorized, so you can't take a bust," I said. They said to a man that they understood. They told me that they had cased the hospital and worked out a plan. Once they found the floor the targets were on, they could figure out how to get at them and work their way out of the hospital. But they said there was a catch.

"Fly, we need some serious shit just in case we have to deal with the police," one of them said.

I looked at them and said, "How serious?"

"AK serious, and we need three nine-millimeter Browning pistols."

"You got it," I said.

The night the team went in, Bethune and I were at the Lamp Post having a drink. I got the call around midnight and drove to East Oakland to the safe house the team had returned to. How they got in and out to this day I haven't a clue. One of the thugs was in the lobby of the hospital visiting with friends, so they passed on him. Good move. However, they found the other one in his room, shanked him, and evaded the police after the nurses and doctors had sounded the alarm. The young nigger didn't die but was severely wounded. We left it at that and moved on.

• • • I was still going to court for the Fox Lounge incident when Elaine told me one day that she urgently needed to talk with me about my case. I met her in her office at the school complex in East Oakland. She said, "Flores, you need to take this assistant chief of staff position seriously. You have a case, and you shouldn't be carrying a gun or hanging with them niggers in the Party that do."

"Okay, that's fine with me," I said in a low, meek voice. Elaine was a real firebrand, and I could tell she didn't like the way I responded.

"And besides," she continued, "I think I've gotten things worked out on your case. So let me explain. I've spoken with the Servant, and he thinks we should make this deal."

I stiffened and waited and then asked, "What deal? If it's doing the time, I can do that, no sweat."

Elaine shot back, "Look, Flores, you don't have to act tough with me. Remember, this is Elaine Brown. I knew you when you were wearing Chuck Taylors in Watts. I'm on your side, if anybody is in this party, and don't forget that. As long as I'm running this shit, you are the one nigger that ain't going to jail for any reason. I need you out here—not in prison. So this is the deal. We can't save Big Bob; he's got priors and stuff from Pittsfield or someplace near Boston. He will have to go to prison. Maybe he'll get two years at the max. And you know they dropped the charges against Deacon. But as for you, High-Top Watts [a nickname she gave me in LA], I've cut a deal. Lionel Wilson is the presiding judge in Alameda County, and the nigger wants to be mayor. Remember our five-year plan? Well, we're back on track. Lionel says if we back him, he'll trade with us. You for the office of mayor. If the Party puts its full weight and organization behind Wilson, he'll cut you loose. Your charges will be reduced down to a misdemeanor, and you'll get probation and have to do community service at the Oakland Community School." I loosened up after that and gave Elaine a big bear hug. Man, was I glad.

Elaine Brown was my ace boon coon in the Party. She was a real buddy to me. She was the closest thing to an older sister, or should I say guardian angel, that I ever had. She always had my back just like I had hers. I think it pissed off a lot of people in the Party, though. She was the one who had me move up into the Oakland Hills with Roni and the Gladwins. She said the young nigger was too valuable to lay his head down so close to the OPD. That ticked off people, but she just kept hooking me up and didn't care what anybody thought, not even Bethune. Even after I became assistant chief of staff, I kept getting into trouble with other people in the leadership, including Bethune, and all Elaine would say to them was "I don't care what he does, ain't nothing ever happening to him." In any case, I knew she needed to clear this with the Servant, and I felt blessed.

20

THE DEAL WAS CUT in the spring of 1975 and I avoided prison again. Now, since I had a fire lit under my ass, my motivation to be serious about things unmilitary in the BPP was up and running. So with that behind me, I settled in and began to take my role as assistant chief of staff more seriously. Elaine was trying to reform the Party's antiquated disciplinary procedures and graciously dumped most of it in my lap. A judicial process had been created a couple of years earlier to adjudicate internal infractions of the Party's rules called the Board of Methods and Corrections. Originally the two judges were rotated about every two months with a member from the rank and file and someone who had a leadership position. Elaine made this a permanent appointment for Ericka Huggins and me.

Most of the really serious infractions, such as hitting women or pulling guns on people, as I was aware, involved members of the security cadre. They would usually get off by pleading that they had been hyped up because of some operation they were not at liberty to discuss, so they got off light. Well, that was about to stop. These guys needed to know that they couldn't get away with inappropriate acts of violence with impunity. When they walked into our chambers for the first time, most of them were shocked. They realized then that they were going to

WILL YOU DIE WITH ME?

have to shape up or ship out. After sitting in judgment of these guys for several months, Ericka and I were able to curb a lot of their cowboy and rowdy ways.

Another aspect of the Party's business that I got deeply involved with as part of my expanded duties was the everyday fund-raising from our field operations, which raised somewhere in the area of $10,000 per week. The Party raised money in many ways. At one time the newspaper was the largest source of revenue, but with the reduced number of chapters and branches, along with fewer subscriptions, that source needed to be replaced. Major sources of revenue in the 1970s came from our business ventures like the Lamp Post, the Fox Theater, and our concert promotion company. This business made big headlines when we had to mud-hole the entire Ike and Tina Turner Revue for breach of contract on the stage of the Oakland Auditorium. Elaine and the sisters had created a multifaceted 501(c)(3) nonprofit apparatus that was bringing in bundles of cash from philanthropic groups, government grant programs, and large private contributions. And there was the money from the illegitimate capitalist. But our everyday bread and butter was the field operation. Scores of comrades would go into the streets collecting donations for our myriad programs such as the Oakland Community School, Seniors Against a Fearful Environment (SAFE), the Sickle-Cell Anemia Research Foundation, and many others. They went to shopping malls, downtown central business districts, and I added overnight trips to other cities in California and Nevada. Being involved with this operation meant keeping regular office hours at our central headquarters. I worked on developing field operation strategies to find new locations, rallying the troops around my new plans, and working closely with our graphic arts department on the creation of up-to-date donation receptacles that people would trust and put their money into.

I felt like I had come full circle with my life in the BPP. The excitement of the military stuff was not something I would enjoy again, I thought. But the day-to-day tedium of managing a program was losing its luster. I was a Panther official who was working in what was comparable to a 9-to-5. This took getting used to. While I was on probation I couldn't carry a gun, and Elaine had made it clear to Bethune that I was never to go on another operation. She told me one day when I was complaining about my new role, "Look, nigger, you're not some Panther gunman anymore; you are the assistant chief of staff and you need to act like it. The Servant said you must also be an administrator. Well, comrade brother, that's what you are now—a Buddha administrator, and your goddamn Samurai days are numbered."

21

OST OF THE PEOPLE who made up the central committee from 1966 to 1974 were part of the organization's original leadership structure. They were, with only a few exceptions, mature men who had lived some before joining the BPP. But with the ascension of Elaine Brown as the new chairman of the central committee, they became a diverse mixture of men and women who were both young and mature and all with considerable experience in the BPP. The first central committee had two or three people with a strong responsibility in the security/military side of the BPP. Six of the members out of thirteen were the highest-ranking military officials in the BPP, and all six had substantial firsthand experience with BPP military operations. In the early days, the BPP openly brandished weapons, while the current group would deny owning a switchblade. I believe this balanced the political and military nature of the BPP in the composition of the central committee, reflecting the sophisticated understanding and development of the organization: that we were political and military at the same time.

The central committee met once a month at Elaine's house and sometimes in other locations, like the school complex. We were five women and eight men. Between 1975 and 1977, the number of men was just six because two of the brothers, both Buddha Samurai, were serving short prison terms related to the stern stuff.

The women were Elaine Brown, chairman; Ericka Huggins, director of the Oakland Community School; Norma Armour, director of finance; and Joan Kelly and Phyllis Jackson, who ran the Party's non-profit apparatus. The men were David Du Bois, stepson of W.E.B. and the publisher of our paper; Michael Fultz and Emory Douglass, both editors of our paper and responsible for other press-related work; Comrade Bethune, chief of staff; and the Buddha Samurai contingent: Big Bob Heard, Ellis White, George Robinson, and me, assistant chief of staff, coordinator of the security cadre, and armorer. The sixth brother was Wiley "Simba" Roberts, who was added to the central committee after he was transferred from our underground operation in LA. And ever present, taking copious notes on her yellow legal pad, was Elaine's secretary, Janice Banks.

Most of the time this group was very civil. Elaine chaired the meetings, and just about everyone participated fully in the lively discussions except me. There was this weird vibe, like an undertow in the room. We would talk about everything under the sun, solve all kinds of problems, and even decide the outcome of political contests on the local and state level. But we would never talk about the stern stuff. I thought that was rather odd, given the composition of the group, but it never happened. I thought that was our biggest drawback, like we had this dirty little secret about all of the bad niggers in the organization and the guns in our closets. And until that discussion was held in the open with this group, I would be a silent member. I chimed in on stuff that concerned me, and I was usually on the defensive.

A big topic—that is, with Phyllis Jackson—that caused my defensive posture was what I did or should do about my folks who doubled as maintenance personnel, cooks, and executive staff at the school complex. Strategically placed at our most valuable asset were some of our top security people. Some did wear concealed weapons, but the untrained eye would think they were just janitors, cooks, and staff of the nonprofit arm. It was important that our school complex was well secured. But the topic that got me into heated discussions with Phyllis was these guys' movements. As their coordinator for the daily work they did at the school complex, she complained that she could not account for their whereabouts, as most coordinators in the Party demanded of their staffs. She would start talking about this in the meetings and I would just tighten up and shrink in my chair. I would say, "You need to talk to them and get them to understand." After the meeting I would go and see Phyllis and tell her on no uncertain terms, "Please don't talk about that there anymore. If you have any beef about that, let's talk and work it out." But she kept talking about it, I kept going to see her about it, and we went back and forth.

Most of the issues discussed in the central committee meetings were political. We discussed the Party's participation in the Wilson for Mayor campaign. Things were going well and it looked like the judge had a clear shot at winning. We talked about dropping the name Black Panther Party and becoming a purely political organization that accepted members based on a monetary contribution basis. In essence, the name associated with the political-military group would disappear from the landscape. We talked about this a lot, but it never came to be. At one point, we made a move to stop using titles in the organization, especially those with military connotations. And then we began a series of discussions that I thought had significant ramifications with regard to my work and the future of our military-underground operations: consolidation!

Elaine started talking about consolidating the balance of the BPP. There were several chapters that had been left open for various reasons, and now Elaine wanted us to consider closing them down and moving the personnel to Oakland. The two most prominent chapters were Seattle, which had a strong and productive free health clinic, and Los Angeles, with its abundance of security personnel and other resources. Other chapters we discussed closing were Winston Salem, North Carolina, with its Free Ambulance Program, and a very small operation in Dallas, Texas.

The discussion about LA moved out of the BPP boardroom and into Elaine's bedroom with Bethune and me present. I told them that this would be a difficult move. I knew the LA operation better than anyone. Jimmy was going to be the biggest problem. He had severely beaten Elaine back when they were lovers, and I knew for sure that he had expected Huey to name him to the central committee with significant responsibility over the military operations. I knew he did not respect Bethune or Elaine or, for that matter, me. We kicked this around and I told them point-blank, "I know these guys. Once Jimmy's gone, they will fall into line, pack up, and move up here."

"So," Elaine said. "Okay, Flores, how do we do this?"

I responded emphatically, "We either take him out or incapacitate him. That's it, there's no other way."

Elaine and Bethune thought this was odd, coming from me, and Elaine asked, "I thought you loved Jimmy and the people down south. How could you be so harsh, Fly?"

"Because I do know them, that's why. Anyway, I love the Black Panther Party more, and I think removing Jimmy and bringing the other comrades up here is what's best for the Party."

Bethune asked, "What will we do for an underground operation? Where will we send our folks when they get hot?"

"We got the Duke in Chicago, and he says those white guys, you know the ones that worked with Fred, could help. I have actually discussed this with the Duke." (The Duke was in Chicago, working to reopen the Illinois chapter.)

They looked at each other and then at me, saying, "Let's do it."

"Okay," I said, "I'm down with this."

• • • Bethune and I began to map out our strategy. The first thing we did was invite Jimmy to come up to Oakland so that we could explain to him the way the Party had been set up in the Servant's absence. This was more of a ruse than anything else. We really wanted him to see the vastness and depth of the BPP's operation in the base. So when Jimmy arrived with this entourage, we wined and dined him, taking him around to the speakeasies and giving him a tour of the Party's facilities, taking great pains not to leave out the fact that we had forty Panthers operating on a broad military scale as opposed to the ten Panthers he could bring to the table. But we were serious; we needed those ten Panthers because they brought a great deal of institutional knowledge to our setup. When they were ready to return to LA, Elaine told Albert Armour to wait around and catch another flight because her schedule did not allow her to meet with him that day. And, like I thought he would, Jimmy told Al that he didn't have to listen to Elaine because Huey had told him he was to answer to no one but him. This was the last straw. Anyway, not only was Huey not here, but he probably had told people all kinds of stuff during those sessions up at his house that he wouldn't even remember. The Black Dog just fucked up.

They returned to LA, and two weeks later, Bethune and I flew down to talk to the troops. We really didn't care about seeing Jimmy; we just wanted to talk to the other folks one-on-two to get the feel of the situation and to ascertain if we were wasting our time in bringing them up after Jimmy was dealt with. These were ten strong comrades, tested and firm in their commitment to the struggle and the Party, and we needed them. Also, they had some good TE that we could use. Bethune and I met with each person. We didn't talk about the entire plan. We just wanted to see where their heads were. Most would love to be in Oakland, with the exception of Jimmy's harem of dedicated women. So the plan was set in motion. It didn't take a rocket scientist to tell that Jimmy was arrogant and would probably overestimate his status and his future position with the BPP. On the other hand, I was sure that he believed he was smarter and more cunning than we were. But with his ego and a hell of a high opinion of himself, we didn't have to venture far for the ruse to get his ass up to Oakland. We told him that he was being brought to Oakland to be installed on the central committee with the rank of field marshal. He called Elaine's secretary, Janice, to inform her that he would be in Oakland on the day of the appointment for his installation.

We weren't taking any chances. We may have had the upper hand, but we would not underestimate him. First we made sure that Jimmy and the two people traveling with him, Simba and Al, were flying up.

FLORES A. FORBES

This way we were sure that they would not be armed. But we had been invited to a place before and an ambush was set. We told them we were flying too. But I took the train with a satchel full of TE, met our people at the airport, and when we walked into the ambush, we turned the tables on them and they got the waylay. So we had to anticipate some form of trick or ruse on his part. Because if I knew anything about Jimmy, Simba, and Al, it was that they were three of the best gunfighters in the Party, and in order for us to do what we planned to do, we needed to make sure that the conditions were in our favor. We set the meeting at my house. I had moved from the Oakland Hills and was now living on Fairmount Street. Elaine lived in the same complex just three floors above me. This was a move I had wanted to happen, but I was a little uncomfortable because my younger sister, Katherine, was up for a visit during this time. I would have to work around her.

Jimmy arrived on time, just like we thought he would. The trap was set. Two brothers would be in a back room with riot shotguns. This was more for effect than anything else. Then we had two people who were great with their hands and feet to do the mud-holing. And then there would be Elaine, Bethune, and me. My sister was hanging out at Elaine's with her roommate, Joan Kelly. Jimmy walked in all arrogant and talking shit. I could sense that he was no more aware of the situation than my sister was. When the meeting began, Elaine made it clear that this was not a central committee meeting and that he was not going to be anointed, but that this was a disciplinary hearing. The Black Dog tensed up. He realized that we had tricked him, and that probably pissed him off more than the fact that he was going to get his ass kicked. But sister Elaine was in her element. She went over the fact that Jimmy had countermanded her order for Al to wait. Jimmy said this stuff was personal and petty, and because Elaine and Jimmy used to have a relationship at one time, it didn't have any basis for a hearing. I was sitting there and thinking, This nigga is not sufficiently up on his Sun-tzu and just doesn't get it: the war was over when he walked through the door. I looked at Al and winked and then at Simba sitting next to Jimmy on the couch. I thought I saw both of them inching away from Jimmy.

Jimmy may not have gotten what was going on, but those two sure as hell did.

I flashed back to when Jimmy's goon squad had come to Riverside. Damn, I thought, I had better odds then than he has now.

"Expelled," Jimmy blurted out in astonishment. "How in the fuck can you expel me for this?" He turned to plead with Bethune. "This shit is personal."

Then things happened real fast. One of the brothers collared Jimmy, yanked him from his seat, and practically carried him to the center of the floor. And then the mud was slung. I moved out of the way, grabbing one of my lamps so these niggas wouldn't break it. All I could think about was how I was going to get this blood off my carpet before my sister came back downstairs. (A few hours later I rented a carpet cleaner to do the job.) Because at this juncture, Jimmy was not worth thinking about; he was old news.

I have never seen Jimmy again.

With that done, we instructed Simba and Al to go back to LA and prepare to move the operation to Oakland. They arrived almost one month later. I sent Texas, Santa Rita, and Aaron down to LA to dig up the TE and move the weapons up to the Bay Area. The irony in this was that the same weapons Shabazz had purchased that day in Riverside from the marines were part of the cache coming up north.

• • • In 1976 we delivered on our part of the deal with Lionel Wilson. We sent out every single Panther, Panther sympathizer, and Party volunteer to work for his campaign, and he became the first black mayor of the city of Oakland. Elaine had come back from visiting Huey in Cuba and announced that we were going to begin planning his return. She worked her side of the street organizing Wilson, Fortune 500 CEOs, and other power brokers in the Bay Area to promote our plan to take over the city of Oakland. (Of course, they didn't know about the plan.) We worked our side of the street. We were organizing many of the local dealers and bringing them into the fold. Some we armed with top-flight weapons, while others were given their own turf that was sacrosanct. Not only did we work the local crowd, but we even expanded to LA and worked with some of the original Crips. Some of them had come up to work on Wilson's campaign, and we hit it off and started working on an idea that Elaine and I had been kicking around for some time: reopening the LA chapter.

The chapter was officially reopened in February 1977. I went down to LA for the project, taking about fifteen people from the base to assist. I met my family for dinner at a local restaurant. I saw them maybe every six months or so, when I traveled down to San Diego for a quick break. My mother and father had finally accepted my life choice. In fact, I believed they were rather proud of me. They could see that I was successful at doing something worthwhile with my life, even if it was dangerous. I had no way of knowing it, but this would be the last time I saw my father alive.

BOOK
TWO

• • • Huey P. Newton was the Servant of the People in his own eyes and in ours, his comrades in the Black Panther Party. He was our leader, so organizationally we attended to him in big and small ways, from following his directives to lighting his cigarette.

22

TEXAS AND I DROVE to a park at the top of the Berkeley Hills. We came here often to smoke weed and to discuss our current and future military operations on the streets of Oakland and Berkeley and our work with the Black Panther Party's arsenal of weapons. Where I parked gave us a panoramic view of the San Francisco–Oakland Bay Area. The time was around 11:30 A.M. and the late-summer-morning overcast had yet to burn off, blurring our view of the Bay Area. We smoked a couple of joints and discussed some immediate business before I changed the subject.

"Texas."

A moment passed before he responded. "What, Fly?"

"Will you die with me, comrade brother?"

Texas looked at me for a few seconds, got off the hood of the car, and walked toward the edge of the mountain. I humorously thought that the question wasn't supposed to make the nigga jump off the mountain. He finished his joint and walked back toward me. He looked me straight in the eye and said, "Yeah, Fly, of course, brother. You know I'm down with you to the end or the day of liberation, whichever comes first, my brother."

This was the answer I had expected, but you never know. Like Huey always said, "Shit happens."

"Texas," I continued, "you know the Servant is coming back from Cuba in a few weeks?"

"Yeah," he replied, almost standing at attention.

"And you know we got a lot of work to do, getting things ready and stuff like that?"

"Yeah, right on."

"Well, you know, there's his case and that dope-fiend bitch that's testifying against him."

Texas remained silent for a while, looking down at the dirt, kicking pebbles around, before he asked, "Fly, do we have a mission?"

"Not quite, but it's something like that." I stood up and walked a few paces away, thinking about how I should put this to him. I turned to face him and said, "Texas, we don't have orders, but what we do have is the 'right to initiative.' "

This term was derived from our reading and interpretation of *Wretched of the Earth,* by Frantz Fanon. He states that it is the oppressed people's right to believe that they should kill their oppressor in order to obtain their freedom. We just modified it somewhat to mean anyone who's in our way, like the woman who meant to testify against Huey. The first part of this phrase dealt with the right to do it. The second part, which relates to the initiative, just meant that we would do the operation and once it was successful, we would report it to the central committee.

Texas smiled and said, "Come on, Fly, what kind of bullshit is that, something from Mao or what's-his-name?"

"You mean the guy who wrote *The Minimanual of the Urban Guerrilla,* Carlos Marighella?"

"Yeah, that's him, and the rest of them motherfuckers we've been reading."

"Shit, Texas, that's some good shit, man—you know, Sun-tzu, Che, the whole nine yards. It puts hair on your brain, man. Look, man, we don't have to wait for someone to tell us what to do."

"We don't?" he replied.

"Look, man, we're Buddha Samurai, and besides, we ain't never been caught. You know we plan this shit out pretty good for some regular old niggas."

"Okay, I'm in, but what about Bethune or Elaine or the Servant?" Texas asked.

I walked a little closer to him, put my hand on his shoulder, and said, "Texas, don't you notice how nobody in the Party questions what you or I do, where we go, or, for that matter, what technical equipment we move and to where? Shit, man, they wouldn't even notice if we planned an operation or not, you know. We could assemble a team, and nobody would question whether we got orders or not. The brothers and sisters we pick will never question me. You know they will never question me because I run the fold. Whenever I speak, comrades assume it has come down from on high, you know what I'm saying?"

Texas laughed in agreement and said, "Yeah, Fly, you're right."

"Look, man, me and you can save the Servant's life by dusting this snitchin' bitch off the planet."

"Who is she, Fly?" Texas asked.

"Her name is Chrystal Gray or something like that, and she was this whore's pimp. The jasper says she saw the Servant shoot her stuff out on San Pablo, and now she wants Huey to pay. Well, we'll fix that shit, T."

"Right on, Fly, right on," he said as we slapped hands and snapped our fingers in the latest dap-style handshake.

I probably could have come up with another plan that didn't involve an assault team, or I could have just done nothing and let it go. Huey always had top-notch lawyers. I could have let them handle the situation, but that was not our nature. I had been instilled over the years in the Black Panther Party in the belief of our righteousness—as Huey used to put it, the belief in our brand of theater. This theater included the use of guns, rhetoric, and bravado and the willingness to use them, even if we were wrong as two left shoes.

Before we got back into my Volvo, I asked Texas to make sure he didn't discuss any of this with Bethune or Big Bob, because they might pull rank on him and jam him about what we were up to. My rationale was simple: if they didn't know and things didn't work out, they could honestly tell Huey and Elaine that they didn't know a thing. Telling the truth in the BPP was important, even though the higher up you got in rank, the less it was adhered to. As we drove off, I told Texas a code phrase I would use on the phone if the operation was a go: "Leave your wallet at home; I'm coming by to pick you up."

This conversation took place in June 1977. We would not mention the subject again until October 21, 1977.

23

Huey had been in exile in Cuba for about three years following an incident in which he was alleged to have murdered a prostitute on San Pablo Avenue in Oakland. He skipped bail, and we had set up his return to the States to stand trial.

"The Servant will be back the first week of July," Elaine Brown said with a proud smile. Her efforts in particular were bringing Huey P. Newton home from Cuba. I was startled because that was about two weeks off. I smiled and began to beam, Bethune smiled, and Elaine started to get emotional. We hugged and congratulated ourselves on a job well done, though I felt that deep down, his return would not be that happy an occasion. We discussed some preliminary details in regard to his coming back, like where he would live and how the Black Panther Party would be organized and structured once he returned. We could not fathom what he might want to do, and that was not good because we—Elaine, Bethune, and I—were the chain of command. Huey was unpredictable. He had that edge on everyone: you could read all about him and be around him and still not be able to predict how he would act or treat you as a person. Because of this unpredictability, most people, including Party members, were afraid of him.

Elaine had received a credible death threat from a former Panther military official. So for the next couple of weeks, during the evening, I assigned different brothers from the cadre to stand watch at her house. On several occasions I went myself. Elaine and I stayed up most of the night talking about the Party, the past, and Huey. I was able to elicit from Elaine information that the legal team had put together to defend Huey against charges of murder. I had to inquire without her getting suspicious about my intentions. Bethune and I had set up several covert operations in the past where we told Elaine about them only after they were completed. She was pretty pissed off and told Bethune that the next time we pulled something like that, she would have his ass nailed to the front of central headquarters on East Fourteenth. He chilled, but I could not. I needed to get the location of the witness; time was running out.

My plan was to kill the witness, the dead prostitute's female pimp, or jasper, on the morning of Huey's preliminary hearing.

Huey was charged with shooting seventeen-year-old Kathleen Smith, a prostitute, in the head on the morning of August 6, 1974. Even though it was believed that other streetwalkers may have seen the incident, only her female pimp had stepped forward as the state's star witness against the Servant. Ms. Smith was in a coma for several months and eventually died.

During the week when Huey was to return, I spent a lot of time with Comrade Bethune. We planned the reception for Huey at the San Francisco airport during the evening and worked on our houses and the school complex during the day. We were renovating many of the properties in our real estate portfolio. We also talked about the status of the security cadre inside the Party.

The security cadre had expanded far beyond our expectations. Most of the brothers and sisters were now trained and deeply entrenched within the Party's everyday apparatus. Bethune, Bob, and I were pretty much settled into what we were doing and were very happy with the progress of the brothers and sisters in the fold. (*Fold* is a word to connote the BPP's inner circle and was also used for the group of people involved with military operations.) Moreover, there was not very much happening on the streets, especially the stern stuff that was related to our earlier work in North Oakland and Berkeley. So as Bethune talked, he began to divulge that there was a new menace afoot: the Felix Mitchell Mob.

Mitchell was operating a large heroin operation right across the street from the school complex. Bethune also said that the Servant was aware of this situation and that he would probably make it a priority on his agenda. I assigned Texas and various brothers to start gathering data on this guy's operation—right away. I figured we had time to plan, so why rush things. I told Texas this was something that was sure to get our attention in the future. I suggested that we confine ourselves to looking at Mitchell's operation and tagging his key people for future reference.

"We'll get to this guy sooner or later," I told Texas. "Besides, we've got more important things to worry about."

"Yeah, you're right, Fly. He'll be here when it's time to move on him and his people. That nigger ain't got nowhere to go anyway, you know, except them goddamn projects." We kinda laughed about this, put it on file, and then let it go for another time.

The planning for Huey's return had hit a feverish pitch by the day of his arrival. He had already left Cuba and landed in Canada. The authorities there flipped and placed him in custody. He was released, though—with the help of a Canadian member of parliament—and was scheduled to arrive at San Francisco International Airport on the evening of July 3. The logistics of putting this together was a unique experience. We had to transport approximately 150 to 200 adult Panthers and half that many kids to the international arrivals area at the airport and get them all back to Oakland after the event. We negotiated with the Oakland Police Department to allow us to drive Huey from the airport in Bethune's Town Car and deliver him to the police once we arrived in Oakland.

Bethune and Elaine had flown to Canada to make the flight back home with Huey and his wife, Gwen. I rode to the airport with Big Bob. We had every little detail of the Servant's homecoming worked out, all the way down to the music. Bob organized it so that when Huey got in

the car, a tape of his favorite song—"I Believe," by Johnnie Taylor—
would be playing.

When we got to the airport, there were thousands of people besides us to greet Huey: comrades, family, friends, the press, and the
Oakland police. We had arranged with the OPD's dignitary protection detail to park the Town Car in the front of the international arrivals door. Bob stayed with the car. It was my job to find the car and to
direct Huey's entourage to its location. One of the OPD officers said,
"Forbes, when we walk out with Huey's people, don't forget about
reminding Bob that you should follow our car to the Alameda County
jail, after we cross the bay." I didn't recognize any of them, but they
knew who I was.

"Right on," I said in reply, while flashing him a clenched fist, Panther
Power.

Cooperating with the OPD was blowing my mind. But for Huey,
anything could be done. Huey was about five to ten minutes away from
deplaning when I decided to build a human gauntlet with the comrades
so that he could walk through the crowd unimpeded. By the time the
gauntlet was finished, the plane was pulling up to the gate. The crowd
started to get loud and press toward the designated gate. I moved with
the brothers to be closer to the Servant, as did the OPD detail. This was
the closest we had ever been to the police, and they were really checking us out. It was one of those rare occasions when that tension between
us was gone. We were cooperating for a good cause.

The door burst open. Elaine and Bethune emerged, followed by the
Servant and Gwen. I felt like a witness to a last-second shot in an NBA
championship game that wins the series or something like that, when
someone does something that is unexpected and it works. It was a
moment of pure joy that comes with goose bumps and watery eyes. I
was close to the kind of tears that you might shed when someone makes
an emotional speech that touches every major and minor point you
believe in. I was truly psyched, but I did snap out of my trance. I had to
move; I could not stand around teary-eyed. The police clearly didn't
want Huey to go through the gauntlet. The head of their detail said we

should go through a special door when it was time to leave. That was cool with me.

Huey got on top of the baggage counter, and the throngs of people began cheering and waving as he bent down to shake hands and dap with familiar well-wishers. It was then that we made eye contact. He gave me the Buddha Samurai nod, and I nodded back. I jumped up onto the counter and we embraced. I then got down to greet and hug Gwen.

"Fly, where's the car?" Bethune asked.

"It's this way," I said, pointing in the direction of the OPD special door. As I started to steer them in that direction, Bethune grabbed my arm and asked who were those white men following us.

"They're the police, man. We've been kicking it with them all evening," I replied with a touch of sarcasm.

"Oh, okay, that's right, we have to take the Servant to the jail," he said.

"Right," I said.

Before we could leave, the Servant jumped back onto the baggage counter and held up his hands, gesturing for people to be quiet. I didn't hear most of what he said, but I did hear him say, "Comrades, we are declaring war on the drug dealers, and we will rid Oakland of this new menace."

I was stunned, to say the least. We never made policy statements in public like that, not without careful planning. But he had done it now, and that meant we were committed, and I didn't like it. Huey had changed! He never would have made such a statement in public before, especially with the police around. As we pushed through the door, I looked at Bethune and he looked at me. He was stunned too. We made our way to the car out front, and before I got in, the OPD sergeant said for us to follow them again. "Right on," I said. Those guys were really nervous, and who could blame them? After all of these years of fuckin' with us and us fuckin' with them, I guess they couldn't really believe that we would hear a word they said.

The ride back to Oakland was a quiet one for me, except for the stereo blasting Johnnie Taylor. All I could think about was this declaration of war that Huey had tied us to. Huey spoke briefly to Bob, Elaine, and Bethune. He then turned around in the front seat and said, "Flores, how are you, comrade brother, how have you been doing?"

"Fine, Servant, I'm doing fine." Man, was I distracted.

He had that look in his eyes, as if to say: "I am different, but how? You figure it out, Fly; you think you're so goddamn smart." You know, it was like he was laughing at you, from deep down inside. From the very first time I met Huey, in 1972, he was always kind of spooky. He was born with a veil over his face, and that's supposed to connote some type of mystical power. That could have been some bullshit, but he was always pulling a rabbit out of his hat. He was doing it now, with this almost impossible return to America. He was finally back, safe and sound, just like I prayed he'd be. We went directly to the Alameda County jail and turned Huey over to the OPD. He was bailed out two weeks later.

The Black Panther Party that Huey left in 1974 was not the same one he returned to in 1977. We had grown in some significant ways. We had gotten Lionel Wilson elected mayor of Oakland, thus completing one of the major objectives of our five-year plan to take over the city of Oakland. Elaine had worked effectively to establish links with the governor, judges, and many of the Fortune 500 companies in the Bay Area. And our centerpiece program, the Oakland Community School, was considered a serious innovation in alternative education and had reaped the public kudos to prove it. We had expanded our operations on all fronts. The people who were in leadership positions were relatively new to the Servant, even though most of them had been in the Party for some time.

I began to hear rumblings from Phyllis Jackson, Norma Armour, and Ericka Huggins. Elaine was absent from places where I usually saw her—a telltale sign of something not going well. There was this new tension in the air at festive parties, meetings, and other types of events. You could cut the shit with a knife. I thought things were still swell, but I sensed some uneasiness at the top, especially where our chain of command was concerned. The reason for this tension was obvious to me. We had a disciplined organizational structure or chain of command upon Huey's return. Before Huey left, the chain of command wasn't adhered to strictly. He might talk to you, a comrade, about some very deep shit that we would be involved with. But now the chain of command was adhered to strictly. Conversations now with him were usually about casual topics and not the stern stuff, as in the past. Everyone, including Elaine and me, was dealing with a buffer like Bethune or Bob between Huey and us. I was still the main link in the chain of command to the central committee for the fold and the rank and file. I wasn't very comfortable with that role, but I had to learn how to work with the new circumstances.

I was working on our housing projects, the Felix Mitchell stuff, and responding to whatever new things the Servant wanted done. One day, while I was working on the house on Tenth Street in North Berkeley, Bethune, Bob, and the Servant came by. Huey was reviewing our work on the houses and the school complex. He was still peripatetic and walked around the property greeting the brothers and inspecting the work. He didn't stay long, and as we shook hands, he nodded in approval, asking me if everything was okay. "Of course," I replied. We walked Huey to the car, all except Bethune, who told the Servant he was going to stay. It was not customary for us to leave the Servant's company until we were dismissed. There was something afoot. Huey and Bob drove off. Bethune directed me to the front porch of the house and offered me a seat.

"Fly," Bethune began, "I have some bad news."

"What is it?" I asked with that confident sound you try and make when a surprise response on your part could mean your ass or your life.

"Well, Joan Kelly has filed charges against the Pearl, Fly."

Joan Kelly was a member of the central committee who was in charge of the Party's expansive nonprofit organizations, and Frances "Pearl" Moore was my live-in girlfriend and a rank-and-file member of the BPP. We had been together for three years.

"What? What for?" I was shaken. Bethune stood up and walked onto the sidewalk approach to the porch and then turned on his heel.

"She's a thief, Fly; she stole some stuff from Joan Kelly's purse. And you know she's been suspected of this kind of thing before. The Servant says she's got to be expelled." I was numb, but I didn't say a word. "Fly," Bethune said, "are you okay?"

"What do you think?" I said as I got up to walk away. I hit my forehead with the palm of my hand. Damn. Shit, this is fucked up, I said to myself. I couldn't believe they would fuck with Baby at this juncture. It seemed as if they didn't give a fuck about nothing. After all of these years of dedicated service, these niggers choose now to fuck with me by fucking with my woman. I knew how the shit worked around here, and that meant it wasn't Joan who had come up with this scam. It was probably the nigga I was trying to save. Yeah, I was certain, because this was the Servant's style. I should've known because I was usually in on the scheme, but not this time. And here I was planning to lop off this bitch's head to save the Servant. Man, the shit could get thick around here. I was schooled by the movement to subordinate my personal relationships and my feelings for the business of the fold. This was hard because I loved this woman.

I must set an example, I said to myself. So at her board hearing, at which I did not preside because of a conflict of interest, I showed my support for the executive decision. I did not try to defend her. I did not say one word. Bethune read the charges and she started to cry, glancing in my direction. I averted my eyes because it was hard not to help, seeing those big beautiful brown eyes filled with tears. I would not help because this could be a test, knowing how many games Huey could play with a person. I believed the Party came before my personal life, and now was my time to practice what I preached. After reading the charges, Bethune told Frances, "You have been officially expelled from the Black Panther Party with no appeal possible. You must go to your apartment and remove all of your personal belongings." And then he added, "Oh yeah, don't call Flores, because as you can see, he is in agreement with this move." Bethune then nodded in my direction. I got up, took Frances by the hand, and left. I drove her to our place to collect her things. I did not say one word to her in the elevator, car, or even as she walked out of the door and out of my life.

Over the next several weeks, other people left and or were expelled from the Party. It was reminiscent of the purge in 1974. We lost several people from the security cadre who had committed only minor infractions but split because they were afraid that with the Servant back, their discipline would be harsh. David Du Bois, the editor of our paper, left because of his mother's terminal illness, and about a dozen other people left for other reasons. I was hurting at the loss of many of them, but losing Frances hurt the most. Not once did I contemplate leaving or scrubbing the mission, though. I would not allow my personal problems to interfere with or overcome my fealty to the Servant. That was the way I had been trained.

One evening, Bethune called me up and told me to meet him at the school as soon as possible. I parked in the school complex parking lot, and before I could get out of the car, Bethune came over, motioning for me to keep the engine running. He said he wanted to drive around and talk about the Felix Mitchell situation. We did, but then he changed the subject. "Fly, Elaine has left the Party," he said in a sad voice. I didn't say a word for a minute or two. I just sat there thinking that something was terribly wrong.

"Is she okay, I mean, physically?"

"Yeah," said Bethune, "she's okay." He continued, "She left last night, you know. She had Aaron leave her the car here at the school, and she picked up her daughter, Ericka, and went to the San Francisco airport last night." We continued to drive around Oakland discussing other issues, but I drew a blank on everything else he talked about.

I had known Elaine Brown longer than anyone else I had considered a friend in the Black Panther Party. I had learned many things from her over the years, and desertion was not one of them. So for her to leave, I knew she had to have a damn good reason. At least she was safe and sound, I thought.

The Black Panther Party was a male-dominated organization. Until

157

Elaine came to power, and even after her ascension, one male-centered policy had not changed: women in the Party were not allowed to date men who were not Party members. The reasons given for this prohibition were as varied as the men who might have answered the question. The rule was made to control the influx of men into the Party, as far as I was concerned. Most government agents known to have infiltrated the Party were men. So, if you asked me why we practiced this caveman policy, my response would be for reasons of security. Women in leadership positions, though, could date or marry whomever they liked. This, therefore, became a burning issue among the sisters in the rank and file.

The women led by Ericka Huggins called for two central committee meetings to discuss, first, the issue of women dating outside of the Party and, second, Elaine's leaving. Ericka Huggins, like Elaine, Norma Armour, Joan Kelly, and I, was from Los Angeles and had been through the early wars together. They were known as the LA clique because they stuck together on many issues and because they were the women who ran most of the BPP. Ericka was the director of the school and well known in the black/women's liberation struggle in this country. In addition, she was just about as well known as Huey during certain periods of our history. And on top of that, she was known for not taking any shit. Tall, tan, and beautiful, Ericka projected a fun-loving exterior that many people mistook as meaning she was weak. We knew better. Ericka had been through more than many of the brothers. Phyllis Jackson and Joan Kelly ran our major nonprofit operation, Educational Opportunities Corporation (EOC). Joan was from LA and had dropped out of UCLA to join the Party in 1969. She was one of the major movers and shakers during Bobby's and Elaine's first campaigns, Elaine's second campaign, and in the successful election of Lionel Wilson in 1976. Phyllis had been a major player during the previous campaigns and, along with Joan, ran EOC with an iron fist. Phyllis was also one of the first women recruited by Masai for the security cadre. She hadn't been active in the last couple of years, but Phyllis was on many of the early military operations we ran in the early '70s. And let me tell you, she was slinging and banging like she had been doing this street thing for years. Norma Armour was down like most of the brothers when it came to using technical equipment. She was our finance director, and when I needed money to get down or something, Norma was not a "rubber stamp." I remember one time Bethune and I came up with this scheme to rob the Black Knight (a local speakeasy), and Norma made us run through the plans with her and even take her down to the joint so she could see if the take we estimated would be worth the cost. I'll be damned, this woman was doing a cost-benefit analysis to determine whether the job was worth it. She didn't back it, so we dropped the whole thing.

Huey's wife, Gwen, had literally saved his life. As the story goes, when Huey was a fugitive, Gwen and he were on this boat getting ready to land on the Cuban coast. The boat hit a reef and went down. Huey couldn't swim, but Gwen was a strong swimmer and she rescued him from drowning. He wouldn't have survived if it weren't for Gwen.

The meeting was held on a bright, sunny day. Many were in good spirits with Huey back, especially the kids at the school. They mobbed him when he arrived, and during the entire meeting they were milling outside of the classroom Ericka had selected for the meeting. Traditionally, the central committee meeting was run by the chairman, but since Elaine was not present and Ericka had called the meeting, Huey deferred to her as the host. We were all sitting around talking and acting like everything was cool when Ericka started off the meeting. She got right to the point.

"Huey, we want to make some changes around here," Ericka said.

"Fine, comrade sister, what kind of changes would you like to propose?" Huey responded.

"Well," said Ericka, "we carry quite a bit of the load around here, and we want some equity, you know, the kind of stuff that you and Bobby used to talk about when you first got out of prison. We are the ones with most of the skills in the Party. We write the grant proposals, teach most if not all of the classes at the school. We run the lion's share of our programs and yet we are treated like some motherfucking Pantherettes."

Wow! I said to myself, she was getting deep and she was just getting warm. I glanced at Big Bob and Bethune, who were noticeably moved. The sisters sat there as if this were their own in-house theatrical presentation. And it was. Ericka shifted in her chair and turned toward the rest of the sisters as she continued. The chairs were arranged in a semicircle: the men on one side and the women on the other.

"We have fought and died just like you guys have. My husband was killed by those faggots in LA. Joan Kelly has lost two men here, one dead and the other in prison. And there isn't one brother in this room or in the Black Panther Party who can ride or shoot better than any woman in this room."

When Ericka said that, she eyeballed all of the brothers, roving up and down the pistol-packing assemblage. "Shit," she said as she crossed one of her long pretty legs over the other, "the women here should be able to fuck whomever they want to. We have earned it." The room was silent. I looked at the Servant, and if looks could kill, Ericka would have been dead on arrival.

"Does anyone else have anything to say?" Huey asked in a reserved voice.

Hell no, I could hear everyone except Ericka saying to themselves. No one responded.

"Fine," said the Servant. "What Comrade Ericka said will be taken under advisement. This meeting is over." The room cleared in about thirty seconds.

The brothers on the central committee were just regular guys. Emory Douglass was the only person left in the Party who had gone to Sacramento in 1967 and defined what our revolutionary culture was from day one. It's been said that the San Francisco police wanted to cut his hands off because of his artful depiction of them as "pigs."

Big Bob, Bethune, George Robinson, Ellis White, and I were just ordinary everyday Panther gunmen turned administrators. Everything the sisters didn't run, we ran. Michael Fultz was the editor of *The Black Panther* and wrote a lot of the press that we disseminated. I also believe that Fultz was the only brother on the central committee with a BA.

Even though the entire central committee—Ericka, Norma, Joan, Phyllis, Gwen, Bethune, Bob, Ellis, Emory, Fultz, George, and I—were present, it was clear that it was just a rubber-stamp committee with very little power and that Huey P. Newton was the sole decision maker of the body. Or, if you were viewing this from my side of the room: all of the brothers on the CC would naturally back the Servant.

The next and last central committee meeting I attended was held at Huey's house. The purpose of this meeting was to address Elaine's leaving and to take a vote on the dating issue. There was a great deal of tension in this meeting, especially after Ericka's performance at the school. It was obvious that the women had gotten together and discussed their strategy. Afterward, I got together with some of the brothers on the CC, got fucked up, and talked shit about the show that the sisters had put on. And it appeared they had organized a plan for this one too.

The men sat on one side of a long table while the women sat on the other. Huey came down from his bedroom dressed in a silk robe; not even street clothes. It was clear that he had no respect for this so-called august body any longer or, for that matter, even the people in the Party. Ericka, Phyllis, Joan, Norma, and Gwen were on one side of the issue, and Huey, Bob, Bethune, Ellis, George, Fultz, Emory, and I were on the other side. And that's the way the vote went, along gender lines.

When the discussion turned to Elaine's departure, Phyllis broke down crying. She cried for the entire meeting—something I know they didn't plan on. She said that since she was one of the last people to talk with Elaine, she thought she would be accused by remaining Party members of complicity and get beaten up or something like that. Huey told her that her fears were ridiculous. As one of the most trusted people in the Party, she had nothing to worry about. I thought I heard a silent collective snicker. But Phyllis kept crying nonetheless. She was a member of the security cadre, and I had to relate. Phyllis wasn't just another innocent attracted to the leather and guns; she was here to really help her people. So I felt deeply for her concerns. She was among the few real friends I had left. And they were growing fewer by the day.

Huey said he had talked with Elaine and she might be coming back, but if she didn't, we should move on, because this was an organizational collective and not an organization of individual personalities. Just like in the prior meeting, the collective voice of the women came from Ericka Huggins.

Ericka said, "I know all of these brothers here. Their reputations would make Bumpy Johnson* shit in his pants. How do we know sister Elaine is alive, even though you've said you have spoken to her? Where is she, Huey?" Man, she was pushing some real buttons. Ericka then leaned over the table and in her harshest voice said, "Phyllis, will you please shut the fuck up, I can't hear myself think." That moved everybody. A few of us actually jumped in our chairs. And then Ericka sat back and stiffened, awaiting Huey's response.

Huey shifted in his chair and reached into the pocket of his robe and produced a piece of paper. "Sister Ericka, I'm sorry you no longer trust us, but I would never harm a hair on Elaine's head." He then tossed the paper across the table toward Ericka, saying, "She's at this number in LA."

Without remorse, Ericka said, "Can I keep this?"

Before she could finish, Huey rose, bowed toward us, and said, "Of course." He then stood up straight, said, "Power to the people," and, turning quickly, left the room. This was a gloomy moment, and the rain outside seemed to underscore matters. I sat there, thinking that never before in my life had I seen so many tough people so uptight or nervous. This time the room cleared in twenty seconds. More and more I began to wonder what this all really meant for my future and me.

---

*Bumpy Johnson was a notorious Harlem gangster involved in the policy rackets during the 1930s.

24

Elaine never returned to the Party, and after that meeting, I never saw Huey P. Newton again.

THE NEXT DAY WAS October 21, 1977. I had secured the intelligence data needed for the operation to get rid of the witness against Huey about two days before the last central committee meeting at Huey's house. The preliminary hearing was scheduled for this Monday; we would strike on that Sunday morning, just as the target was rolling over. So on this day, as I woke, I contemplated doing my disappearing act for at least the two days it would take to set up and execute the plan. I looked at the phone and thought about calling Texas, but instead I got up and paced around my living room, trying to get at what was bothering me. Maybe the Servant wasn't worth this effort. But I was committed and wouldn't turn back now, even if he wasn't worth it. I went back into my bedroom and took the phone off the dresser and into the bathroom and shut the door behind me.

I needed another safety net. I figured that the only brothers in the fold outside of Texas whom I could trust were the brothers in the cadre from LA. I decided to call Pookie and Stubbs. They were both down with the Buddha Samurai, and besides, I knew they would kill grass if I told them to. The phone rang about four or five times before Pookie answered. I could tell he was just waking up; it was about 7:00 A.M.

"Right on, this is Pookie."

"Pookie, it's me, man." I waited and hoped he recognized my voice.

"Yeah, right on, Fly."

Good, I thought. "Listen, Pook, I need you to be ready for a phone call. When you get it, listen carefully to the person on the other end. It probably won't be me, so don't trip on that, okay?"

"Okay, right on."

"It will probably be within the next few days."

"Right on."

"When you get the call, go and get Stubbs and tell him everything that I'm telling you now, in addition to the information from the phone call that you might receive."

"Right on."

"And do everything they tell you to do."

"Right on."

"Also, Pook, check this out. If you get the call and have to hook something up for me, you probably should keep going after you finish." There was a pause on the other end, but I knew he was still there because I could hear his breathing.

"Fly," he said after a few seconds.

"Yeah."

"I'm down with you to the end, my brother, or until the final day of liberation." I just sat there on the phone and took in what he had just said. Man, I thought, it was kind of overwhelming to hear someone say that to you. I guess the thing that really rocked me is that he was deadly serious about who and what we were. Just like I was.

"Right on, Pook, I knew I could count on you. And there's just one more thing to remember about the call."

"What's that, Fly?"

"That we will always be brothers in life and brothers in death." I almost thought I was going to cry when I said that. Damn, I thought. I had to say that. What else could I say? Something stupid, like "Thank you, my brother, for backing me in the blind."

"Right on, Fly, I got it," he said and hung up.

I hung up and just sat on the edge of the bathtub. I got up and headed for the picture that hung over the couch in my living room. I knelt on the couch and took the frame off its hook. I sat on the couch and carefully slid the armory list out of the back of the frame. Then I picked up the phone to call Texas.

"Right on, this is Naomi."

"Hey, Nai Nai, this is Flores."

"Hi, Fly, how are you doing?"

"I'm fine, baby. Is the Twister there?"

"Yeah, hold on."

"What's up, Fly?"

I paused, contemplating again how to say this. "T, ah, leave your wallet at home, I'm coming by to pick you up in about an hour."

"Right on, Fly," he said, and he hung up.

I hopped off the couch and walked back into my bedroom with the list. As I was looking for something to wear and intermittently checking the list for the best locations for the TE and a main staging area, my mind began to drift, and I wondered about the lack of fear. I was not bothered by the fact that I was on my way to assassinating someone. I wondered why then, and now.

I think that most Black Panther Party members—especially those comrades who had been in the Party for longer than five years—were in some kind of a "confidence zone." We thought we could do almost anything to achieve an objective—a revolutionary objective. This was the result of years of ideological and philosophical conditioning. We comrades were constantly bombarded with slick and catchy phrases that expounded on the greatness of sacrificing all for the cause, struggle, revolution, or whatever term was in vogue. We were taught that you should subordinate your personal life and all else for the goals spelled out in the Ten Point Platform and Program of the Black Panther Party.

What we were about to do, though, had nothing to do with the Ten Point Platform and Program.

In the final analysis, what I really believed was that Huey P. Newton was my "prince." I would kill or die for him at the drop of a hat. The brothers in the fold had pledged an allegiance to me in much the same way. We were down for this or that, and the only thing that mattered was that it worked. When we were attacked, we counterattacked the best we could. If we needed to change our rhetoric in order to fool the opposition, we did so. If we needed to change the way we dressed in order to deceive the local police and other law enforcement agencies, we did so. We had announced that we were laying down our guns in order to cut back on police attacks and murders, though we did not mean it. It was just another urban guerrilla adaptation. We made political statements for military reasons that would buy us time until we regrouped for another push against the system and society.

I got to Texas's pad, which was in the lower part of East Oakland, about five minutes later than I had expected. We started to plan our agenda for the next forty-eight hours. I had already selected several locations where we could pick up the TE that we would need for the job. And I had picked out a staging area at one of our places in North Oakland. It was near the freeway and about a twenty-minute drive from Richmond, the city where the witness lived. As we drove around, I explained to Texas about the location and that there was a slight possibility that the police might be there. I had this suspicion because the intelligence for this operation came from secondary sources and not our own due diligence. Upon hearing this, Texas just said in his own low-key style, "Fuck the police," and we pushed on.

I really liked Texas; he was a very talented brother who didn't get much credit, especially from the women in leadership positions. He was originally from Beaumont, Texas, hence the nickname, but had grown up in Detroit, which was where he first joined the Party. Louis Talbert Johnson was, to me, the prototypical Black Panther Party street operative. He was about six-two and weighed between 180 to 200 pounds. He was smart, and some considered him slick. He knew his weapons and

could shoot equally well with a handgun or automatic rifle, but he preferred a riot shotgun to any of them. He was good with his hands and a
buck knife and was probably one of the best "wheel men" in the Party.
He was a lover of jazz, especially fusion, and specifically Weather
Report. He was also a marijuana connoisseur of the highest order. But
what made him stand out the most, besides the large Apple Jack hat he
used to wear, was his dedication to duty and the Party and his fearless,
almost swashbuckling, style on a military operation. He always wanted
to be the first person through the door. He was my ace boon coon—
always there—making the right moves and having a good time doing it.
We had a deadly serious trust in each other, you know. Deep down
inside of me, I even wished, because I felt this impending doom, that I
had gone to Bethune and said the Party should support this thing and
make it one of those deep underground operations. But in order to do
that, we would need the Servant's nod, and I didn't think we would get
that. So there we were, making our move, as wrong as two left shoes.
Anyway, Texas was my main man, and we were going down for the
cause together. We were going down for our prince and not the people
or the Party or some other abstract notion of liberation. Yes, we were
idealists and too aggressive for some people, but we were not stupid
enough to think that what we were doing was tied to the Ten Point Platform and Program or any of our 1960s rhetoric. We believed we had
"the right to initiative," to take matters into our own hands. If things did
not work out, we were also willing to suffer the consequences.

We swooped into Richmond just to take a peek at the spot and locate
a secondary staging area. We looked long and hard and didn't see any
police. "Looks good," I said to Texas.

"Yeah, looks good, Fly," he replied.

We then set off for Oakland, to choose a team, pick up the TE, recon
the site, set up our staging area, plan a little more, make our move, and
go home. We decided that we needed about four more people to fill out
the team. One more brother to be with us on the initial assault, another
brother to drive and drop us off, and a man and a woman to pose as a
couple on a one-night stand to hold down the secondary staging area.

We stopped at a phone booth in Berkeley to call central headquarters. Henry "Mitch" Mitchell, who was the officer of the day, told me that Bethune and Bob had called, looking for me. I told Mitch, who had been on the housing rehab crew, to say he hadn't heard from me and not to sweat telling a lie. Everything was cool with him, he said. I asked him about the location of Elmo Black, Randell Jefferson, Stephanie Hopson, and Joe Jackson. They were the additional people we had selected to fill out our crew. I told him to contact each of them and have them meet me at the staging area in North Oakland. I further instructed him to say that this was extremely important and that they should not speak to anyone about this, which included their coordinators, Bethune and Bob. We were to meet in North Oakland at 11:00 P.M. The time now was 8:00 or 9:00 P.M.

Texas and I made two stops in Berkeley and grabbed an M16 automatic rifle and put it together and taped two 30-round banana clips full of .223-caliber ammo together. We then picked up two Riot 20 Standard, 12-gauge pump shotguns with 00 buck rounds for the tubular magazine; three dark jumpsuits; three pairs of leather gloves; and three ski masks. We would use the M16 as a backup for the police if they should show up or for anybody who could outgun the Riot 20s. The reason we used shotguns as the primary assault weapon was because they left no land or groove tracing that could be detected by a ballistics test. And the jumpsuits, ski masks, and gloves were used to prevent blood from splattering on our clothes, faces, and hands. The gloves were also used to hold down the prints we might leave behind and to shield our hands from the blast residue emitted by firing a weapon. But if anything at all went wrong, we had the option of leaving everything behind, because we knew that nothing could be traced back to us, unless it was one of our bodies. And as another precaution, everyone on the operation was instructed not to carry any ID. It would take the police several hours to trace you with only your prints.

We packed the trunk of the car and drove to the staging area in North Oakland to drop off the stuff. We then left to recon the spot. There were no changes. We drove around to time and measure the distance between the spot and the hotel we would use as a secondary staging area. We also looked for a good location to park the second car, in which we would leave the area after the operation was over. We returned to our primary staging area at about 10:30 P.M., and everyone was assembled. I spoke separately with everyone. I instructed Elmo Black to take Joe and Stephanie to the hotel staging area, where we would rest and lay low after the operation so that we would not have to drive back to Oakland until the next day. We went over everything again and again until 1:00 A.M. We set an alarm clock for 2:30 A.M. and then settled down to take a short nap. Texas and Randell were up and dressed in their gear, strapped down, and ready to go when the alarm went off at 2:30. I was the only one still asleep.

We left North Oakland in two cars. When we arrived at our location in Richmond, I instructed Randell, who was driving the second car, to park on the next block over and leave the keys in that car. He then hopped into our car, and we drove around for another hour or so to get familiar with the street movement. It was time.

Elmo dropped us off in front of the designated house at around 4:00 and then left to return to Oakland, as instructed. We walked up the driveway and knelt down in the dark below a window facing the street. I looked toward the front of the house just to see what I could see. Nothing. No movement, no sign of anyone. We pulled down our ski masks, and in a duck-walking crouch, we moved around to the designated door. This was a duplex with two doors facing the sidewalk with a backdrop or open area the size of a racquetball court. We went to the second door and stood up. I was on the left and Texas was on the right while Randell was kneeling on the other side of the sidewalk facing the front door. I motioned to Randell to rip the screen door off. Texas would reel around and kick the door in.

I gave the signal and everybody moved. With that done, I started in the door, closely followed by Texas. Randell remained outside to cover us. I saw two muzzle flashes and heard two sharp reports as I entered the door. I thought they had come from within. But I wasn't sure. They were followed by several sharp and rapid reports from outside. I began to raise my weapon to fire, but found that my entire right side was not working, it was numb. I couldn't feel a goddamn thing on my right side.

I had been shot.

A copper-jacketed .223-caliber bullet had banked off the right side of my shotgun stock and slid underneath the back of my glove and entered the crease of my wrist, just below the heel of my hand. Tumbling and slashing, it had exited out the top of my knuckle, ripping through my leather glove and leaving my gun hand useless but still wrapped around the stock. Damn, I thought. I cradled my weapon as more shots rang out from outside. I tried to retreat back through the door, but Texas, who seemed to be moving in slow motion, blocked my path. He was slumping near the entrance.

I said, "Texas, are you okay?" (Even that came out in slow motion.) There was no response. Randell turned and was facing the backdrop with his weapon held from a squatting position. Texas continued to fall in slow motion. Randell turned to see Texas falling and jumped toward him, trying to break his fall. He then struggled to pull Texas away from the door. Texas had been hit with a .223-caliber bullet in the back of the neck. It exited through his throat. I reeled outside, dropping my weapon and looking down at my right side. I felt my right arm with my left hand. Nothing. I raised my right hand with the help of my left hand. I couldn't see my fingers. Damn. I had been shot in the hand and I couldn't see my fingers anymore. Damn. I ripped at the glove. My hand started to burn and sting. I pulled the glove off, flinging it to the ground.

"Help me with Texas, Fly! He's hurt bad!" Randell shouted.

I grabbed T's left side as Randell grabbed his right. We attempted to drag him toward the street, but as we got to the driveway, I could see that he was gone. He felt like he weighed a thousand pounds.

"He's dead, man, we gotta leave him," I said.

"No," said Randell, "we gotta take him with us."

He continued trying to drag Texas, who was dead on his feet. I could not hold him up anymore, so I let go. The weight of T's body was too much for Randell alone, and he let go too.

"Come on, Randell, let's go," I said sternly.

We ran up the street toward the curb, peeling off our outerwear as we went. We had been trained long ago that if an operation gets botched, you must leave everything behind—guns, jumpsuits, and dead comrades. We made a left turn and headed for the next block, where we had parked the other car. As we got to the corner, I could see two police cars nearing the intersection from our right. We crossed the street and went to the car. I turned, while standing on the driver's side of the car, and faced the oncoming police car. The lights were flashing, but there was no siren. The police were about twenty feet away when they made a sharp left turn and headed down the street we had just left. Randell and I stood still there in the early-morning darkness. I popped the lock with my left hand and got into the car. Randell jumped in on the passenger side. We drove off. We swooped back to the hotel and picked up the couple at the secondary staging area; we wouldn't need it now.

After leaving the hotel, we drove down the street that intersected the street where we left Texas's body. There were police cars everywhere, but as I had guessed, there were no roadblocks yet. So we just drove by the police and headed back to the main staging area in North Oakland. As I drove away from the scene, I looked down at my bloody nub of a hand. Damn, I thought, I have to get medical treatment.

We were quiet in the car until Randell nervously said, "Fly, do you want me to drive?" I didn't answer. I just drove on, thinking, I have to get away. We have to get away. The cold reality of the situation set in and I felt a shiver throughout my body. Cold-blooded fear was riding me now. As I maneuvered the car back toward North Oakland, I kept repeating these short phrases to myself as if I were counting sheep, trying to go to sleep and forget about everything that had just happened. It didn't work.

What will I do now? What will I do? What will I do?

I will get away. That's what I will do. I will get away.

But regardless of what I said to psych myself up, I knew that from this moment on, my life as I had known it was over.

25

WHEN YOU EXPERIENCE a near-death occurrence or someone close to you gets popped and you're there, it forces you to focus in on where you have been in your life. Because, baby, that moment could be the last thing you remember. It could be the last taste of life that you get.

We made it back to Oakland from Richmond without any further incident. Jefferson helped me out of the car and into the house. I paid no attention to whether I was bleeding to death or not, I just wanted to lie down and go to sleep, hoping that when I woke up, this would all be a dream. It was hard to fathom that Texas was dead and still lying out there in the street being examined by the police, poking him, taking pictures of him, and then finally zipping him up in a big green bag.

Several people were home when I got inside the house. Jefferson helped me toward the back where the bedrooms were, and at Nelson's insistence he took me to the largest bed. Nelson was one of the best emergency medical technicians (EMTs) in the Party. As they positioned me on the bed, he started shouting orders: "Get me some hot water, peroxide, towels, and sheets, and something hard but flexible to make a splint with." He didn't appear nervous, but everyone else sure was. They started rushing the stuff in, and as they dropped it off, Nelson told them to leave the room.

My eyes stopped spinning and my mind cleared up as I looked down at my hand. I had no feeling from my shoulder to the hand. It looked like a big red catcher's glove with lots of white, black, and streaks of some other colors in it. I was lying there feeling all fucked up, while Nelson, with the skill of a field combat medic, calmly and efficiently wrapped my hand and arm around a makeshift splint. He then placed it in a sling. I guess after a few minutes I went to sleep or passed out. When I woke, Jefferson was lying at the foot of my bed and Nelson was sitting in a chair next to the bed.

I told Jefferson to wake up Elmo, who was asleep in the room next to mine, and ask him to come here. It was around 6:00 A.M. on Monday. Huey's arraignment was scheduled to begin at ten. Elmo came into the room looking a little disheveled and disoriented. I snapped into my assistant-chief-of-staff act to get his full attention. I told Jefferson and Nelson to leave, and as the door closed behind them, I began to disclose to Elmo the truth about this botched operation.

"Elmo, listen, and listen closely, man. I need for you to go to Bethune's house ASAP. Tell him I'm sorry but I thought we could pull this off without an incident. The shit did not work and it's my entire fault. Tell him Texas is dead and that I'm hurt real bad. I know they will be mad, so tell them that I will do whatever they want and that I won't cause any trouble. Elmo, they did not know about this, so they'll be pretty pissed off while you're there."

Elmo stepped back for a minute as if he had been shoved and said, "They didn't know—shit, are you serious, man?"

"Yeah, nigga, I'm serious," I snapped. "Look, motherfucker, go give them the message and tell them I need their help. I'm hit real bad and I might not make it, so get going."

Elmo snapped his head to attention and said, "Right on, Fly." He turned quickly, leaving the room, and a few minutes later I could hear his car zooming away.

After Elmo left, I called Nelson back into the room and asked him what he thought. "You need a doctor, Fly, that's all I can say or recommend." He said don't smoke and I did; he said don't drink any alcohol and I did. I was lying there helpless, like a wounded animal that wanted to survive.

I guess the kicker was that I really believed that for the last ten years I had been training and waiting for this day. The big challenge. The can't-win situation. The scuba-diver scenario: I was two hundred feet deep, my oxygen tank was punctured, a fifty-foot white shark was bearing down on my ass, and the bends were setting in as I swam to the surface too fast. And you really think you're going to make it after all.

If the Party would help, I could get away, because I thought I knew this stuff well enough to elude capture. My biggest problem was being wounded. I knew that no Panther in our history had been wounded and escaped capture because they were usually busted at the hospital. I really thought I had it together, though. At least I would if Huey would help, or maybe he might trip out and think I was part of a plot to fuck up his defense. If he thought that about me, I was sunk. But if he went deep into his heart and remembered how dedicated the "Fly" was, he would know that I was just taking the initiative and it didn't work. Huey was down. He was a Buddha Samurai too, and I was sure he would appreciate the effort, even if it cost the life of one of his very best soldiers.

The knock on the door was soft. I could tell it was not Bethune or Big Bob or Huey. None of them would have knocked. I also gathered that given the situation, none of them would be coming by. I told whoever was at the door to come in. It was Albert Armour, a Buddha Samurai and one of my homies from LA. I told Nelson and Jefferson to leave, but I consoled Jefferson as he left by saying, "Don't worry, brother, it wasn't your fault." But I said to myself, Yeah, you just panicked and shot everybody the fuck up.

Bert, as we called Armour, walked in and stood right by my side. "Fly, are you okay?"

"Yeah!"

"That's all they wanted to know. Bethune said it's no big deal, except for Texas, anyway. He says we all know that shit happens."

"Yeah," I said, moving myself into a more comfortable position but still keeping my no-feeling hand and arm across my heart as Nelson had instructed. Bert moved a little closer and took Nelson's chair near the bed, but he didn't sit down.

"Fly, are you willing to go to a hospital for an X-ray, and if we could hook it up, will you go to a hospital to get fixed up?"

"Yeah, sure," I said. I guess I would have said anything at this point because I could see Bert was nervous, and this made me nervous too. He said they would hook up a doctor and the trip to San Francisco for the X-ray and get me into a hospital afterward on Pill Hill, a neighborhood in North Oakland. He said the doctor would be here soon and then we'd drive to the hospital for the X-ray.

While we waited, Bert sat down in the chair and asked, "Is T really dead?"

"Yeah, Bert, he's really dead."

Texas and Bert had been pretty close.

In an hour or so Nelson came to the door to announce that the doctor had arrived. Bert jumped to his feet, motioning to Nelson to bring him in. A white guy with a beard, dressed in a shirt and jeans, came through the door with his little black bag. He walked over to me with Nelson following. He examined my splint and tourniquet from a distance without touching it. He then got a little closer and began touching part of Nelson's handiwork.

"Who did this splint?" he asked.

Nelson said, "I did."

Looking at Nelson as he removed the bandages, he said, "Nice work."

"Thanks," Nelson replied.

Once he had removed the bandages, he began to examine my hand. It appeared that he was looking for the entry and exit wounds. All I knew was that my hand was really fucked up. Finally he saw a small hole at the crease of my wrist. "Here it is," he said, pointing to the back of my wrist. I asked him if he thought the bullet was still inside, and he said he didn't know but that I should definitely get an X-ray to determine that. He stepped away from the bed and looked around the room at Bert and Nelson. "I don't know if the bullet is still inside, but what I can tell you

175

is this: you must get him medical attention within the next thirty-six hours or gangrene will set in, and young man, you will die if that happens." That was enough for me.

Bert got the directions from the doctor for the hospital trip. Nelson rewrapped my hand and strapped it over my heart, and Bert, Nelson, and I left for San Francisco to get the X-ray.

The X-ray was negative, meaning the bullet left my hand and didn't look back. When we returned to the house, Bert said that he needed to leave and make his report. However, before he did, he came into my room with some last words from the top.

"Fly, they said for me to wait until we checked the X-ray before I told you this."

"What?" I demanded.

"They will help you with the hospital and, if necessary, with the network, but you must leave the Bay Area on either account."

I just sat there. "Okay," I said. I really didn't have a choice in the matter. I had gotten what I wanted. I needed the underground network of extraordinary forces to get medical treatment and to navigate the network of underground contacts.

Bert added, "You can't come back." I nodded. And he spun on his heel and left.

When Bert returned to take Nelson and me to the hospital, things were starting to hit the fan. First of all, the Alameda County district attorney, Tom Orloff, announced in the courtroom that there had been an attempt on the star witness in Richmond this morning and that the operation was botched and the body of Louis Talbert Johnson—Texas—had been found in the driveway.

We had worked out a story for the ER doctor that involved my hand, a jackhammer accident, and getting high on the job. Nelson concurred that this made sense, given the condition my hand was in.

Bert drove Nelson and me to the ER at Piedmont Hospital on Pill Hill. He dropped us off and sped away. Little did I know that I would see Bert very soon, but the circumstances would be very tense and in a "get out of town" style. Nelson and I moved through the hospital with ease. I registered at the ER desk and was ushered immediately, with Nelson at my side, into an ER room with a young white male doctor and about five or six other attendants standing nearby.

Without asking any questions, the doctor started to remove my dressing. Halfway through, he asked, as the other doctor had asked, who had done this work. I said, "It was him," motioning toward Nelson.

"Great work," the doctor said. "Now, what happened?"

"I was working on a construction project in Petaluma when my jack-hammer got away from me and stuck me in the top of my right hand." I stopped talking and glanced at Nelson for his eye-contact feedback.

But before we could register, the doctor said, "That can't be the case."

"What?" I said.

"That can't be the case," he repeated. First pointing to the entry wound on my wrist, he said, "This is where it came in—and this is where it left."

I said, "Where what came in?"

"The bullet," he said. "This looks like the wound the police said we should be on the lookout for and that we must notify them." I moved away from the doctor, Nelson at my side, and backed toward the door.

The doctor said, "Look, if you don't get treatment, you can die; besides, I must tell the police about all gunshot wounds I treat."

Yeah, right! Nelson and I turned and started running out of the ER section of the hospital and into the parking lot. We didn't look back, but the doctor and his attendants were at the exit, watching us leave the scene. We broke through the parking lot, dodging cars and finally crossing the street and tumbling down an embankment that took us out of their sights. We stopped running and began to walk quickly when we heard the police sirens heading toward the hospital. I knew this area extremely well, so I decided the closest place to hide and make a call was our house on Santa Rosa; it was currently used as dormitory for the kids. We slipped into Santa Rosa through a window that was always open, and when I saw the oven mitt on the counter, my mind began to free-associate and it finally hit me. Damn, I said to myself, banging my left hand on the kitchen counter. I forgot that I left my motherfucking glove at the scene.

• • • I sat down in a chair in what used to be the living room when this house was occupied by the chairman. I was dumbstruck and had to fight real hard against coming unglued. I looked over at Nelson and thought about the last several hours. He had saved my life, but had he been honest? Maybe he was overwhelmed and intimidated by the situation. He was an experienced EMT and I'm sure the brother had seen numerous gunshot wounds. And then I thought about the doctor. Shit! What medical school did he go to? Damn, I went to the hospital to get an X-ray to see if the bullet was still in my hand. What was that all about? At this point, with all of the folly, I began to realize that not only was I doomed, but I didn't know if up was down or left was right. I just couldn't believe what was going on. The saddest part of this entire drama was that I was the star and a sure flop on opening night.

26

THE TRAUMA OF THE GUNSHOT had taken its toll on my young brain. I never would have missed the glove. I now knew it was time to put some distance between me and the Bay Area, and fast. I was so confident of my mental condition regarding the entire incident that I didn't even bother to give a false name at the hospital. Sure, I thought, I had produced ID to confirm who I was, and I really didn't need to show them anything. Man, was I fucking up, big time. Wow! I was fucking up real bad and I better get the fuck away from these guys before they think I'm doing it on purpose, or that maybe I am just incompetent. The glove. I forgot about the glove. Damn.

I told Nelson to call Bert and run down the situation, minus the bit about the glove. I figured by the time they found out, I would be long gone anyway. I arranged for Bert to pick us up and take us to the San Francisco airport, and from there we would fly to Las Vegas to make the medical move. Bethune told Nelson via Bert that they would have money brought to us at the airport and that the folks in Las Vegas would be there to pick us up. In addition, the message I received was that I could use the network until I was well. That is, if I got away. It was now time for me to make my call to Pookie and Stubbs.

When I reached them by phone, I explained in detail what I needed them to do and what the consequences of their actions would be. I made it clear that they shouldn't tell anyone, and if they did, they would be classified as AWOL from the BPP.

Pook said, "Fly, don't worry, baby boy, we're with you, man." So I told them to contact Bert (he would go along with my plan if I needed him, and I needed him) after I left. He would have the money for them to rent a car so that they could meet me in Las Vegas when I called for them. But until I called, they should sit tight and wait. Bert arrived at Santa Rosa and promptly took Nelson and me to the airport, where we caught a flight to Vegas. At the boarding gate, Bert said he would call Bunchy in Vegas, per Bethune's instructions, to give me the network information after they heard I had been treated and released without incident. This bit of information was like morphine for my ailing and painful hand, because without Huey's imprimatur, I would have been anathema to the folks who were part of our "underground railroad."

The flight to Vegas was smooth and uneventful. I guessed that I had about a week on the West Coast before I would be apprehended. But according to the medical people, I would have definitely been dead if I hadn't checked in to a hospital by then. In the Party, we realized that the United States is made up of regions and clusters of states. When you go to the Midwest, you get Midwest news, incidents, police dragnets, et cetera. The same applied for the South and the East. So I believed that I could get away if I got out of the West as soon as possible. This tactical belief bore itself out because one to two weeks after I was identified, the feds and other police were checking for my whereabouts at my parents' house in San Diego. Anyway, when my plane landed in Vegas, Bunchy and Houseman met me at the airport. Both were Buddha Samurai and were standing with their mouths agape when they saw I had been injured.

Apparently, the news media had not gotten into the story here in Las Vegas, and when the brothers were contacted by Oakland, no one told them who they were picking up. We drove from the airport and checked in to a hotel. I asked Bunchy and Houseman about the hospital situation here. Namely, could a black man go to the trauma unit with a gunshot wound and get treated without showing ID and reporting to the police? I was getting desperate and was at a point where it might not matter. I wanted to live as much as I didn't want to get caught. The first thing they said was not a problem, but the second was a must-do at the hospital. On the other hand, even though we may have stumbled and bumbled our way here, we still had the element of knowing what not to say. We would tell the police at the hospital that we were playing in the desert with a gun and I accidentally got shot.

Once we decided on the hospital, I was prepared to go there immediately, because my thirty-six hours were winding down. Bunchy and Houseman dropped Nelson and me off at the hospital and we walked straight through the door and headed for the trauma unit check-in station. I told the doctor it was a gunshot wound. He examined it, and with the help of a nurse, I was led into a room with a bed to wait for the police interview. I'm not sure if this was some freakish Freudian stuff, but the name I blurted out in response to the policeman's question was Jimmy Johnson. Don't know why, but I did. The policeman who showed up was a tall redheaded white guy with this little smirk on his face.

"Okay, fella or Jimmy, what happened?" he asked as he flipped opened a long notepad and began to write.

"Well, sir, we was out in the desert shooting a twenty-two at a snake or two when one of the guys that was doing the firing hit a rock or something and it must have bounced off one of them rocks and jumped up and hit me in the back of the wrist," I explained. Nelson looked at me and I concurred with his look. That story sounded stupid enough to believe.

The cop stopped writing and examined my hand while looking over at the doctor, who obviously believed that regardless of how dumb my story sounded, it could have happened. The cop said jokingly, "Shit, those twenty-twos sure make some ugly little holes, don't they?"

"Yes, sir, they sure do, Officer," I said.

He looked up at me and scribbled something on his pad and told the doctor, "Looks okay to me. Next time, you should be more careful, son."

"Yes, sir, I will," I responded.

He turned and headed back to the police room in the hospital. I looked at Nelson and he looked at me and we both let out a controlled sigh of relief, especially me. The doctor said I would need to be admitted, with surgery planned, for at least two days.

I was checked in, and two days later, a tall white male doctor wearing blue scrubs and a surgical hat came over to my bed and examined my hand. I asked if he could hook me up, and he replied like he was God or something, "Piece of cake, son. You'll be as good as new." I went under the knife a few hours later, and when I woke up, my hand looked like a huge stitched-up glove. The doctor came in and told me that I could be released in a couple of days but that I needed to return in two or three months so he could remove the wires. No shit, I thought. There was no way I was coming back here to get my wires pulled. I had these deeply neurotic nightmares over the next two days. Each time I woke up in a heavy sweat, I thought I was handcuffed to the hospital bed and that there were dozens of police standing around with notepads waiting for me to talk.

The day I checked out was a busy phone day for Bunchy and Houseman. I had them call Bert to tell the brothers in the fold that I had been treated and released and was doing fine. And that I needed a hookup for a doctor to pull the wires in two or three months. I then had Houseman call Pookie and Stubbs, two people he was really tight with, to tell them they should start their trip to Vegas so that they could pick me up.

I left the hospital promising the doctor I would return. I didn't. Two years later, I found out the policeman who conducted the interview was fired for not following standard operating procedures: "Damn, those twenty-twos make some ugly holes."

Pookie and Stubbs showed up the next day in a rented car. Bert had wired me $2,000 and given Bunchy the name and address I should go to in Chicago, which was my first network stop. Pook had brought some of the newspaper articles that were being printed in the Bay Area about the "Richmond incident." He also told me that the police were having a field day. They had kicked in the door to my place and arrested Emory, but he was soon released. I wondered what happened to the armory list behind the picture in my living room. They had raided Texas's pad and Norma's place in Berkeley, a location that Texas had used as a mailing address in the past. The papers were saying that I was head of security for the Party and that Texas and I were closely connected to Huey. Huey released a statement saying that Texas and I were renegades involved in some overzealous act. It was true!

Before I left, I had a private word with Nelson. I told Nelson that even though he was not directly involved, he should go home to North Carolina and not return to Oakland. Furthermore, I admonished him about leaving with anyone in the Party whom he didn't know. "Nelson," I said, "you don't have to trust someone like me, but you should definitely listen to me when I try to explain the nature of some people. You should not leave here with anyone from the fold, I mean the guys I worked with. Don't do it. Just take my word for it. Go home alone, and let's leave it at that."

We left and I never saw Bunchy, Houseman, or Nelson again.

27

POOKIE, STUBBS, AND I left Las Vegas and got on the interstate, destination Chicago, Illinois. We would ride "Pony Express style" all the way to Chicago, which basically meant we would not stop to sleep but just for gas and to pick up food. When Pookie was driving, Stubbs would sleep and vice versa. I was very paranoid because I wasn't sure what it would look like to state troopers, highway patrols, and local police in small-town America when they saw three black men driving through their state or city in somewhat of a hurry but trying not to show it.

At the beginning of the trip, I was cold and didn't have enough pain medicine, but I knew I had to make it with what I had because we would not stop to look for more. I started to feel the pain of my recent operation as the medicine wore down. I could feel the wires that had been inserted inside what was left of my fingers and right hand. My hand was throbbing and at times I thought I could actually hear it beating like it had a pulse. But I refused to show any effects from the pain as we moved along at the speed limit, though it seemed as if we were traveling much faster.

Stubbs took us north from Las Vegas and headed toward Salt Lake

City. This part of the trip was somewhat pleasant because I was getting away and that made me feel better. It seemed the farther we got away from Oakland, the better I was able to mentally negotiate the pain shooting through my hand as it started to come alive again. When we reached Salt Lake City, it was dark, and this was good in my estimation because not many brothers were in this part of the country. We stopped for fuel and to get some food. I could not eat or sleep. Pookie took over from here, and after checking the map, he swung us east in the direction of Ogden, Utah, and Cheyenne, Wyoming. This part of the country was flat and appeared barren for miles and miles. All I could see was either something growing with no people around or just flat wide-open spaces.

As Pookie and Stubbs wheeled me to freedom, I couldn't help but wonder how, like me, these guys were able to deal with this type of existence. The BPP was long past that period of its history when the issues were just black and white. And as for us, we were involved with the type of work that you didn't get much praise for anymore. In fact, the last words I had read about me said that I was being called an outlaw by the very man I was trying to save. But that was part of the territory. You got down, and if you were killed or on the run, like I was, you paid the price with anonymity. I knew of dozens of comrades who had disappeared and were never heard from again. They were still alive but seemed to be gone from the face of the earth because they had accepted this type of life in the BPP.

We were all from LA and had seen quite a bit in a short life. Pookie and Stubbs had come up from LA after Jimmy Johnson was expelled and were used to doing things without having all of the information. A couple of times during the trip I tried to explain to them what had happened and why I did it. Pookie spoke up, and that ended my guilt trip and the discussion.

He said, "Look, Flores, you are the man. We don't care who it is that you were trying to hit. I'm down with you, and Stubbs is down with you, brother, so don't trip about us; we got this covered. We understand that this is it for us, and we had a good run, you know. You made things real cool for us when we were moved up north, so don't sweat it, man. We're down with you, ain't that right, Stubbs?"

From the backseat Stubbs said, "That's right, Fly, man, until that day, my brother, I'm with you, man."

"Listen, you guys," I began, "I hate to tell you this, but that day is here and passed."

We talked a lot of shit after that exchange, about past operations and comrades we all would miss. But what they said was something I needed to hear, because it definitely eased the pain in my hand and my heart. But something struck me as we motored along. Our conversations, as well as my thoughts and beliefs that had become part of my thought process for maybe the last two or three years with regard to the Party, were personal and narrow-minded. The bigger picture of helping our people had been subordinated. Maybe it was something that came with the lifestyle. I wondered about it and even raised it with them. Did the Party's Ten Point Platform and Program mean the same thing to us now that it did when we were idealistic younger people whose super objective was to help our people? When I asked, the car remained silent. I'm not sure if "the people" provided our motivation anymore.

When we arrived in Cheyenne, Stubbs announced jokingly, "Everybody better hurry up and look over to your left because we just entered and left Cheyenne, Wyoming." Pookie and I looked over to our left and we both said, "Man, you mean to tell me that's it?" All three of us got a good laugh out of this, and given the situation, a good laugh really helped. All I saw were trailer park homes and small detached homes and a few buildings that were three or four stories high on what seemed like an embankment.

We whisked through Wyoming and into Nebraska and saw more flatland with stuff growing in rows upon rows of fields. There were these gigantic balls of shit stacked up along the highway that Pookie said were fertilizer that the farmers used. Not knowing anything about this stuff made me feel awkward about living in urban areas most of my life. Nebraska was also barren for miles, and when we hit civilization in

Omaha, it was dark and all we could see were lights from a few cars and the city's silhouette in the background as we passed through.

The closer we got to Chicago, the colder it got and the more my hand was hurting. Several times we pulled over so that I could clean my wound with peroxide. The fizzing from this stuff started to sting my wound so badly that I wished I could cut my hand off at times. It was painful, but we continued to move rapidly across the country, out of Nebraska and into Iowa, as Pookie said, "Fly, we're more than halfway there."

"Right on," I replied. I laid my head back on the headrest and just daydreamed about my life and what my future might hold. I tried not to think about the present. The best thing I had going for me was an uncertain future. I kept repeating to myself the doctor's instructions, "Keep your hand above your heart at all times and don't forget to return to the hospital in several weeks to get your wires pulled." Shit, if they picked up my trail, the police would be waiting for me to come back and get my wires pulled too.

Those words were troubling because I needed a doctor to pull the wires or, as the doctor had reminded me, "Or your bones will grow around the wires and remain there for the rest of your life." I think it was something like that. That was pretty scary to think about. My mind flashed backward and then to the present as I began to nod off. Then the flashing lights from the oncoming traffic would snap me back to consciousness again. I was in and out, in and out. I would not think about Richmond that much because I had really fucked up, especially Texas and that motherfucking glove. I kept saying to myself, If I had remembered ripping off my glove, I would not have tried to go to the hospital in the Bay Area. Oh, man! What a fuckup I turned out to be. I thought about my family. What would they think? I was sure they would get over this episode and get on with their lives. But what did I know about a respectable family who hears the news that their son or brother is either dead or missing after the fact? And then I thought about Nelson. I hoped the brother had listened to me. I started to get this nerve-tingling feeling in my hand, so I kept looking down at it, imagining what it would look like in a week, a month, a year. Damn! What if I didn't make it?

And then suddenly, the front of the car hit something, and this was followed by a thud, a jerk, and then a lurching motion as Stubbs struggled to control the car, wheeling to the right and then to the left with one hand, while using the other to pin me against the seat. Pookie reached up to the front to keep me from hitting the dashboard. When Stubbs got control of the car and pulled it to a stop, he asked, "Is everybody all right?" Pookie and I both said we were okay. Stubbs got out quickly to see what happened. He came back to the car and reached under the seat for a large .45 automatic. He got out to look at the car again and so did Pookie. Vision-impaired by fog, we had hit a deer. Stubbs said it looked like we had hit the back of a deer that was almost across the highway. I hit the front of my head with my left hand and said, "Man, wouldn't that be a bitch. The headlines would say three Black Panthers on the run got run down by a fucking deer." I settled down and asked Stubbs if he knew where we were at.

"Yeah, Fly, we've been in Illinois for some time now. We should make Chi-town in a few hours."

When we arrived in Chicago, Stubbs called the number I had gotten from Bert, my connection to our underground railroad. The people on the other line directed us to an address on the North Side, near Uptown. Pookie and Stubbs drove carefully through the streets of Chicago at my insistence, because I still wasn't sure we were safe. The address we went to looked like a public housing project. Per our instructions, I was the only one who should get out of the car and enter the apartment. I got my suitcase out of the trunk and with some difficulty lumbered around to the driver's side window. Looking at Pookie and Stubbs, I said, "Looks like this is it, fellas."

"Yeah, Fly, you take care," Pookie replied.

"Look," I said, "I might not see you guys again, but I want you to know that I have always respected and loved both of you and I will never forget what you've done because you guys have given it up for me and I'll never forget this." I wasn't teary-eyed, but this really got to me.

They had sacrificed so much. In fact, my future was probably more certain than theirs. Both Pookie and Stubbs got out of the car and we embraced for what would be the last time. I grabbed my suitcase, turned, and walked to the stairwell to ascend to the apartment. I would never see Pookie and Stubbs again.

28

I KNOCKED ON THE DOOR and Slim Coleman, the head of a group of friendly white radicals, answered it and greeted me with a big smile.

"How you doing, Fly?" he said in his deep Texas drawl.

"Fine, Slim, I'm just doing as fine as I can be." I raised my wounded hand. Man, was I glad to see him. He introduced me to the lady whose home this was, and then he explained the plan. I would stay here for a couple of days and then change locations. Sometime in November I would be driven to New York City, where there was a doctor who would pull my wires, and then I would begin my extensive rehabilitation. Slim stayed for a while and smoked a joint with me as we discussed my situation, the conditions here and on the coast. Slim said that the word he had gotten from the coast was that it was hot. He said they told him that I had really affected the fold's capacity because I was gone, Texas was dead, and the brothers I had gotten involved, some four or five, had deserted. But he said they said to tell me that they weren't mad and that I would understand this.

I didn't feel shit at this point. I was not upset at the botched operations or the desertions—shit happens. I didn't give a fuck because I was a fugitive and my life as I knew it was over. This was it for me and I couldn't see it any other way. Slim seemed to be concerned with help-ing me and not the situation on the coast.

Slim left, and two days later, Jack Hart, Slim's right-hand man, came by to move me to another location that I would get to know well during my fugitive years. This new location was the home of Pat Spalding, a pretty white woman with red hair and icy blue eyes who, as my lover, offered me the only real warmth and physical intimacy that I would experience while in the wilderness. I stayed at Pat's for about two weeks. During that period a doctor came by to remove my stitches and instruct me on how to clean my wound with peroxide. Nothing hap-pened sexually between Pat and me during this first stint in Chicago because I was distracted by my immediate situation and by getting the wires pulled.

I tried to keep my mind occupied with anything I could. Pat, who was a law student, had several books that grabbed my interest, most notably one entitled *Race and Law in America* by Derrick Bell. Slim had gone out and bought me some records by various artists, but the one I lis-tened to over and over again was by the Emotions, "Best of My Love." It was a good distraction for the reality of my life.

But the distance between Richmond and me was not far, and I was depressed and overwhelmed with what had occurred and how it was affecting my shaky brain and psyche. It's times like these when a person can easily go over the edge, but I did not have the energy to do anything of the kind. From what I saw of the Second City at the time, it was cold and dark, and this fit well with my depressed state of mind and body. When I was outside, transferring from one house to another, I just felt like closing my eyes to block everything out of existence. I was drawing a blank, you know, as to where I would go and what I would do. Every-thing was up in the air, and even further down the line, if things went well, would I get my hand fixed up? And the big one: would I get caught? Because at this time, turning myself in was out of the question. But what if I wouldn't get a doctor to pull my wires? Man, was I in a fix. All I had were questions with no answers in sight.

It was Thanksgiving night when Jack came by with some weed and turkey. However, something else was afoot. Jack said I wasn't safe here anymore and I was being moved to New York City. "Okay," I said, "when do we leave?"

"Right now, Fly," he replied without a blink. I liked the way these guys worked.

I said my good-byes to Pat, not knowing if I would see her again, and then Jack, and I split in his car for New York City. I didn't know at the time what had spooked Jack, Slim, and anybody else enough to think I should be moved. Jack pulled off a serious feat that would leave me impressed and respectful of him to this day. He drove nonstop except for gas and food, in the rain, sleet, snow, and windstorms for approximately a thousand miles in order to get me to New York City.

It was not until we got to Pennsylvania that Jack told me they had found a brother in the desert and he wasn't dead but was in very bad shape. I was a little taken aback, but my intuition about my comrades was right. No one needed to tell me who the person in the desert was: Nelson. I didn't think the move made sense, and I still do not understand or condone the narrow-minded decision process that cost a dedicated person like Nelson the use of his body. This was one of those moments in my life when I didn't give a fuck, but what happened to Nelson was wrong. Shit, the stuff I did was crazy, but that was my nature. What happened to Nelson was unnatural.

As we motored along, I wasn't sure why I was still alive at this point because my brain was foggy. I was a downbeat, a deadbeat, almost like a zombie. Everything kept repeating itself, except me. I hadn't taken a shit in almost a week, or was it two? And it seemed as if the radio station—or was it a different station?—played the same tune over and over, by Crystal Gayle: "Don't It Make My Brown Eyes Blue."

Jack was Slim's main guy in their operation in Uptown, Chicago. We had met several years ago when Jack ran some guns out to the coast and we hooked up so that I could stash them neatly into one of our armory nests. He was slightly built and wiry, with a deep bass voice that defied his skinny boyish exterior. We talked about everything under the gray sky as we drove along. We never saw the sun. We encountered every type of inclement weather nature could provide. The climate control in the car was working fine, but it seemed cold, especially to my hand. When we reached the Holland Tunnel and entered New York City, the potholes were out in full force and our ride to the first safe house was bumpy. Jack got me there safe and sound nevertheless. I was first holed up in an apartment in Greenpoint, Brooklyn, and my main runner was a guy named Curly. Several days later I was moved to the West Village in Manhattan. I was set up in an apartment at 113 Christopher Street with a live-in runner named Cathy. I would remain in this apartment, not leaving for any reason, for the next seven months. It was not like jail, but it gave me the solitude one might get from jail and the time to contemplate my existence as a fugitive. It was the first break I had in ten years.

29

IGUESS I REFLECTED ON AND REVIEWED my life twenty
or thirty times in just one day. I thought about the operation and
how it could have gone right, and how, if it had, I wouldn't be
here now. I did that also twenty or thirty times, but the kicker was all
we had to do was get the right address, and that didn't happen. All of
my thoughts were futile, make-believe, after the fact. Maybe it was
just time to hang it up. I even fantasized about returning home to
Oakland and beating the case in some ridiculous scam. Shit, it was
ridiculous to even think about that because the case was in Richmond, not Oakland, and that was Co Co—Contra Costa—County,
not a good place to be wanted in if you were black and especially a
Black Panther.

I read books, magazines, and newspapers, anything that would
occupy my mind. I also began to teach myself how to write with my
left hand, just in case the right one didn't respond to therapy. I would
become completely and totally obsessed with the condition of my
hand from then on. It was hard for me to imagine life without the use
of all of my body parts. I heard an interviewer ask Stevie Wonder if he
was upset because he could not see and therefore could not enjoy life
as much. Stevie told the interviewer he did not have a problem with
being blind because he'd been blind all of his life and didn't realize

what it would be like to see and so didn't worry about it one minute. But I was acting like a big baby and was mad about not having a hand that I'd been used to having all of my life. Even though there's no real comparison between your eyesight and one hand, it was having a devastating effect on me because I had lived with two hands all of my twenty-five years and now I was faced with the realization that I could lose one of them. That was deep to me.

Every time I washed and cleaned my hand with peroxide, I would think about the things I used to do with my right hand and how maybe, just maybe, I would never do those things again. I was having trouble just buttoning my shirt, so I stopped wearing one. I could barely get my pants on and negotiate putting my belt through the loops. I was very depressed because I had been such a physical person most of my life. And while I was learning to write with my left hand, the thought of actually developing this skill was very daunting. It was hard at first; I would try holding the pencil like a left-handed person, and that was awkward. So I gave it up. I just tried to hold the pencil the way a naturally right-handed person would, struggling with this process until my hand got used to holding the pencil. My hand felt weak and painful after each try at writing numbers and letters. Nonetheless, I stuck with it.

The location of my safe house on Christopher Street between Hudson and Bleecker afforded me a great view of life in Greenwich Village. I spent a lot of time watching the tourist and gay populations strolling the streets on weekends. It was the weekends and watching the people walk by that helped distract me from my isolation. It was being here on Christopher Street, going over my situation day after day, that finally brought me to the realization that I was a fugitive who had gotten away. I began to think as a person who was a fugitive and come up with a plan to fit that life.

I guess what really got to me was the finality of it all. I had been with the BPP for ten years. I was twenty-five years old, and as far as I was concerned, I had been at the top of my game, and in thirty seconds it was over. My best friend was dead. My right arm from my hand to my elbow was also dead. On one hand (no pun intended), my belief in a "right to initiative" probably had a great deal to do with the demise of what I loved most in my life: my work with the Black Panther Party. On the other hand, at the top of my concerns was my family. I loved them. I had had no contact with them since February of this year, when I spent some time in LA. I hadn't had much contact with them in the past ten years because my lifestyle made it prudent for me not to fraternize much with them. Nonetheless, the FBI and others still dropped by my parents' house to inquire about me. They were never in jeopardy because of me, and for that I am grateful.

This was my rest period. I was wounded and taking a rest in the bushes. That's how I saw myself. Whenever I watched a movie or read a book about someone on the run, there always seemed to be that period when the pursued got a chance to take stock, regroup, and get his head together. This was mine. But unlike that of my fugitive slave ancestors, my rest in the bushes is a cozy pad in an exclusive West Village neighborhood, not the backwoods of Mississippi. Why not? No one would have expected me to be here in the Village, in New York. Anyway, as I was taking stock of my situation, I realized things didn't look that discouraging. I wouldn't dare use my real name. I needed a new ID, but the network would provide that as well as money, housing, medical care, women, weed, food, and almost anything else I needed within reason, at least during my rehabbing period. So in my estimation, for about a year or two I would be okay. Or would I? It had been only two months since Richmond. How the fuck could I believe everything was going to be all right just because I had a cozy pad and wasn't stuck outside in the winter cold?

And so I tried to project my thoughts about my situation forward, which caused me to worry even more about each phase of my anticipated journey. Would I ever get the wires pulled? Shit! What if I had to go to a hospital here in New York City to get it done? Would I get arrested? All right, I thought, I should go to the post office to check and see if they have a wanted poster up. It was bad to think about this stuff. I was flustered, confused, worried, and scared. I could barely think sometimes. Yeah, I thought, if I get my wires pulled, what about rehabilitation? What will that consist of? If I leave the network, how will I live? Shit! I have never had a job as an adult. What in the fuck will I do to survive? So if the network is not here, how will I get ID? A real ID, that is. What about a place to live? What about food? Damn, what about money? These negative thoughts and, conversely, the positive ones, constantly bombarded my fragile psyche for the first few weeks, and I knew they would continue until things started to break, started to become clear and focused. The ultimate question or issue was: had I really gotten away?

Huey always used to talk about the trilogy of alternate reality that any revolutionary would face in this country: death, imprisonment, or exile. It seemed for the moment that I had escaped the first, but as Huey would say, "We never escape life alive." Being a fugitive—a form of exile—was upon me. He talked a lot about the law and how it affected what we did as fugitives and how in many instances it was in our favor. If that was the case, then I guess history was on my side. Many people became fugitives in the United States, and many of them returned to face the criminal justice system. I knew that if I surrendered, I would be charged with felony murder. So I had to be willing to face trial and a little or a lot of prison time. The other charges, not murder-related, had a statute of limitations. These thoughts didn't make me rush to the airport and book a flight for the Bay Area, but they did put things into perspective for the future.

I decided as a result of my wound and the fact that I had put thousands of miles between me and the scene of the crime, I would not need to carry a gun. If confronted with the possibility of being arrested by the authorities, I would take the bust. Before, I would have been inclined to get down with the authorities, if caught, because I had nothing to lose. But from now on I would no longer behave like a roughneck, talking shit and challenging people. Because I would not be able to use my hands or my gun. Armed struggle was definitely over, at least until I had fully recovered. I developed an exit strategy with regard to my hand. I would not step one foot outside of this apartment until I could use my hand again or until it stopped looking like a catcher's mitt.

Once my hand was well, I planned to relocate and start my new life as a fugitive. I needed to create a new identity with a birth certificate from someone who died when he was around one or two years old and who fit my age range. Then I could get a Social Security card, library card, et cetera. I would get a job doing casual labor or construction until I could establish a work record and history résumé and move on to a better-paying job. I could sell drugs or something like that, but that would bring the gun issue back into play and break one of my new rules. I planned to be low-key and underpaid so as not to attract any attention. Most of this I would accomplish, I thought, with the help of the network. In any event, I had time. I needed to use it wisely to think deeply about what it would take to solve this long, drawn-out problem. One conclusion I came to was that I needed the network and its chain of safe houses around the country. If I broke with my network too soon it could mean trouble, especially because I was wounded and needed medical treatment.

When Huey went underground, he had his own network working for him: the Hollywood crew. But when one of us got shot, like Huey, Bruce Richards, Deacon, or many other brothers and sisters, we usually had to give them up because the network did not accommodate such drastic assistance. I was lucky, because some things had changed by 1977. So when Slim showed up in December to announce that the doctor would arrive soon to start preparing me to have my wires pulled, I was good to go once again.

Slim told me that the doctor was a homeboy of his who, after playing professional football in Canada, went to medical school and became a trauma surgeon. The doctor showed up to just check my hand and ascertain what kinds of equipment he would need. He then returned in a week. He was a real cool customer. Solidly built, like a linebacker, he had a gentle style when he was inspecting my hand. He held my hand and asked how this felt and that felt, doused it with peroxide, numbed it with a shot, and deftly pulled the wires with the precise skill of the surgeon he was. We did have one problem, though. One of the wires was real snug, so he had to tug and pull me around the pad until it shook free. I thanked him and he protested, saying, "No, thank you. I'm glad that I could be of assistance."

"Well, thanks anyway, both of you," I said, nodding and glancing between the doctor and Slim. The doctor gave me my rehab instructions: work the hand, squeeze the ball, wash it with peroxide, and in several months it would be fine. But it would never be like it was before.

My schedule was set. I would spend the duration of my time—until June 1978—rehabbing my hand and lying low at 113 Christopher Street. I settled in and propped myself up on the couch and bed. I slept on the couch because I was afraid of rolling off the bed and onto my hand. I watched stuff on television I had never seen before, like the Super Bowl, NBA play-offs, and college national championship games. I saw soap operas such as *The Guiding Light, All My Children,* and almost every late-night movie that was shown on TV. I got drunk and dumb on wine and beer almost every other night—I needed that extra day to recover. I smoked cigarettes and Curly's good weed in the morning, afternoon, and at night. I tried to read every book that Cathy brought home. Many days and nights after the weather got warm, I crawled out onto the fire escape to watch the Village scenes and the large gay crowds that hung out at Ty's across the street. This pad was small compared to an apartment in Oakland. It was about four hundred square feet, with a small living room, a kitchenette, a bedroom in the closet, and the type of bathroom you find on an airplane, but with a shower.

My day was pretty simple and basically evolved into a routine that helped me to survive the boredom and loneliness that a fugitive must endure, especially if you can't leave your hiding place. I was alone and had to learn to live with myself. And I did. I would wake up in the morning to the sound of the garbage trucks around 8:00 or 9:00 A.M. I did not take a shower every day because my hand and arm were still quite a hassle, so I took a "bird bath" most of the time and showered three to four times a week. Cathy slept in the closet bedroom and would usually get breakfast together and leave for the day to take care of her business, returning in the evening with loads of newspapers, books, and magazines. On the days I didn't drink so much I would cool out by reading books like W. E. B. Du Bois's *Black Reconstruction,* which took me several months to get through. My mind was blown; I had gotten pretty tight with David Du Bois when he was on the central committee and I really didn't know who his stepfather was until I read that book.

The New York Times got my attention when it ran this story on the so-called Richmond incident and how the prostitute's female pimp recanted her testimony, thus setting Huey free. This caused a peculiar feeling in me that drove me to drink that day. I was trying to convince myself that my role in this stuff was over and that my life in the BPP was also over. It was a pitiful and deeply depressing feeling that overwhelmed me that day. Texas had been my friend, someone who trusted me while I trusted him, but I felt like I had abused my friendship with my aggressive attitude about what we did for a living. I had made this operation sound like something we had a right to do, and I just fucked up. After all of this shit, I had still led them to the wrong door and almost killed this middle-aged black woman who had never harmed a soul, let alone Huey's soul. Shit! From what I read in the papers, she was a tough old bitch. With one hand on the phone, she was calling the police and, with the other, firing at us with her .38. I should have been smarter, but I wasn't.

In the meantime, while I was wrecking my brain and liver, I was also working out by squeezing various balls to build the strength back up in my hand and forearm. It was painful at first because I hadn't used this hand in months. It was remarkable to see my hand shattered by one form of technology and repaired by those who used another to heal.

30

THE MORE I EXERCISED MY HAND, the better it got. Each time I washed it with peroxide, the wound got cleaner. In fact, it got so much better and cleaner that by the summer of 1978 I was raring to go somewhere, anywhere. I was ready to leave the Big Apple. Something deep inside gave me the courage to move. It was almost like a dare or challenge to my dignity to come out of this place and get on with my life. I honestly did not know if my drunkenness, remorsefulness, or sanity and sense of purpose were driving me to move on. The better my hand got, the less I drank. The better my hand got, the less I smoked weed. The better I got, said Curly, "The more you start to act like the person we heard you were." I felt less sorry for myself, and that told me I was turning the corner. For the past seven months, I'd been banging my head up against a wall. Now the wall was giving way and I could see that I could make it. Knowing that I was going to have the use of two hands brought my black ass back out of personal purgatory.

I conferred with Slim, and he decided to move me to Boston. The network had connections there, but what it would really do was change any travel patterns he had been developing when coming from Chicago. Slim was cautious and that was good. We both believed I had gotten away, but there was nothing wrong with changing up your moves to make sure no one was following you.

We left for Boston on a muggy summer day and I was scared to death. I had trouble breathing and even focusing my eyes. This was sheer fright. The walls in the hallway of the building seemed to be closing in on me. I braced myself against the wall as I navigated the stairway leading to Christopher Street. I hadn't been outdoors for over six months and was paranoid, jumpy. As we made our way to the taxi stand on Seventh Avenue, I believed that every person I walked by on the street was a police officer with my picture etched in his brain. It was sickening. I almost told Cathy twice that we should turn around and go back. Several times, my legs felt like they were going to give in. Ultimately, though, we made it to the taxi stand.

We took an Amtrak train to Brookline, Massachusetts, and stayed at Cathy's mom's house for a while. A couple of weeks later we moved to our own place. I was to remain here for four to five months. I had needed this change, but I still stayed inside for the entire time I was in Boston. I was taking baby steps in my rehabilitation to the outside world. Boston was kind of a stopover, a change of pace that would allow me to catch my breath and organize my life somewhat. I stopped drinking for weeks at a time as things really began to clear up and the fog lifted. I finally completed reading *Black Reconstruction,* which was symbolic to me because finishing the book signaled the removal of one of my last great obstacles that I had brought with me from New York City. I was ready to start moving back into things after graduating from these big balls to a smaller racquetball as my hand began to resemble a regular-looking one that people wouldn't find unusual. I told Cathy to call Slim again. It was time to get outside.

In our conversations over these past months, I had kept dogging Slim about going back to Chicago to start my life over. He finally capitulated in September, when Pat Spalding showed up out of the blue to take me via train back to Chicago. Pat was beautiful, strong, great company, and we enjoyed terrific sex together. Shit, I hadn't had sex since Richmond, which was almost a year. However, hooking up with Pat was not just about the physical intimacy, but more about the fulfillment of my fugitive fantasy of moving from woman to woman or house to house as I worked my way back home. It was just a fantasy because the relationship I had with Pat was the only one I experienced as a fugitive. I was getting home-cooked meals instead of every kind of takeout one could imagine. It really didn't matter if she liked me or not. I believed she was just doing her duty as one of Slim's operatives. That was fine with me. I just felt better about myself, and with her positive reinforcement, I believed there was something to my future. I cut back on my reading and hanging inside and started going outside in the Chicago sunshine. Pat's apartment was in a pretty good location on the North Side of Chicago, approximately three or four blocks from the Gold Coast. I was proud of the fact that I was educating myself about my locale. Chicago is one of the most segregated cities in the country, and I learned that I needed to be careful when hanging out with a white woman in the Second City. A brother could get stoned if he was sporting a white woman on his arm in the wrong neighborhood. I was also getting my street smarts back, which meant I was thinking with my big head instead of my little head. I alerted Slim that I would need to relocate to a neighborhood with a few more black folks.

I stayed with Pat until mid-1979, and then Slim arranged for me to move in with Harold Bell, a former Panther and a survivor of the police raid that killed Fred Hampton. Harold Bell was a cool brother from Tennessee who was then a small businessman. While staying with the Bells, Harold and his wife, Bobbie, I was treated like a part of the family, which made me sick for my own. My alias at this time was Carl Tribble of Tennessee, courtesy of Harold, who made the trip to his home state to acquire the birth certificate.

Harold, showed me around Chicago, introducing me to many of his friends and local acquaintances. But Harold and Bobbie worked during the weekdays, so I had plenty of time on my hands, as did many of the brothers in this North Side neighborhood. I met several local brothers who did nothing all day long but hang out, get high, and talk shit about everything under the sun except how to get a job. Man, these guys were a gas, but I wouldn't trade their shoes for mine, regardless of how entertaining they were. Most of them had been to prison in either Illinois or Michigan, and they had plenty of stories—or should I say tales—to pass on. One brother, who looked like a thirty-year-old, said he'd just gotten out after doing thirty years in Jackson State prison in Michigan for a police murder. His street name was Killer, no shit! He said he used to wrestle bears while in prison to entertain the guards and inmates.

All of them had this theory about how the white man and black woman had it made and were going to hook up to get rid of the white woman and black man. I never understood their logic, but I'm sure the drugs we smoked had a lot to do with it. Anyway, that was some pretty wild shit. But the wildest was when one of these guys' woman, whose name was Akkeeba, came around dressed in black and sporting this large hat. We were standing around getting high, and she was calling me this funny name and I asked her what was up. She told me I looked just like this guy from the P Stone Nation, aka the Blackstone Rangers, and she thought I was hiding out in another part of Chicago because Jeff Fort had a contract out on me. Well, that prompted me to quickly call Slim because it was time to get the fuck out of this neighborhood. This arrangement with the Bells lasted a few more months until I got my own place and began moving around town in another circle of people, but still with network support.

As time went by, I began to acclimate to the outside world, which gave me more confidence to be sociable and outgoing. I started taking long walks all over the North Side of Chicago but stayed away from certain neighborhoods. My new place was on Greenleaf, which was several blocks from Lake Michigan. I walked along the walkways bordering the lake and really enjoyed the view, with the park land on one side and the rough waves on the other. I guess a guy could start tripping out there and forget who he really was, but I thought zoning out like that was good for me, at least for a short time. This was in a way the calm before the storm, a period of inner peace when I believed I was safe and that my future was actually in my hands for the first time in years.

I had been underground for almost two years, and it was closing in on 1980. I was rethinking my situation with a clear mind. I needed to really be on my own, but I also understood that I was going through a transition of sorts, moving from one type of dependency to another while searching for the common ground that would make me feel safer and more secure as a fugitive. Currently, my biggest dependency, or my safety net, was Slim. Moving away from him and his people was the ultimate move that would no doubt signal to me and to them that I was ready to go.

Lester "Slim" Coleman was a towering figure in a six-feet-four frame and was called Slim because he was truly a tall, slim guy. But he was also a towering figure in the liberation movement and the steadfast conductor of this modern-day underground railroad. I had known him for several years prior to my downfall, and he was extremely popular and very trusted by the Party's leadership and by just about anyone else involved in the movement. Slim had organized many of the poor white residents of Uptown into a strong political machine. He referred to his core group of members as "Revolutionary Hillbillies." He was intelligent, which was obvious, and I remembered Elaine telling me that he was one semester short of graduation at some Ivy League school but had dropped out to join the struggle. He was down-home and somewhat folksy. I remember him with his guitar, singing political hillbilly songs at his office in the '70s during a trip we made to Chicago. He seemed sincere then, and all my interactions with him this time had confirmed that.

During the spring of 1980, I changed IDs and became John Wesley Tate, also of Tennessee. My situation was mellowing out. I was still living off the network money, Pat was still my girlfriend, and I had all of the time in the world on my hands. And then the Duke came back into my life.

31

THE DUKE WAS BACK IN THE MIDWEST. He'd been
transferred to Chicago in 1976 to reorganize the chapter.
Apparently, things didn't work out because when the Duke
heard about Richmond—and then about what had happened to
Nelson—he got mad with the folks on the coast, assuming I had
suffered a more severe fate than Nelson. He told me that the word
in the underground and on the street was that I was dead and buried
somewhere in a Nevada desert. Coming from the Duke, the retelling
of the incident was more like receiving intelligence on the operation,
so at the time it made no impact on my psyche. He was always a good
and loyal friend. We started contacting each other via Slim and Pat
and subsequently began discussing a business deal that would relocate me to his hometown of East St. Louis, Illinois. We were putting
together an operation to sell grade-A weed out of Rush City, a small
neighborhood in East St. Louis. In January, I said good-bye to Pat,
packed my bags, and boarded a train to East St. Louis with the Duke.
In the baggage compartment was a suitcase with twenty pounds of
marijuana inside. It was a new business venture between old friends
and also what I hoped would be the beginning of my new life. I never
saw Pat again.

I was very upbeat and comfortable about this move, which made me feel that I was getting my land legs back. I guess what goes around comes around, because I was not totally surprised that I had hooked up with the Duke again. I had known he was somewhere out here but didn't know how to reach him. Luckily, he found me. The Duke was a real piece of work, a survivor of the Vietnam experience as well as the Black Panther experience. On the train ride we talked about old times, past successful operations, and what had happened that morning in Richmond. The Duke was the first person since the botched operation whom I trusted enough to confide in. "Fly," he said, "you know if I was there, things would have turned out for the best and you wouldn't be here now all shot up and shit."

I said firmly, "No, it wouldn't, man, because we went to the wrong door then and we would have gone to the wrong door if you were there too. It got fucked up, man, and we can't change none of it. Besides, nothing we say will bring back the dead, you know?" We laughed about the discussion even though there was nothing at all funny about it.

I moved in with the Duke and his wife, Carolyn. They lived in a typical East St. Louis apartment building with six to eight units. His building was across the street from the great dancer Katherine Dunham's old house, which was currently used as a museum dedicated to her work in the arts. The Duke had been working on the railroad but was recently laid off. The majority of the brothers I met through him did not have regular jobs either. They were hustlers and in various stages of gangster-hood. One brother named Buzzard, a former Panther, broke this stereotype and was the only guy I met who had a regular job at the railroad. Arnold Stewart was the Duke's point man on the weed operation in Rush City; he was a hope-to-die gangster. And Dirty Red: he did something for a living and I was pretty sure it wasn't a 9-to-5. He had been involved in a shoot-out with the police, killed a cop, gotten wounded, and beaten the case. And it showed. The Duke's crew was fierce and nobody was fucking with them, not even the police. We set up our weed operation at Arnold's in Rush City, a section of East St. Louis located near the banks of the Mississippi. Customers could drive up to this single-family detached house, which had a window just a few feet from a dirt road that ran by the house. They could place their money in the window and have the weed handed back out to them in seconds without leaving their car. Just like a drive-through burger joint.

East St. Louis, directly across the Mississippi River from the city of Saint Louis, was a city on the outside of America looking in. This place had been devastated by America's atomic bomb of socio-economic deprivation and corporate white flight. Even Monsanto, a Fortune 500 company, had created its own municipality in order to distance itself from the depleted East St. Louis tax base. There were vacant storefronts, vacant land, and boarded-up buildings for blocks and blocks. There were a few gas stations, but most were closed down; every other supermarket was boarded up, their parking lots occupied by abandoned vehicles. The few small retail stores that were open sold liquor and Chinese food. People from Missouri came here to purchase alcohol because of their blue laws that restricted the sale of booze after 1:00 A.M. and on Sundays. Even the *Whirl,* a local tabloid that chronicled the exploits of the area's black underworld, said the most appropriate use for East St. Louis was as a dumping ground for the bodies of the gangsters that came up a dollar short or late on their debts. The city's most notable offspring were Miles Davis, Harry Edwards, and Tina Turner. And almost every single football season, the local high school football team was ranked in the national polls. The Duke and I spent a lot of time attending girls' basketball games at his alma mater, Lincoln High School, watching a skinny black girl named Jackie Joyner lead her team to the state championship. The place was a real drag, but the Duke had sold me on a story that there was hope for the future of East St. Louis.

The Duke had a lot of political connections within local government and with local businessmen, so he was telling me that there was a big group of investors seriously interested in building luxury hotels and casinos on the East St. Louis side of the Mississippi because the land was cheap. You know, the Duke was talking about economic development and big opportunities that would bring this place back from the dead. In addition, he said we could get in on the ground floor with the local jobs and some of the construction contracts. This sounded real cool at the time, but as far as I was concerned, there was one huge problem. "Why would anyone want to come to East St. Louis and stay in a luxury hotel when they could go somewhere else?" (This so-called investment bonanza turned out to be an elaborate scam.)

Then again, if you were a fugitive like I was, East St. Louis was the place to be. I didn't have to try very hard to blend in because everybody here was black, and on top of that, the Duke was a local player who knew everyone, so my association with him was proof enough as to who I was. No one would question my being in this part of the country. Shit, the Duke knew the mayor, the police chief, and most of the cops, who kind of looked up to him. This was definitely not a hotbed of fugitive or radical activity like New York or Chicago. When I was in the Big Apple, shit was jumping off all the time. There was the Black Liberation Army robbing armored cars and banks. They even had a couple of shoot-outs with the police while I was in town. It stayed hot there. But this place was really cool—rest and relaxation all day and night. My days and nights had radically changed. I had gone from the shut-in days and nights in New York and Boston to getting out and about in Chicago. But in East St. Louis I sensed that I was safe and that I could probably begin to stabilize my life in this community.

Our little operation in Rush City allowed me time to focus on building a new history for John Wesley Tate. One of the ways I had decided to do this was to create an education history that would eventually yield a paper trail. First I would get a GED and then go to college or just get training in some trade so that I could assimilate into the East St. Louis social and economic structure. So almost every day I would get up and walk the couple of miles to the downtown library and study for the test. I thought the best way for me to prepare was to take the practice tests they had on file down at the library's reference section. I never thought it was difficult because I had aced it as Flores A. Forbes. I would do this most of the day, but the real cool thing that helped me was that I could now write with both hands. After I finished at the library, I would return to the Duke's stomping grounds and hang with him and his homies, getting high and drinking beer. Things were very laid-back in East St. Louis.

Socially, the Duke and his wife were always trying to hook me up with some young lady who they thought could help to domesticate me. They wanted to see me settle in this quaint little place. So I was courting a young sister who was about nineteen or twenty years old. She had three kids and lived with her entire family in a two-story house on a street where the streetlights didn't come on at night. Anyway, I was hanging out on the porch of this young lady's house. We were sitting on a dingy couch when her mother came outside to tell her that it was her turn to get her hair done with the hot comb. She said to me, "Do you want to come inside and wait?" And I was like "Cool, no problem."

We went inside and it was dark, but I could see the silhouettes of furniture cluttered in the large living room. Over to the left was the kitchen, which was well lit and full of women and kids getting their hair done. There were no men in sight except me. So I walked over to the kitchen doorway and stood there watching this group of women and kids moving about in the kitchen. Near the kitchen sink and counter, a movement caught my eye. Now, this kitchen was big, with a large table and chairs and maybe nine to ten adults doing hair and kids crawling all about. Everyone was talking and listening to some new rap music on this Saint Louis radio station, and I just couldn't believe my eyes. Over by the kitchen sink, where you could see the U-shaped pipes extending down from the sink's tub, I saw first two and then three and then four and five or six large rats jumping over and between the U-shaped pipe as if it were a contest. I looked at this baby crawling on the floor near the sink, and then I looked at the other people in the kitchen, and nobody seemed to notice or care. They were just blindly desensitized to the existence of these huge rats holding an equestrian-like jumping match under their sink.

I stood there in the doorway for about fifteen more minutes, and when no one said or noticed a thing, I eased out the doorway and walked out of the house. For some reason I couldn't speak to save my life. I was mesmerized by this scene—shocked at what I saw and how it made me feel and react. All of a sudden, as I was walking home, it really started to hit me like some kind of religious epiphany. I felt depressed and ashamed at the same time. Not because I couldn't stand it and walked out, but because of what it really meant to me. That house was a symbol with three generations of family poverty in the kitchen. That house, that neighborhood, the people, and this city—this was what the struggle was all about. The Party's Ten Point Platform and Program focused on these issues. And this was what I started out fighting against but not what I was doing now. Man, was I out of it. A staggering realization came over me and I knew for certain that in principle I was no longer a member of the Black Panther Party. The Flores Forbes I started out to be would have almost cried at seeing this family in poverty. It would have made me want to fight harder to overcome these ills of society, but not now. I was too far gone, and I felt okay about feeling like this. Or maybe I would find another way to help, because the old way—the Panther way—was not in me any longer. The fire was gone.

• • • At first I thought my decision to come to East St. Louis was going to be my final stop on the underground railroad, and in theory it was. But my last stint as a fugitive and my association with the Duke were probably what convinced me to change my life. The Duke was a gunslinger at heart and conducted the majority of his business with a gun. I understood this because we were conspirators from way back in the day. So given the Duke and his roadies' lifestyle, what took place one afternoon was inevitable.

We were driving down the street, heading to Arnold's house to check on the weed operation, when this other car almost sideswiped us. They didn't hit us, and we, as anyone else would have, should have let it go, but not these guys. In the car were Perkins, Dirty Red, and me. Red was driving, and Perkins told him to pull up alongside the car that almost hit us. As Red accelerated and began to pull even with this car, I saw the Duke pull out a .45 automatic Colt Combat Commander from his holster. Perkins instructed Red to pull up next to the driver's side and hold it steady. As we approached, the Duke started rolling down his window. I started to get that old feeling and I shouted to the Duke, "Stop it, man! What in the fuck do you think you're doing?" I put my hand on his shoulder from the backseat. "Duke, this is not 1973, and we ain't in Oakland, California. This is 1980, and we are in East St. Louis, and I am a fugitive. You can't do this to me, man." I told Red, "Pull up, man, we don't need this kind of shit, man."

He eased up, and I could see that Perkins was fuming. He wanted to shoot these people because they cut us off. This was the kind of thing I was concerned about, and it made up my mind.

I was committed more than ever to returning and facing the consequences. It was just a matter of time before I would take a fall, given my current environment and associations. I would never go anywhere with the Duke and Red together again. I didn't need that shit. I decided I had to do something else to survive and to do it somewhere else. I was convinced that I needed to explore how to go back. I was getting tried of dragging this fugitive scene out. So I asked the Duke to get in touch with our old friend and attorney Charles R. Garry in San Francisco. I needed to talk to a lawyer about my situation as a fugitive.

32

T HE FIRST TIME I MET the attorney Charles R. Garry was sometime in 1968, when I was just sixteen years old. I had been assigned to the security detail for Eldridge Cleaver, David Hilliard, and Emory Douglass while Eldridge was in San Diego for a speaking engagement at UC San Diego. Garry had accompanied them, probably because he was Eldridge Cleaver's and David Hilliard's attorney for the April 6 shoot-out in which Li'l Bobby Hutton was killed.

Perkins's lawyer had contacted Garry while he was still in San Francisco, and we arranged the meeting to coincide with a business trip that Garry was making to Chicago. The meeting was set for the morning, and I was to meet Charles in his hotel room in Chicago. Jack Hart picked me up at the train station and drove me to Garry's hotel in downtown Chicago. As Jack pulled into the parking lot of the hotel, I assumed Garry had seen us through his window because he cracked the door and peeped outside. Jack let me out and drove away. I wasn't as paranoid as I was when I first went underground, but being with Garry made me a little more comfortable.

Garry greeted me with a traditional hug and then sat back and said, "Flores, you're looking well."

"Yeah, I'm okay, Garry," I said with a nervous smile as I slowly began to accept the imminent changes in my life.

He held up my hand to see how my old wound was and then offered me breakfast. I accepted the offer, and while we ate, we talked about current events, old times, and as usual with an old warhorse like Garry, the current mental status of Huey P. Newton. Garry said that the Servant was out of his mind, using drugs and drinking gallons of cognac every day and night.

He then quickly changed the subject and, with a grimace, asked me why in the hell did I want to turn myself in after three years. I said that I was tired; I needed to speak with a lawyer to assess what my chances were for acquittal or conviction. And if the latter was the result, how much time would I face?

Garry was silent for a moment. Then, with a touch of surprise in his voice, he said, "Everybody—Huey, me, and others—don't understand why you want to turn yourself in."

"Why?" I asked irritably.

"Because the authorities—federal, state, OPD, Richmond PD, et cetera—think you're dead," Garry said in the same surprised voice. I was a little stunned at first and then as it quickly sank in, I was overwhelmed by these hot and cold feelings. This was the first time I had spoken with someone from my old world. I had left the Bay Area and Las Vegas three years ago, and it was hard for me to comprehend what Garry had just said.

"Dead," I said.

"Yes, dead, Flores."

The difference between Garry and the Duke was that the Duke's message was from the underground while Garry's words were from the daily news, which meant my family thought I might be dead. What Garry was saying had much more impact on my psyche. This was not shop talk between operatives.

"The police dragged the desert after they found Nelson, believing you were there too, especially when you didn't return to get your wires pulled. They found nothing, and so they stopped looking for you. I assumed, they presumed, you were dead."

"Dead," I said again.

"Yes, dead," replied Garry.

I didn't have a problem with what Garry was saying, but what really bothered me was that if the police thought I was dead, then so did my family, and that's what gave me the hot and cold flashes again.

Garry said, "Let me bring you up on what's happening in the real world."

"Sure," I said.

Garry continued, "Flores, the Party as you and I once knew it, in all of its splendor, swagger, brashness, and power, is over. You know, you guys had a pretty impressive run, and you frightened a lot of people in this country, but things have run their course, it appears. I mean, look at you; you're here, not there. How effective are you nowadays? Most of the really effective people are gone. I think Ericka is still there because of the school, but I doubt whether she will last. Flores, you and your people really made a mess of things. Bodies were showing up everywhere, and all Huey could do was say that his main people—especially you, Flores—were now renegades. I spoke with him personally about the situation and he just said, 'You know the brothers are high-strung with all of that Frantz Fanon stuff.' Most of us in the know understood that something was terribly wrong. And then, you know, Nelson in the desert, well, that was the straw that broke the big cat's back."

Garry said all of this with that lawyer's grin of his, while mockingly raising a left hand that sparkled with the gold Panther ring that had been a gift from Huey. If any one lawyer or person, black or white, knew us, Garry did.

He had defended everyone: Huey, Bobby, David, Eldridge, and the entire Buddha Samurai at one time or another. He knew where most of the bodies—metaphorically speaking—were buried, and I knew that because Huey had told me. So here's this elderly, gray-haired

Armenian man who knows the deal, and I don't have a choice but to believe him.

He said, "Flores, you guys possess a type of loyalty that is scary to us white people and I'll bet to most black people. What is this stuff that you and Huey call the 'right to initiative'? That is some very deep stuff. Because when they first discovered Nelson, half-dead but alive in this badly dug grave, he stuck to his story. He wouldn't implicate you in anything. But I think the police convinced the doctors to tell him that he was going to die, and he broke down. Did you know that he would not give his real name and insisted on using an alias?"

"No," I said. "I don't know what happened. Honest, I don't."

"Hey, Flores, that's okay. Look, I'm your lawyer, and what is said here stays right here in this room. Do you understand?"

"Yes," I replied.

"Good," he said. "Now, these two Panther gunmen came to Las Vegas and told Nelson they were going to take him to a safe place to hide until the heat got cooler."

I flashed back to my ride with Jack on Thanksgiving. I got another chill.

"Nelson, according to his statement, said they were driving this rented U-Haul truck and, after driving for a while, stopped in the desert so that they could stretch their legs. When he got out, they waited until he got off the road and then they shot him several times. Dug a grave and left him in it for dead. He was discovered by tourists and taken to the hospital. That's when the story broke. Huey had to run for cover." Garry stopped and looked at me sternly for a minute. He seemed to be having some trouble getting out the rest of the story.

"Flores, you know the Servant was trying to help you, just as you were trying to help him. He said you were his most trusted shield and his deadliest sword and that he would never abandon someone who was so loyal and true to the game."

I hit a wall. This wasn't Garry talking, but Huey.

"I'm going to borrow a sports metaphor when I explain this to you, Flores. You left everything on the field that morning, and so he felt that he could sacrifice just as much. All of his political and community support was up in arms. It had never looked so bad." Garry stopped.

"So what about the thing in Richmond, did that fuck things up?" I asked.

Garry waited for a moment before responding. His answer was guarded. "No. Because they knew who you guys were, and when the real soldiers die, nobody is going to cry or scream. After Richmond, shit, that bitch recanted and nobody even blinked. But Nelson—come on, Flores—he ran the Party's ambulance program in North Carolina. That's the stuff that people liked about you guys. We could always live with the guns and stuff; after all, this is America. But it was only when you and your people were involved in community stuff that made it acceptable. How in the fuck do you think I was able to make those deals that kept you and a lot of those guys out of prison?"

Garry was telling me that parts of society would put up with some of this shit because we dressed nice and didn't slur our curse words. I was chilled. Huey used to say that the line between the state and us was very thin. I remember when the Oakland police chief leaked it to Garry that the local mobs we were shaking down had placed a contract on the Servant. Who would have guessed that the police really wanted us to win?

Pointing at myself, I said, "You mean when we died, it was okay?"

He paused for a minute and said, "Yes, Flores. That was your job, wasn't it?"

"Yeah," I said weakly. "I guess so." I had never thought about it like this. I made a mental note before I said anything to call my family ASAP. Besides, the police didn't know where I was anyway. I looked up at Garry, and he asked if I was all right. "Yeah, I'm fine." I paused and then asked, "So will you take my case?"

Garry replied, "Of course, Flores, my retainer starts at fifteen thousand dollars plus our hourly fee."

I didn't have any money, but I said okay, that sounded cool to me. It was close to the time for me to leave, and as I did, I asked Garry how much time I was looking at if I was convicted and "maxed out."

"Ten years," he answered.

"Yeah, okay, I could do that," I said. I would be thirty-eight when I got out. That was cool with me.

I was shaken after Garry's revelation, but I was able to leave under my own power. For the next couple of weeks and up until the time I surrendered, I was disconcerted and clearly fucked up. The problem wasn't whether I could do ten years, but when someone tells you that everybody you know and love believes you're dead, well, that can be pretty devastating. Especially if you're not dead.

33

AFTER RETURNING TO EAST ST. LOUIS, I didn't know if I was going or coming. But what I did understand was that I was going to do something, even if I only spit. I wondered if I had it in me to turn myself in and face the California criminal justice system alone. I think the real problem was that I was truly alone out there and that I was going to have to deal with this by myself. Since 1968, I had never been alone in doing anything that was related to the struggle. I had my family, the Party, and now the network and the Duke. But from what Garry was telling me, the Party was gone, which made the network an illusion. Maybe that was the source of my loneliness. It was like I had lost someone or something close to me. Was it the death of the Black Panther Party, that Garry had prophesied, or something else? Regardless of how I may have felt at that moment about the Party and how far I had drifted, it was all I had known for the past decade. This was like the death of a parent. Garry was in the know and he loved Huey, so I didn't think he was bullshitting me, because that wasn't his style. I was depressed. I was a lost son, but that was no big deal—I would have to pull myself out of this funk. I thought seriously about what I should do. If I stayed out here, I had nothing to look forward to. But if I turned myself in and did the time, I could look forward to something other than the wilderness. I would be thirty-eight when I got out. I also wanted to see my father, mother, brother, sister, and their families.

I told the Duke about my meeting with Garry and what he said about me being dead. The Duke thought that was hip.

"Shit, Fly," he said, "you're really gone now, man, you really beat them this time."

Yeah, right, I thought sarcastically. If I was true to the game, as we used to say, then I should be jumping with joy, but I was not happy about being dead to the unknowing public, especially my family.

My years in the Party and my three-year stint as a fugitive all started to back up on me. It was like throwing up your hands to surrender to your conscience, to yourself, and telling the Urban Guerrilla God and Lord Buddha Samurai, "I've had enough of this shit." For three years, I thought only about getting away, healing my wound, and creating a new identity so that I could assimilate into society and live the successful life of a fugitive. My mental and moral stand on these issues started to change. I was thinking more about my family, about living a regular life again. I had not been a regular guy since I was sixteen years old. I was locked in this zone, the zone that people become embroiled with when they decide early in life to give all for some cause. I was so involved with this cause mentally that I had blocked out all other things, except saving my prince. During that moment in my life, there had been nothing more important than killing that bitch to save the Servant. I got seriously depressed as I began to recite my parents' phone number over and over, trying not to forget it. So in early October 1980, I told the Duke that I was going to call my parents and let them know I was alive. I hadn't completely made up my mind about turning myself in yet.

I dialed and let the phone ring. I was startled at what I heard: "I'm sorry, but the number you have dialed has been disconnected, and no other number is available at this time." What? What in the fuck was this? I was concerned that this was some kind of police trick at first. I tried the number again; I thought maybe I had dialed the wrong number. Same response. I called directory assistance in San Diego County, and they informed me that this number had been disconnected and there was no forwarding number. I was discombobulated, completely. What was wrong? They never would have changed their number. But maybe it had something to do with me. Garry said they had dragged the desert looking for my body. Maybe that was the reason they had changed their number. My parents were strong, but maybe this was too much for them and they disconnected with everything around them. There had to be an explanation. So I decided to go to my second option and call my older brother, Fred.

I sat for a while thinking about how I would start off my conversation with my brother, who probably thought I had been dead for approximately three years. I didn't know his number by heart, so I called directory assistance to get it right. I got the number and waited for a reasonable time to call. Fred answered the phone, and when I said his name, he recognized my voice immediately.

"Flores, is that you? Oh man, it's good to hear your voice, are you okay? How's your wound?"

"I'm fine, Fred, got it all taken care of," I said as I relaxed from the prior disappointment. We talked about everything except our parents for about five minutes, catching up on the news. He told me how the press had written me off for dead, as had the police. He said he had gone to Las Vegas when they were dragging the desert for my body, so the stuff about being dead was real to my family. Then I popped the question: "Fred, how's Mom and Dad?"

"You mean you don't know?" he replied.

"Know what?" I started to get the same feeling I'd gotten when Charles Garry told me that everyone outside of those in the "know" thought I was dead.

Fred said, "Daddy died of a heart attack in July 1978."

Fred waited for my response. I was numb, but after a few cold and hot flashes went away, I felt lonely and cold.

"What happened?"

Fred began to run everything down. The night of the heart attack; the phone call Fred got from the police; the drive from his house to San

Diego, et cetera. He said the FBI and other police agencies were hovering around the house and the hospital room, waiting for me to show up. He told me that they were even at our father's funeral waiting for me. I had him tell the story twice. I was completely floored, but I had made up my mind.

"Fred," I said, "I'm going to turn myself in, probably next month."

Fred asked if I was safe and would I be safe when I turned myself in. I told him not to worry and that I would be just fine. We agreed that I would not contact my mother and that he would do that just in case she freaked out. We decided that I would drop by my mom's before I turned myself in. I hung up the phone, and for the first time in my life, I cried like a baby.

The news of my father's death coupled with my bad experiences with the Duke marked the turning point. I was tired and homesick. I was now twenty-eight years old. I had never been married and I had no children. I had never held a 9-to-5 as an adult. I told myself that I had been raised in an environment of struggle and so was able to justify turning myself in and continuing the struggle by other means. I did not know what was going on with the Party during this deliberation, but what I did know was that I was finished. My feelings about the BPP and what it had been for me would never change. I felt the experience had made me a man, giving me the ability to make crucial decisions. It may have taken me several iterations to finally make up my mind, but it didn't take that long for me to realize that this run was coming to a close. I did not discuss the pros and cons or my process, I just told the Duke I was leaving and thanked him for his help. I loved this crazy nigger and always would, so our parting was an amicable one.

34

I LEFT EAST ST. LOUIS and traveled by bus to Chicago. My plan was to hook up with my cousin Carolyn Forbes and stay with her and my baby cousin Andrea, until I got up the courage to get on the bus and travel back to California. I met with Slim and Jack to explain my plan and to thank them. These guys and their organization had been terrific throughout my ordeal. If anybody can be given credit for my survival, for my making it through this phase of the operation, it's them. I stayed with my cousin for two weeks, as planned, and then got on a Greyhound bus and began my journey back to California.

The bus trip from Chicago to San Diego would take about two days. That was enough time to change my mind, not that I had anything else on the drawing board. The decision was so hard to make, I couldn't leave myself room for any other choices. I did not have the will or desire to remain a fugitive. I knew that all the evidence the authorities had against me was circumstantial. So I concluded that I had a fifty-fifty chance at beating the case. There was a statute of limitations for all but one charge against me, and that was murder. Even at that, I did not believe that I would wind up doing life, though the probability remained.

The bus ride also let me put other things into perspective. As I took in the scenic views of the Midwest, Southwest, and finally Southern California, I considered how I would build my life over again. I wanted to go to school, get my degree, a decent job, and raise a family. I stayed mostly to myself during the trip, reading newspapers, magazines, and just daydreaming, playing out in my mind my move from my mother's house to when I turned myself in. This was going to be my last operation of any kind.

I was still, in the face of it all, unafraid—a quality I had become less and less proud of. I had come to the realization that a little fear is okay every now and then. I believed that "Fear will keep you honest with yourself." As we came through the mountains surrounding the county, I could see San Diego. It was around October 20 or 21, and according to Garry, the three-year anniversary for my case would be up sometime in the latter part of October. That meant that if the statute of limitations held up, I would have to contend with only the felony murder beef. I was on with my move.

The twenty-minute cab ride to my parents' house was pretty tough. I was back in San Diego knowing that I would not get the chance to see my father alive again. I ran through several scenarios that I thought might take place when I saw my mother. Would we both break down and cry, or would she rebuke me for not letting them know where I was and that I was still alive? I planned to run through here quickly because whether she was upset or just happy to see her son, I was still a fugitive, and if I was captured or put into any compromising situation around my mother, things could go bad. So I planned to stay only two or three days and then take a bus to the Martinez County jail and turn myself in.

When my mother first laid eyes on me after believing I was dead, she didn't cry but attributed my living to her nightly and daily prayers to God. We embraced at the front door, and then, like a mother helping her fugitive son, she furtively looked behind me and said, "Please, come inside." We ate and talked for a while about my father and the details of his death. She told me about the FBI being at his bedside and how they had hung around the house believing I would show up to see him even after he was released from the hospital. It dawned on me that even had I known, I could not have shown up.

I had to keep this short. I loved my mother and my family very much, but regardless of how hard I tried to convince myself, I was still in that "zone." Visiting my mother's home and calling my brother were cardinal sins to a fugitive. But after conferring with Garry, I felt it was a safe gamble. I hung around the house feeling that any minute I would hear this bullhorn outside demanding that I come out with my hands up. But instead of that happening, my mother snapped out on me, and this wasn't the first time in my life that it had happened. I definitely knew it was time to go and hook up my shit.

I was all burned out and most of the fight had left me. I didn't have to face a confrontation with police, but I did have to take the wrath of my mom. She started to blame me for my father's death. I just took it. She said the rest of the family also thought the shock of hearing about my death had killed him. "It was a heart attack, Momma, not me," I said. "Besides, why didn't you pray to your God to turn things around and save his life, if you think He's so great?"

She swung at me and then she said, "Boy, God will punish you for speaking of Him like that. Do you hear me? He will hurt you."

"Shit," I said. "He already has, if you hadn't noticed." I left the next morning.

The Greyhound bus ride to the Martinez County jail would take from twelve to eighteen hours—more than enough time for me to change my mind again. In the meantime, I was trying to contact a lawyer who could help or be there when I turned myself in. I could not afford Garry, and I knew he would not change his fee demand just because of the old days.

I failed to hook up with a lawyer, and every firm I spoke to suggested that I not turn myself in until I had one. I decided that I would follow my own counsel and follow through with my plan to surrender, lawyer or not. I walked confidently up the stairs to the Martinez County jail under the cover of darkness, before sunup.

BOOK
THREE

35

IWALKED UP THE STAIRS and to what I assumed was the watch sergeant's desk. "My name is Flores Alexander Forbes," I announced to an officer who was staring down at some paperwork, "and I think I'm wanted for murder in Richmond."

I wasn't sure what to expect. Would this officer leap over the counter and wrestle me to the ground and cuff me, or would some dipshit officer pull his gun in panic and say, "On the ground, nigger. Oh, I mean put your hands up before I blow your head off"? Well, there was no immediate response. This cop reminded me of the police in Las Vegas: very laid-back and probably thinking, This nigger is crazy for messing with my time. I just stood there watching him and waiting patiently. Taking his own sweet time, the officer got up and walked over to confer with another officer, also seated and doing some paperwork. After about a thirty-second conversation and a phone call to someone, the officer did an about-face and, with one hand in the air and the other near his sidearm, he walked toward me, saying, "Mr. Forbes, please stay right where you are."

Right, I thought. Does it look like I'm trying to break out of here after announcing I'm back after three years on the run? The other officer in the back came through the gate and asked me to be seated at a table directly behind me. I saw I would have to be patient with these guys. I must have sat there fifteen to twenty minutes until a blond athletic-looking white man came rushing through the door wearing a jogging suit. He had Richmond PD detective written all over him. He walked over to the two sheriff's deputies and said a few words while glancing over at me several times. Then he walked over to me, extending his hand and saying he was Richmond PD and that I was under arrest for the murder of Louis Talbert Johnson. Damn, these guys are polite, I thought.

"Yes, right," I said.

The detective was handed a tape recorder by one of the deputies. He placed it on the table, turned it on, and moved the microphone toward me. Before he could speak, I said, "Look, read me my rights and turn off the tape because I have nothing to say." I think he was a little shocked, but he read me my rights and turned off the tape. They cuffed me, searched me, and led me to a holding room to be fingerprinted. I was processed and then led to a holding cell, or, more aptly, a dungeon.

In all of the years I was with the Party, I had never seen a lockup or holding cell that resembled a dungeon. It was something out of the movie *Caligula*. Caligula snaps after his freaky sister Drusilla dies, and he hits the streets and gets busted in a Roman police sweep and lands in a holding cell just like the one I was in. It was dark. I couldn't see a soul until my eyes adjusted to the lack of light. The odor was a combination of urine, solid human waste, vomit, you name it. Suspects were sleeping in this stuff and on concrete benches that lined the dungeon. The ceiling was approximately ten to twelve feet high and the space was about nine hundred square feet. Man, this place was deplorable, but I was on a mission and tried to ignore the conditions. So I settled down. What the fuck, no one dragged me in here kicking and screaming. I took a seat until they came to move me to a cell.

I waited, contemplating Huey's response. He would more than likely send a lawyer to find out if I was a wacko, trembling and scared, or just a mumbling idiot trying to trade years of closely held secrets about the Party and him for my freedom. Huey would no doubt be paranoid.

Even though he had known nothing about the Richmond incident, he knew I was hooked up with the other shit we had been into on the street. So I might want to make a deal. Well, there were to be no deals. I had gotten myself into this, and all of the decisions were mine. I was not going to drag people down with me, because I was taking responsibility for my own actions. But I knew Huey, and I suspected he was concerned. He used to tell the brothers in the Buddha Samurai that if he ever got busted, we were to move all of the stash, cache, and stuff and to clear out of town. He said since we all had a breaking point, he didn't know how long he could hold out before he started to spill the beans on us. He would laugh after saying this, but I could see in his eyes that he thought this sentiment might apply to some of us.

The officer came to get me from my cell for a lawyer's visit. I hadn't hired one, so it was either the public defender or Huey's man. His name was Tabor, and he was a tall white man wearing a stylish suit. He was not a public defender. We talked about a few things like my hand, but I could sense this guy was on a mission that he had not yet completed, so I offered him a way out.

"Look, Mr. Tabor, tell Huey everything is fine. This is my case and I'm the one dealing with this stuff. The DA here and the DA in Oakland won't hear about anything else that happened from 1972 to 1977. Okay? Tell Huey that I'm still at heart a Buddha Samurai and that I will be true to the game."

He gave me a smile, handed me his card, and said, "If you need anything, please call." He left and I never called.

I had been in jail for about three days when they came and got me for arraignment across the street at the courthouse. When I reached the courtroom, this not-so-well-dressed white man approached me and said he was my PD and that until I retained other counsel, he would represent me. My docket number was read by a court officer who then said, "The People of the State of California versus Flores Alexander Forbes." Wow, that sounded fucked up: the entire state against me, and was this lawyer too? They read the charges and then the judge asked, "Mr. Forbes, how do you plead?" I leaned over, making it look like I was conferring with this PD, and he whispered some stuff in my ear. I rose from my seat and said in a clear voice, "Not guilty."

I knew from the beginning that this Co Co County PD was going to be a problem. I was in deep shit and needed some real help. But a few days after my arraignment, I found out that Mr. Tabor had delivered my message. The cavalry was coming to the rescue in the person of a legal giant named J. Tony Serra. Thanks, Huey!

• • • Throughout my life in the Black Panther Party and in my particular experiences with Huey P. Newton, he often surprised me, and on many occasions he would mesmerize me with his worldly sense of the struggle and how we fit within its domestic and international framework. Moreover, my relationship with him was extremely satisfying for a young black man and for a young Black Panther. It was gratifying to know that he trusted me then and trusted me now, even after all of the trouble I had caused with the Richmond incident and its consequences.

So I was not surprised when a young white man wearing a three-piece pin-striped suit showed up at one of my court hearings to let me know that he was standing in for J. Tony Serra, who was seated in the audience with his second chair, Julie Traun. The young white man's name was Guy Gregor Smith. He came over and sat opposite my shaky public defender and whispered into my ear. There's a saying I read while I was a fugitive: "If you whisper something into someone's ear, they are bound to believe it." Well, I believed I was truly blessed and that this was the last time Huey P. Newton would help me or trust me. I knew they were there only because Huey had either asked them or paid them. It turned out to be the former: Serra was taking my case pro bono. Guy said that Tony would be taking my case and I should tell the judge at this time that I was firing my public defender and needed a two-week continuance in order for Tony to get prepared to step in.

My case was moving from the municipal court to the higher superior court, which meant there was no turning back because technically I was being bound over for trial. I asked the PD to tell the judge that I wanted to speak. I stood up and said, "Your Honor, due to the fact that I am firing my present counsel to replace him with new counsel, I would like to request a two-week continuance." The DA was furious and told the judge that this would complicate his calendar and that the continuance should be denied. The judge asked who the new attorney was, and Guy stepped in to say it was Mr. Serra, who was currently occupied with another murder trial and would not be able to proceed for two or three weeks. The judge denied my motion, the preliminary hearing was held, and I was bound over for trial.

At first I thought I was in deep shit, but what Tony had done was use the law to our advantage. I had asked for a continuance of two weeks in order to substitute attorneys, and at the same time I fired the PD. This was denied. So when the judge bound me over, technically I had no attorney. Whether Tony knew they would proceed blindly, denying me my constitutional right of having the lawyer of my choice, I don't know. But in any event, his next move assured me I was in good hands.

Tony visited me in jail a couple of days later to explain his strategy. In his sweeping but flamboyant style, he told me that the judge and DA had fucked up. In their haste to bind me over, they had denied my constitutional right to have the attorney of my choice during the most critical phase of my case. Tony said the next day he would file a motion called a 995, asking that my charges be dropped because of this gross miscarriage of justice. The only way, he said, for them to refile the charges was to come up with new evidence or to indict me using a grand jury, which Co Co County had not done in twenty years for a criminal case. I thought this was too good to be true.

The next day in court Tony elegantly argued for my cause, pointing out that as a young black man, I was being treated as if the Constitution didn't exist, especially since its purpose was to protect indigent defendants like me. The DA was appalled at the motion and the suddenness of what appeared to be happening. I think he could see the case slipping away right before his eyes. It took the judge about twenty minutes to decide in our favor, and for the first time since I turned myself in, I really felt like I had made a good move. I was technically free but for only two days. On the third day, the DA took my case to the grand jury and the charges were reinstated. I was to spend the next two years in jail, fighting the grand jury indictment, because I couldn't make bail, set at $150,000.

• • • In the meantime, I was receiving a flood of visits from comrades still in the Party. It was good to see them again, but etched in them was a premonition that sent a chill up my spine. This foreboding was so startling that it almost overshadowed my current fight for my freedom. The Black Panther Party, as I knew it, was fading away. From what I could learn from my visitors, the two hundred–plus people who were there at the time of my "demise" was down to a handful. People were becoming disillusioned and leaving every day. When I spoke with the guys in the leadership, all they talked about was getting high and hanging out. Huey never came to visit me, but this did not disturb me. He had hooked me up with J. Tony Serra, and that spoke volumes to me about how he felt. I had visits from Frances, Roni, and some of my other lady friends. Frances had been struggling since her expulsion, and Roni had left the Party and was pulling herself back together.

An entire phase of my life was passing away right in front of my eyes. While I was still a fugitive, I had decided to separate myself mentally from the Party and its directives. I needed to put some closure on my past life, and I knew this would be difficult. I never planned to leave the Black Panther Party alive. I was currently twenty-eight years old, and twelve of those years had been with the Party in some capacity. I had given of myself, every weal and woe I could muster, for twenty-four hours a day, seven days a week. I had conducted my life during this period as if there would never be another calling in my life. But the visitors kept coming and I kept up a good front. They were, after all, the only real friends I had ever known.

But I was fighting for my life now—not theirs and not Huey's. I decided that I wanted to live my life the way I wanted to. No more directives or chains of command. No more rights to initiative and stuff like that. I wanted to be Flores A. Forbes, a person, and not Flores "Fly" Forbes, the Black Panther. I decided to live and re-create or reinvent myself out of what was left.

36

THE JAIL I WAS SENT TO was filled up with guys—black, white, and Chicano—that Donald Goines or Chester Himes could have conjured up. Most of the black prisoners were from Richmond or Pittsburg, California. The whites and Chicanos were from some of the same cities and others, like Dublin, Vallejo, and Sonoma County. The brothers were all "touch hogs," prison slang for a penitentiary hoodlum, with at least one or two prison terms under their belts. Most of them either used drugs or sold them. They were tough, with several arriving after high-speed chases and gunfights with the police. They were to become my friends and primary source of information on how to conduct myself in prison. The cell block was on the second floor. The jail was rectangular, with the cell blocks located on the east, west, and south sides, while the north side served as a combination dayroom/chow hall. Each cell held four inmates, and because of the racial strife and killings inherent within prison life, the inmates were segregated by race. These particular facilities were at 200 percent capacity, so the county had raised money and was soon to complete the building of its new high-tech jail across the street. The new jail would offer a single room per inmate, so many inmates were looking forward to passing their time there.

The transition from being on the street to being in jail was extremely difficult. I felt homeless, living out of a box, dependent on my captors for everything I received. From the time I woke up until the time I went back to sleep, I had to depend on some third party for some form of subsistence. It was humiliating and almost infantile, like a baby in its crib shaking a rattle to get its mother's attention. Breakfast was served to you in your cell. The most common dish was appropriately named "shit on a shingle," a beef concoction poured over potatoes. There were no tables or chairs to eat on, so you sat on your bed to eat, read, and talk. Normally there was nothing to do after breakfast but return to sleep until the next meal. The space between the two sets of bunk beds was not enough for two people to stand at the same time. And if you had to shit, you did it in public because the commode was located at the end of the lower bunk. When the dayroom opened around noon, there was still nothing to do short of playing cards, checkers, chess, or talking and listening to each other.

Boredom can be painful, I found out. The idleness and lack of mental stimulation were very hard for me. I was coming off a three-year stint as a fugitive, and now I was facing murder charges with no real hope of beating my case. Nevertheless, I still believed that I had made the right choice in turning myself in, yet working through this stuff seemed so intense. The hardships were more mental than physical. I was really in limbo now. I was like everyone else in jail—either awaiting trial, unable to make bail, or just passing through between jail and prison. My brain was not being used, because I couldn't get enough information to stimulate the goddamned thing. During the day, I longed for nighttime so that I could put the day behind me by sleeping. Sleep was the only pleasure I found during my early incarceration. It was a great substitute for staying awake without any mental stimulation. Everyone—especially me—waited in anticipation over the next few weeks for the new jail to open.

• • • The move to the new jail meant many things to the inmates doing time here. It meant you might have more privacy while taking a shit, but most of all it meant that you would have your own cell and not have to share yourself with three other people. The real big deal about this new jail wasn't, in my opinion, the fact that you would have your own room, but that Co Co County had spent millions of dollars on a high-tech, color-coordinated modern dungeon so that the local inmates could suffer peacefully. I heard from some of the guards that psychologists had been consulted, prison design experts and people who could tell them that if they put these designs, colors, and environmental controls in one jail, the inmates will be passive and laid-back while waiting for trial or whatever their fate might be. The thing about the new jail that excited me (if one is allowed to get excited about this shit) was the fact that the library services would be upgraded, and that meant more mental stimulation. I was happy to walk outside and cross the street. But that doesn't mean by any stretch that being incarcerated is enjoyable.

This new jail was out of the ordinary compared to other detention centers. It resembled a modern college campus, with all of the latest high-tech gadgets actually developed to house men and women who are presumed innocent until proven guilty. It was divided into sections called quads. In each living quad there was a large common area with about three or four cozy cul-de-sacs with couches surrounding a thirty-six-inch TV. There were tables and chairs, which were used for dining and recreation. And there was a large courtyard with a basketball court and handball wall that could be viewed from the inside through a large reinforced glass window. Surrounding the entire common area were rooms instead of cells, with real doors that were locked and unlocked electronically from the main guard station. Each door had one elongated window that was about six by twelve inches so the guards could peer inside your room. The rooms were ground level and on a mezzanine. There was a comfortable bed, a toilet, and a washbasin with a special mirror that was made out of some type of metal. In the three different corners of the quads were shower rooms.

In the old jail, visiting had been very difficult. You met your visitor through small windows in the dayroom, and you spoke to them via little speaker systems. But in the new jail, there were large private visiting stalls with glass partitions, and every thirty days you could have a contact visit in one of the rooms with a table and chair. It was during these contact visits that inmates often had sex with their wives and girl-friends, and on many occasions drugs were smuggled in by slipping a balloon full of weed or something else up your ass. Or if you were in cahoots with someone on the inside while you were visiting, they would distract, or "turn," the guards and then you could pass it under the door to be picked up by another accomplice. Believe me, this was a serious psychological improvement over the dungeon across the street.

• • • I tried to do something that most experienced cons recommend you don't, and that was find a woman to run for me while I was incar-cerated. I must have reached out to every old flame I could remember. Roni started visiting and we hooked up again, promising each other everlasting love, and then something went wrong and she stopped showing up. Frances came back into my life—shit, we even had a jail-house wedding—but it was annulled when she split on me. I met other guys who tried to fix me up with their sisters, cousins, old girlfriends, et cetera. For much of my time in prison, I was trying to build a life that I thought would resemble the life I had on the outside before becoming a fugitive. But reality outside was elusive and caused me most of the pain I would endure in jail and prison. Doing the time itself is not diffi-cult or the problem. The issue is, will you do time alone? That's what's hard.

37

MOST OF THE GUYS I met in the new jail were young black men between the ages of eighteen and thirty-five. I remember on several occasions hearing some of them mimic the Meyer Lansky character from *The Godfather:* "This is the life we have chosen." And true to this expression, most were hardcore career criminals. They were from all over the Bay Area, but the ones I came to know well were either from Oakland, Richmond, or Pittsburg, California. They thought that I was cool because of my work with the BPP, and others believed I practiced sound street etiquette because I had been through so much without snitching on anyone in order to get out or reduce whatever time I might be facing.

There was Big Yogi, a big-time drug dealer from Richmond who reminded me of a black Sydney Greenstreet, always working an angle and always trying to cut a deal. He was about five-five and weighed nearly 400 pounds. He had three fingers blown off his hand in an old robbery attempt, which caused one of his hands to look like a pair of claws with a thumb and little finger. I felt like we had something in common, given that I, too, had a debilitating hand injury.

Cholly Baldwin, a sophisticated drug dealer who had been one of Felix Mitchell's top people in his drug operation in Oakland, and I became close. Like many of the brothers in here, he was politically mature and understood better than most people not involved in criminal activity what the BPP was all about. We used to talk about the Party's shake-down of the drug dealers. I appreciated learning what it was like with someone who was on the other side from us. Cholly was slim and smooth and conducted himself like a streetwise black mandarin. He, like Yogi, had all of the angles covered, knew who was who, and re-ceived a great deal of respect from everyone he came into contact with. The word around the joint was that Cholly was the guy to know.

Another brother was "Park" Mark Randell from Richmond, Califor-nia. He was a young, aggressive street gangster who divided his street work between strong-arm robbery and playing on a con-man team. For a short while in the old jail he was my cellmate. This brother feigned falling off his bunk one time in order to be taken to the hospital so that he would have a better advantage at escaping. He followed through with his plan to the letter but forgot one thing: the police don't play. They shot him trying to escape, but he was only wounded and returned to the jail as a hero of sorts.

One of Cholly's partners was a brother named Charlie Boo from the Richmond "set" who appeared to be popular as a gofer or scrounger for local black mob guys like Cholly and Big Yogi. Like many of the other brothers I encountered, he was a functional illiterate but still seemed capable of making his way through life as a career criminal.

Mack Slim, aka Steve Johnson, was a loudmouthed, fast-talking, I-know-every-goddamn-thing pimp. About nineteen years old, Steve competed hard in everything we did in the jailhouse but maintained his cloak of "Mackism," as he put it, until the day he died. Steve was in jail for pimping and pandering, and it was amusing to watch the other inmates and me gawking at the parade of women that came to visit him.

There was also a group of hard-core brothers who had done serious time and had strong affiliations with the infamous prison gang the Black Guerrilla Family (BGF). One of these brothers, Kennard Jefferson, had a competitive bodybuilding physique from the waist up, with real skinny legs. He was thirty-one years old, and I remember him telling me that he had spent fifteen years in and out of the Youth Authority and prison. He spent most of his time lifting weights, eating, and reading "shitkicker" western novels by Louis L'Amour. A brother with the same prison connections but almost the extreme opposite of Kennard was Harold "Rip Saw" Washington. Rumor had it that he was a real live BGF hit man. Convicts had a tattooed teardrop near their eyes to signify that they had killed someone from another race. He had the tattooed teardrops to prove it. He was small and buffed physically but had the largest and rowdiest mouth I ever heard. He could rap, toast, cap, play the dozens, and signify better than anyone I ever knew. In fact, Rip was an institutionalized court jester with strong political and prison gang connections. I met him after he was arrested for a parole violation and some other new beefs. He had been free and out of prison for just five days, and prior to that he stayed out just twelve days before catching another case.

And then there was a group of us who had one thing in common: we were the brothers charged with murder. Two in particular that I hung with were Titus Yates and George Hughes. Titus was being held for a much-publicized robbery-murder and was facing life without the possibility of parole. At one time Titus was a recruiting-poster marine who was assigned to the detail stationed at the White House. It was rumored that he had seduced a female deputy sheriff who quit her job to marry him after he beat his case. George Hughes was a career criminal charged with murder and several other counts under the special-circumstances statutes that carried life without the possibility of parole. I got to know George well over the short time we were incarcerated together. But soon after his conviction on almost every count, he withdrew to prepare his mind for leaving and never getting out again. I spoke to him the day he left for Vacaville and the only concern he expressed was, "How long would my woman run for me?" Like I said, that was all that counted in there.

38

THE GRAND JURY INDICTMENT loomed large in my mind, as it would until the special hearing was convened. Tony said, "Flores, they really want your ass." I guess that was true, because for most of our existence, the Party never respected the United States criminal justice system. We didn't give a fuck, because if we did, we would have been paralyzed and never made a move. Our overt contempt for the so-called American system of just-us was no secret. Shit, if there was a witness who had the courage to testify against us, we would bribe them. Or, as we'd tried to do in Richmond, take stern steps to ensure they didn't show or testify. If we got away or out on bail following an incident, encounter, shoot-out, what have you, we would jump bail or just leave and possibly return to challenge the authenticity of the allegations. But that did not happen much because there were still dozens of Panthers underground and on the run who had no intention of surrendering, as I had. So here I was of my own volition, a real live Black Panther who had left a crime scene and a dead comrade behind, bloody jumpsuits, ski masks, automatic weapons (stolen from a USMC base), riot shotguns, and a bloody glove that matched a wounded hand. And the witness who was to testify against Huey had been next door. We had gone to the wrong door, but our presence nonetheless gave them motive with a capital *M*.

In any case, Tony and Julie had a plan. They planned to challenge the grand jury indictment based on the composition of the grand jury relative to the demographic makeup of Contra Costa County. The bottom line was a serious discrepancy between the composition of the grand jury, the composition of the jail population, and the racial makeup of the county. Or to put it another way, there were no black people on the grand jury. Tony and Julie said, prima facie, we have a case if you want to attack the composition of the grand jury. But if you do it, it will take time and you must be patient, which means you could be in jail a little longer than you may have anticipated. I told them I was down.

They went to work writing briefs and bringing in Stanley Aronowitz from UC Irvine, an expert witness in analyzing demographic trends along racial lines. The judge selected to hear the case was a conservative named Vukasin. The date was set and the hearing was held. Vukasin responded to our motions with one sentence that basically said, "No. Now get your ass ready to go to trial."

• • • My trial began in the summer of 1983. Like a boxer, I was letting the blow take me in whatever direction I fell. Tony and Julie were ready. Both had told me that the burden of proof was on the state: in cases where the evidence is primarily circumstantial, it is incumbent upon the state to present every single thread of evidence it has in order to sway the jury and convince them the defendant is guilty. That said, the state did not have an eyewitness to point at me and say, "He was the one who was there."

I began to grasp the fear inside of me about the prospects of the trial going forward. I wished it were going forward without me. My biggest concern was the exposure of what I used to do in the Party to the public. My life being paraded in front of total strangers was one thing, but my life in the Party—well, that was something else altogether. What would my mother think when she heard that her baby was a gunman, an underground operative, or whatever term they might use? That was what really bothered me, and I couldn't do a goddamn thing about it.

During the jury selection phase, the courtroom was packed with people. They were not there to support or see me; they were the jury selection pool. I was alone again. But that didn't matter. I had Tony and Julie standing between me and the state of California. I had a strong team. Anyway, as Tony and the DA conducted voir dire, Tony would tell anecdotes that would explain to the prospective jurors what the crux of the case was. But it was one specific story Tony told that I believe set the tone for the entire trial phase.

Tony was tall, an imposing figure, and a very natty dresser. He swayed and almost pranced around the courtroom, spouting legal terms with his own personal flourish, but at the same time brought the case and the issues down to a layman's understanding. His hair was coiffed into a ponytail, and he wore a plaid three-button suit. He polished off this ensemble with a pair of brown "old man comforts." He approached the panel and said the heart of the state's case was built on circumstantial evidence. This meant there were no eyewitnesses, just traces of blood, a few broken twigs, footprints, guns, and stuff like that. Oh, yes, and a body. So therefore, it was incumbent upon the state to interpret what it believed happened that morning. "But," he emphasized, pointing to the jury, "you should be careful of the interpretation, because if there is more than one possible interpretation of what happened that morning, then you must find the defendant not guilty."

He then launched into this story. "Just imagine," he said, "that you are attending a baseball game and that you have arrived late. You are hurrying to take your seat, but before you do, you stop at the concession stand to purchase a beer and a hot dog. You then proceed to your seat, excusing yourself as you move down the aisle." He stopped. Everyone, including the DA, was focused on his next words as he walked back to the dais with his head down as if in deep concentration. He stopped and faced the jury box before continuing. "You take your seat and then you look at the field of play and glance at the scoreboard. There is one out and a runner on first base. But just as you are settling in, your neighbor inadvertently knocks your cold beer onto your lap. You take your eyes away from the playing field as you begin to clean yourself off. At the very instant you turn your eyes from the game, you hear the crack of the bat, the roar of the crowd, and then applause. You look up and the home team is heading off the field and the team that was just batting, having been retired, is in the dugout preparing to take the field."

Tony paused as he looked over the faces of the jurors. "What happened? There was obviously a double play, but what kind of double play combination?" he demanded in a loud voice. Then he closed by saying this story was analogous to the multiple interpretations one can derive from a case that is built on circumstantial evidence. The courtroom was silent until the DA jumped to his feet to protest Tony's correlation between a baseball game and a serious murder case. But I got it, and I could see on the faces of the prospective jurors that they got it too.

The jury selection process ended when Tony turned to me and said that he was satisfied with the current panel and was ready to proceed. There were eight women and four men. Nine were white, two black, and one Native American. The older black men made me think of my father, and I hoped they would view me as their son and cut me loose. The Native American made me think of Tony, and I hoped he had similar feelings. Shit, when your ass is on the line, your analysis of the situation can be pretty simplistic.

My trial lasted approximately three weeks and consisted mostly of the DA parading to the stand every kind of Richmond police officer who was available. They testified about the guns, jumpsuits, DNA (blood and hair samples), ski masks, and finally the glove. Of all the police officers to testify, the one who gave me the creeps was the serologist. He was an Asian man, and he was talking about the match to my blood between the stained glove and the blood from the jumpsuits. He told the jury that the probability of me being at the scene, based on my blood type and the stains on the evidence collected at the scene, was near 90 percent. Man, was I squirming with this guy on the stand. The DA said that this was "as good as" having an eyewitness account. No shit, I could see I was getting my ass kicked in this place and the motherfucker was really rubbing it in.

To rub it in further, the DA went into my past and brought in two Alameda County witnesses. The first guy was Tom Orloff, the current executive DA in Alameda County who was the prosecutor on the Newton murder case and went by the sobriquet "Panther Prosecutor." Orloff was this tall, thin white guy who looked like Mr. Peepers with his large black-rimmed glasses. Orloff took the stand and the DA spoonfed him questions that elicited the kinds of answers that I surely believed would turn the jury against me by painting the portrait of a "hard-core, dyed-in-the-wool Panther" with no regard for the law or human life. With each question I flinched, and with each answer I squirmed, as if someone were jabbing at me with a fist. I furtively glanced over at the jury to check each reaction to the DA's questions and Orloff's answers. Well, you know, Orloff and the DA just went on and on. Orloff said he knew me and that according to Alameda County and other police authorities, I was one of the most dangerous Panthers on the street at that time. I thought, Shit, he's embellishing this stuff, because if they really knew this, I would have been ineffective from the beginning and never would have been the armorer or gone on any missions. He was making this shit up. He continued by saying that I was one of Huey's top people and that each time Mr. Newton was in court for his murder case, I was there with him. (Along with about fifty or sixty other people, I thought.) He went over the Fox Lounge incident and how the Treasury Department was investigating us for racketeering, and said that I was one of the principals being looked into. Orloff was asked by the DA whether I carried a gun. He said yes, loud and clear. I thought, These motherfuckers didn't know shit until Richmond, and now they're acting like they have us pegged.

As Orloff walked off the stand, I followed him with my eyes, saying to myself, Jive-ass motherfucker, fronting like they were really doing a top-flight job. It happens all the time after the fact they make everyone think they had your measure when they didn't even know my name.

FLORES A. FORBES

Turned out the DA was just getting started. The next witness was some undercover operative from the OPD. He said he was the deputy inspector of the OPD Intelligence Division. I mean, this guy could have been an actor or something, or someone they found to come in and make this shit up. He was a tall white man with graying hair, a handle-bar mustache (like that of Rollie Fingers, the baseball player), and he wore a tweed jacket over a sweater vest. He was acting like they had me pegged long before Richmond. In response to a question about his qualifications, he said he was the foremost police expert on the Black Panther Party. I almost fell out of my chair. He still didn't know shit. He was mumbling this shit up there about he knew me, and named a few places I was at, but the bottom line was that he and Orloff, like the rest of them, didn't have a clue until Richmond, and now they were fronting. These guys were shameless. Whether they were faking it or not, though, I was glad to see the guy get off the stand.

Two witnesses in particular—who were not police officers—really shook my confidence. One morning before I had been transported to the courthouse, Tony and Julie came by to see me in the special booth on my floor that was reserved for contact and attorney visits. Tony got right to the point. He asked me if I knew a woman named Stephanie Hopson.

I almost said her name as he finished saying it. I put my hands over my face and felt like I was getting dizzy and was going to pass out. I was totally caught off guard. I said to myself, Ain't this bitch got something else to do, like live her life? Damn. Tony and Julie were looking at me and then at each other. Tony said she had testified at the grand jury hearing and given a statement to the Richmond PD stating that she was at a secondary staging area waiting for us to return and that when we did, Texas was not with us. I just kind of nodded. I was sick. Then I heard Tony say, "Sick." And I said, "No, I'm all right. I'm not sick."

Tony repeated, "No, Flores, *she's* sick." He said she was institutionalized and that he would challenge her competency based on the fact that she was a certified nutcase. A special hearing was held excluding the jury, and when she came in to testify, she looked like a little girl all drugged up. Even before she started to talk, Tony got up with a folder in his hand and asked to approach the bench. The DA, Julie, and Tony had an animated discussion, and when they returned to the table, a recess was called. The next time we came back to court, the judge said he would not allow her to testify.

But it was the older black woman whose door we went to by mistake who did testify, making me feel very bad about my past life. It was not what she said that hurt me but who she was and how she appeared on the stand. She said she didn't see me or know who I was when she was asked by the DA those specific questions. Man, here was this middle-aged black woman, dark-skinned, thin, and wearing the same type of dress my mother would wear to church, with a pillbox hat and that little net draped over her face. Damn, she looked like my mother or Mrs. Stevens or Mrs. Williams. This was someone's mother, and that really fucked with me. I just stopped listening and began daydreaming.

I remembered, during Bobby's campaign for mayor, when we were getting out the vote and we stopped at a campaign office in West Oakland. A call came in from an older black woman who needed a ride to the polls. So the chairman told me to go and pick her up and take her to the polls. This older sister was maybe eighty or ninety years old, frail, and blind. As I drove her to the polls, she told me her story. She'd been in Oakland about thirty years, and her entire family was dead, and the only people who came to her house were the social worker from the agency and her mailman. But since the Party had been in existence, certain sisters used to come by her house and read *The Black Panther* to her, bringing her free food. They also registered her to vote. She said she had never voted in her life. So we got to the polling place and I had to assist her with signing in and then I led her to the voting booth. I pulled back the curtain and ushered her into the booth. She looked in my direction and said, "Son, you have to help me do this, so vote for that boy that works with those boys and girls that feeds them kids and stopped them police from messin' with us in West Oakland."

That image was being projected by the woman on the witness stand. She was like every black mother, sister, and daughter before me all rolled into one. As she continued to testify, I felt sick, hurt, disgusted, and ashamed at what I tried to do that morning in 1977. Man, was I glad when she finished.

The DA wasn't finished, though. I was instructed to walk in front of the jury and show them my hand. This was the most damaging evidence that was presented: my hand and the shot-up glove, which the DA claimed were a perfect match. I didn't testify or say anything, but I knew that this evidence was a match.

When the prosecution rested, Tony Serra rose to address the judge and jury. "Your Honor, we believe that the prosecution has not met its burden to prove that Mr. Forbes was involved in this incident. Therefore, the defense will not present any evidence to refute the state's accusations because we feel that they have not met their burden." After the DA's and Tony's summations, the next day the judge read the jury their instructions and then they were sent out to deliberate. They came back in two days with a guilty verdict on second-degree murder and the arming and use clause (the legal term for using a gun). I hugged Tony and Julie, thanking them for saving what was left of my life. The following week Judge Merrill sentenced me to a total of eight years with time served.

39

THE STARK REALITY I FELT creeping up my back when I first heard those electronic gates close behind me was enough to shake up any bad motherfucker. The medical facility and receiving center at Vacaville, California, was the beginning of my journey through the California Department of Corrections (CDC), not the end. Now they had my ass. After we inmates were unloaded like human cargo, we were stripped, searched, quizzed by the guards, and then told to sit and wait after getting dressed. Then this large CDC officer walked over to me after conferring with other officers and asked me to step aside so that he could speak with me in private. The officer, holding a card in his hand, looked at it, then looked at me and said, "Are you Flores Alexander Forbes, the Black Panther gunman?" I was not surprised at what he asked. I was just shocked at the addition of the *gunman*.

"Yes," I replied.

"Do you have any enemies, or because of your notoriety, would you like to be placed in protective custody while you're here at Vacaville?"

Damn, I thought, this is more of an insult than anything else. What did they think, that I couldn't do my time like everybody else?

"No," I said emphatically.

"Okay," he replied, adding, "there's no need to get upset. It's just routine, okay?"

"Right on," I said. And then he walked toward the group of officers he had left to ask me these questions. He briefly spoke with them, handed them the card, and then walked away. I guessed I would be in the general population after all.

I was placed in a two-man cell with a brother from San Francisco, and just like in the county jail, prisoners were segregated in cells by race. I was to stay at Vacaville for approximately thirty to sixty days. Like all inmates, I received a number that was my ID—C-72851. You also undergo a physical exam and a battery of exams that measure your IQ and your Adult Basic Education level. The CDC has a point system that they use to determine which "pen" you will be assigned to. The amount of points I compiled was too little for maximum-security incarceration and too high for minimum, so I was assigned to a medium classification that would fit nicely with my future plans for going to college while in prison. After your points have been assigned, you're given a list of the prisons that fall within that point range. The only thing I was interested in was which prison had the four-year college program. The only medium "pen" that fit this need was Soledad in Salinas, California. So I selected that. My choice was approved and I was informed that in twenty to thirty days, I would be transported to my new home via the CDC bus prisoners called the "gray goose."

The twenty to thirty days that I was to spend at Vacaville could only best be put to use for acclimating to prison life. My goal was to make contact with the players and in my case the Black Guerrilla Family (BGF), which had been founded by BPP Field Marshal George Jackson. Well, it didn't take long. They found me before I found them. The rumor, or should I say the line on the "yard," was that because of certain bad deals that had gone down in the past—between the Party, BGF in general, and Panthers in particular who went to jail—there was a contract out on the life of Huey P. Newton. With distinct apprehension, I let these six or seven brothers approach me one day in the yard. I could feel that "street thing," or signaling, that this could be trouble. One brother approached me first, and the others made a semicircle and took up positions as if they were on security for me. I was a little moved in a positive way because it was a show of respect rather than a hit move. On the other hand, how would I know? I had never been here before. I just hoped I was reading the situation right.

The brother extended his hand and told me his Swahili name as we shook hands dap style. He then turned to introduce the other brothers, who approached in turn and each one dapped with me. At first I didn't know what to think because this could have been a move they were putting down, but I soon realized that these guys thought I was cool because I did not snitch. The word from other brothers who had preceded me to Vacaville was that Flores Forbes was a serious brother who was really down for the cause. The lead brother began to tell me about the Family in the joint. He said in particular that the thing with Huey had nothing to do with me, unless I was representing him. I assured them I was not representing anyone but myself. He also told me that I should be on the lookout for the BGF in Soledad. Once I arrived there, they would look out for me, just like these guys were looking out for me during my stay here. This was somewhat of a relief, but from what I could see, this place was pretty different from what a regular joint might be like if you had to stay more than thirty days.

Vacaville was not just a receiving center to process incoming inmates who would then be sent to their permanent sites; it was a medical facility and a place for special cons. This was the place where they kept all known homosexuals, freaks, transsexuals, and just plain crazy motherfuckers. It was the place where Johnny Spain, Sirhan Sirhan, and Charles Manson were incarcerated. And if you wanted to cop to being psycho, this is where they would have housed you and filled you up with medication.

Before I was transferred to Soledad, I had what would be called an exit interview with a CDC counselor. He asked me different things about gang affiliation, my sexual preference, and what kind of program I wanted to do at Soledad. He told me that he didn't think I would have a problem at Soledad from the cons, but that the majority of the prison administration there was from the "old school" and didn't take kindly to Panthers walking their yards. I was soon to find out that there was something to his warning. And finally he said he had good news. He told me that because of my time served, coupled with the sentence I had received, that my date for release would be July 28, 1985, provided I either worked or went to school; I would receive a day off my sentence for each activity. This date was eventually recomputed and revised to August 9, 1985, my real release date.

Ever since I had taken that last bus ride to San Diego to turn myself in, I had become one "bus-riding muthafucka." So it was in December 1983 when I was transferred to Soledad prison. I was again shackled, hands and ankles, with a connecting chain to other prisoners and placed on a bus to Salinas, California. This was going to be the most difficult of the many bus rides, with all of the processing to endure, especially at Soledad. The waiting time before processing alone becomes an extraordinary burden on a person. The ride took about three to four hours. When we arrived, we were taken to a very narrow hallway. There was a urinal there that was stopped up and emitting this horrible odor. There was nowhere to sit. We remained shackled and had to endure this for about eight hours.

The stories you hear about going to prison are closer to fantasy than the reality. The myths tend to emphasize how men rape men and other ridiculous stuff. Guys do get raped in the county jail and in prison. If you are weak and seen as vulnerable, the likelihood that it will happen to you will increase. I remember some dumb brother once saying, "If you drop a bar of soap in the shower once you're in the joint, don't pick it up." Well, I and many other people dropped soap bars in the joint and we picked them up because it happens all the time, and not every guy in here is cruising the yard and the shower trying to hook up with your ass. Your mortality is the most fragile thing. People in Soledad get killed, and if no one claims your body, they will bury you in the prison graveyard. People in here successfully commit suicide behind Dear John letters and Dear John visits. And you don't want to get into a thing with a lifer, because when he tells you, "I've got nothing to lose, you get my point," then you've got something to be concerned about.

Friendly relationships in prison are temporary. You try to remain impersonal with other cons because your association with someone could cost you your life, especially if the other guys "gunning" for him think you two are tight. You could get hit too. The loneliness, and the uncertainty about whether you will make it out, is a worry, but the most harrowing realization is how cheap life is in the joint. Cigarettes are the medium of exchange in prison, and it takes only two cartons to pay for a hit on anybody: in other words, to have someone killed in here. And if the two cartons are "Humps"—Camel cigarettes—just forget it, because your ass is grass.

Prison is a microcosm of American society, which means race is the significant variable. This place is segregated by color in the cell block, chow hall, exercise yard, and classroom. The white guards smuggle in weapons for the white racist gangs to use against the brothers, and almost all of the struggles between inmates and administration are along color lines. This place was just one happy segregated camp. But there's another thing that happens that really fucks you up, especially if you get out. The environment in here, which is like a little society, lags behind the big outside society by about ten to twenty years. In prison, convicts sit around during their social rap sessions and discuss what they will do when they get out. Unknown to all of us is the fact that we know nothing of the contemporary real outside world. TV is where you get all of your information, and that's not good. Time stops for you during your incarceration while life and time on the outside move forward. Just look at the hairstyles of those cons who have been down for a while. They would be wearing large afros in 1983 and talking the '60s "off the pigs" rhetoric of the dominant black gangs. The white guys in prison were overt, blazing racists who talked about the old days when a nigger could be lynched for looking at a white woman. They didn't even call the white South Africans Afrikaners; they called them "Boers." (Ain't that a bitch?) The California Department of Corrections' Jim Crow–style segregation was set in stone even in 1983. So in the final analysis it was the real-world racism, cheap life, and the time warp that were the most frightening aspects of prison life that I had to contend with.

Following the excruciating eight-hour wait, the Soledad CDC process began. I was locked down in isolation and moved from one special cell to another until I finally reached the main line and was released into the general population. I was placed in a cell with a brother who was an ex–Vietnam vet from LA, in the part of Soledad referred to as Soledad North, medium security. I was told by one of the guards—or rollers, as we called them—that a Lieutenant Ruth Younger would be visiting me to let me know when my isolation time would be up and then I could get on with my life in the "pen."

She showed up one morning before the cell block was unlocked for breakfast. She was fit and had a permanent suntan and seemed to be very tough. Lieutenant Younger said she had been stationed at San Quentin back when George Jackson was there—her very subtle way of telling me that she didn't take any shit. She said she knew all about the Black Panther Party and had run into many Panthers doing time at "Q," and that the warden for Soledad did not want someone like me here. She further stated that I would be placed on permanent lockdown so that I would not cause any trouble while doing my time.

I was devastated. This bitch was telling me that I was "CDC lockdown public enemy number one" and that until August 9, 1985, when I walked out of here, I would not have met or been seen by a soul except my cellmate. I immediately started sending her these kites, or letters, requesting another face-to-face at my cell. About a week later she showed up again looking tanned and fit but ready to listen. I told her my plans.

"Look, Lieutenant Younger, I can't change what you and your colleagues read about me in the newspaper or in my jacket [file]. But you must understand that I'm here at Soledad because I want to go to college. I'm not a convict. I don't know anybody here, nor do I have an agenda to disrupt your institution or anything of that nature. So you must understand that I will not cause any trouble, and if I do, you can gladly put me in the hole if I break my word."

After I finished, she looked at me for a while and said, "I will pass this on to the warden." She then turned on her heel like a soldier and, with a quick, brisk pace, disappeared down the tier.

I was still in bed, asleep, about one week later when I was awakened by Lieutenant Younger rapping on my cell door. I jumped up, put on my jeans, and met her at the 8½- by 11-inch opening on my cell door.

"Okay, Flores, this is the deal," she said. "We will let you out on the yard. You can go to school and work while you're out, but if you so much as fart loud in the chow hall, you will be sent directly to the hole. Now, do you understand that?"

"Yes, I understand, and you won't regret this decision."

She peered at me closely through the opening and said, "I've known Panthers while at San Quentin and all of them, or most of them, just did their time like everyone else. I told this to the warden and I assured him that I thought you would be okay, so don't front me off." I said thanks, and she turned again on her heel and disappeared down the tier. I thought I could trust her based on my gut instinct and the fact that she had looked into my cell. I discovered that most guards had a problem with looking into my cell. So her doing so told me she was serious and not just some stiff holding down a job. I think it had something to do with seeing another human being caged. After a while the guards either became immune or ignored you, which allowed them the courage to face you as their jailer.

The joint was different compared to the era of George Jackson, Hugo "Yogi" Pennel, the early BGF, and the ethnic prison gangs such as Mexican Mafia, Nuestra Familia, and the Aryan Brotherhood. Many brothers with A and B numbers were from that late-1950s to mid-1960s era. People were rumored to be welded in their cells, inmates were beaten by guards with impunity and murdered, and there were next to no activities that could help you when you got out, that is, if you did. There were indeterminate sentences, so when George Jackson got six months to life for a $70 gas station robbery, he wound up doing ten to fifteen years and never left the joint alive. That was the old California Department of Corrections in classic form. But it was the guys like

George Jackson and his crew who changed the way inmates were treated in the CDC. They fought a revolution behind bars and won. They protested, they killed, and they died, and that's the reason why the joint changed to a place where you could do your time as a man, as long as you respected your peers, paid your debts, and knew how to say "excuse me" when you bumped shoulders with another con while walking the yard or tier.

The yard at Soledad North was probably the same as any yard in the CDC. Most of the activities revolved around a 440-yard jogging track that was laid out in an oval with racquetball/handball courts and various deadweight lifting pits scattered within its perimeter. Literally, you would walk among a sea of blue denim, buffed brothers, Chicanos, and white boys. The ball courts were full of inmates slamming this little black ball, with some doing it at a very high level of competition. And standing constant watch over all of this was a phalanx of CDC guards stationed around the perimeter of the yard and cell blocks in twenty- or thirty-foot towers, toting Mini-14s, or to put it another way, an M16 rifle in the body of a baby-sized M14 rifle. I had used an M16 in my prior Panther business and I knew what they could do, so it was very clear to me that they would kill you if necessary.

There were fashion trends in the joint that, ironically, would spread to the street. One fad still embraced today is the way guys wear their jeans hanging from their asses. Inmates dress that way because the CDC doesn't provide belts. Actually, though, the majority of the brothers inside did not wear their pants like "young lowriders" from Los Angeles.

Similarly, I was really shocked to see when I was released that the hairstyles were back to what they had been during the late '60s and early '70s. Almost every brother who had hair was wearing a natural, afro, what have you. They usually kept it braided and then let it down for visitors. As far as I was concerned, most of the brothers in the joint were frozen in time. It was like everybody here went to sleep in the '60s and '70s and just woke up in 1984. But the guys who were really frozen in time were the Black Guerrilla Family. It was inevitable, and eventful, and kind of a relief when I ran into them again at Soledad. These guys were different from the brothers I had met at Vacaville. The brothers at Vacaville looked the part—big, buffed, rough-looking, and sure enough menacing—but not these guys. In fact, they reminded me of a lot of the brothers in the BPP; many of us did not look the stereotyped part of a "touch hog."

The first BGFer who approached me with an official prison greeting was this small fellow named Coco. He had to be about twenty to twenty-five years old with a baby face and long hair that he wore in a ponytail. I think he was half Hawaiian and half black or something like that. I was going to the lieutenant's office, which was located at the guard station that divided the north yard from the south yard, in order to check my work assignment as a tutor in the school program. I wasn't surprised, but I was a little taken aback when it turned out that Coco was the lieutenant's clerk, which meant he could pull my file and see if I had snitched or had any dealings with the police. They were well connected here and it showed.

He came from behind his desk and kind of slid over to me, motioning for me to walk outside on the yard with him. As we walked, I could see that several rougher, tougher, buffed brothers who looked the BGF stereotype were joining us. Coco said that ever since I hit the joint, the word was out that I was the Panther military guy and that I was a real down brother. He said that I didn't have to take the oath or anything like that, but that if I had any problems here with convicts, I should just let them know and they would help. He was not shocked when I told him that I had a problem with the warden and I would probably try to stay clear of anybody on the yard who was involved with any of the stern stuff. Coco said, "Cool," and turned around to introduce me to a brother named Baby Lynn. He was the BGF shot caller on the yard, and the irony of it all was that I had been transported on the goose with this brother and didn't even know who he was. I guess he was checking me out. He then introduced me to a brother named Spider Webb. Webb, I said to myself, staring at this brother with some recognition.

"Do you have any brothers named Steve or Alfie Webb?" I asked in a nostalgic tone.

"Yeah, Forbes, don't you recognize me, man? I know you from San Diego."

I was dumbfounded. For the rest of my time in prison, I would again and again be shaken by the number of brothers I would meet in prison whom I had grown up with in San Diego. I ran into brothers I went to church with, played Pop Warner football and Little League and Pony League baseball with, tied knots with as Cub Scouts and Boy Scouts, and went to elementary, junior high, and high school with. Some of them were friends of my brother and many knew my parents from their community activities and even in prison referred to them as Mr. Forbes and Mrs. Forbes. I also ran into one of my main childhood rivals named Walter Singleton. The brother didn't even remember me. He blamed his loss of memory on heroin use. I bumped into Ronnie Tyson, someone I knew from the church choir at Mount Erie Baptist Church in Southeast San Diego, the hood. He was a serious penitentiary touch hog, on the weight pile every single day. And even in the library, I ran into a brother named Tony Matthews who went to school with my brother. His brothers were classmates of mine at O'Farrell Junior High School. But what really knocked me out was the conversation I had with the many brothers from San Diego about the other brothers from Diego that weren't here but were in other joints. They told me about the Norman brothers, Lee, Thomas, and some of the others. They were involved in the drug trade in San Diego, big time, and had made several trips to the pen apiece. They told me about Barry and Melford Washington, Skipper Toussaint, the bank robber, and an endless list of homeboys who had found their way to the California Department of Corrections. In a nutshell, this was the kind of story I read about in some Donald Goines or Iceberg Slim novel. Black man from the hood goes to the joint and runs into his entire Little League team, and when he's transferred to another joint, it turns into a neighborhood Boy Scout jamboree or something like that. This experience deeply moved me and made me more resolute about wanting to succeed at what I had set my sights on.

As I made the rounds in Soledad, I could see the huddles of small groups of young black men greeting each other as if this place were the setting for old homeboy week. It didn't seem to matter that much about the location. This was America, and it seemed like this was part of their anticipated existence in this land. What are the odds? That you would fight for your people with unlimited fervor, take shots, skip town, and when you're ready to change your life and get on with the business of looking out for yourself by taking a hit and going to the joint, you run into the very people you thought you were helping. Ain't that a bitch! As far as I was concerned, America had my entire childhood jailed all at once. Shit, if I had been the old Flores—that is, Buddha Samurai— swaggering and dumb enough to think I could convince these guys that this was not the life they had chosen, I would have attempted to edu- cate, organize, agitate, and just plain old start some shit and see how far we could push the system. But I could see that I had changed and was continuing to change. I decided to avoid these guys and get on with my life. I would not tell them that they had been wronged, simply because that was no longer my job or goal in life. My job and goal was to look out for me. I understood now that I would not be able to exist in this place in isolation, but I could exist here in a way that was to my liking.

40

CONSEQUENTLY, JUST AS my childhood and teen years from San Diego came full circle while I was in Soledad, so did my life in Co Co County, in the form of Big Yogi and Charlie Boo. Big Yogi showed up sometime in 1984 and Charlie Boo soon followed. We had met in the time I spent in the Martinez County jail. Big Yogi hit the yard running, which meant not long after his arrival, he was the guy with the big store. Yogi had boxes of cigarettes (the medium of exchange in the joint) and the basic "zoo zoos" and "wham whams." He developed a sophisticated connection for drug smuggling and distribution in Soledad that helped him maintain lines of communications between all of the gangs; this even included the Nazis. That was a first, from what I heard. So in a very short time Big Yogi was damn near running Soledad North. And, as on the street, his main guy in most of his ventures was Charlie Boo.

My job in prison was as a tutor and assistant to the instructor of Adult Basic Education. And Charlie Boo was one of the twelve brothers, Chicanos, and white guys in the class. The relationship I developed with Charlie Boo was one of dependence and trust, because like a few thousand of the inmates here at Soledad, Boo was a functional illiterate. Back during my elementary school days, this would have been called the low group. Anyhow, Charlie Boo came to me one day and asked, in exchange for cigarettes, weed, or anything else I needed, would I read to him his letters from home and then write a response for him. I gladly did this and told Boo to keep his barter because I enjoyed helping the brother out. Besides, I knew that sometime in the future, I might need his help.

The relationship I developed with Yogi, on the other hand, was strictly a penitentiary business agreement. Yogi, who had done time back in the days of George Jackson, was more involved in the politics of prison life than I had realized. So one day this real-life black Sidney Greenstreet character approached me about being his campaign manager. He wanted to run for the Soledad North black prison representative. This position would make Yogi the intermediary for black prisoners in the Soledad North yard, placing him in a powerful and important position relative to the black prisoners and himself. Or, as Yogi put it, "Forbes, it's a great cover for what I really do."

In Yogi's life on the street, he was a drug dealer and local gangster that many brothers had to deal with in Co Co County. He told me he was usually in control and always called the shots, but was pressed to admit that I had an impeccable reputation for honesty and integrity and that if I brought his message to the black inmate population of Soledad North, he would have a good chance of winning. I told him I would do it, but that he owed me, realizing with the way things worked in here, I would need his backing later. But I also told him I had to do it my way. This meant that there would be no public gatherings or small group sessions, but only one-to-one campaigning between me and the con I would be talking to. I preferred doing it this way because of the warden and Lieutenant Younger's admonition for me not to organize or start any shit while I was on their yard. I felt I could control the campaign better by being selective about whom I was meeting because of the snitches on the yard. My pious attitude about staying clean began to diminish the longer I was in prison. In any event, I had always been a risk taker and I would take one more before I left this place. I also understood that helping Yogi would solidify my position on the yard as one of the players to deal with, but it did not really become apparent until I was asked by the Crips to negotiate a peace treaty between them and the Bloods a few months down the road.

I began campaigning for Yogi by hitting the yard and talking to individual inmates. I was also recruiting other brothers to promote Yogi's candidacy by approaching specific brothers on the yard who I had checked out through Coco, who would go into their jackets to ascertain whether they were snitching or not. My rap was simple: if you vote for Yogi, I'll hook you up with Charlie Boo, who will get you everything you need from Yogi's store on credit. But if you don't pay, that's another issue that I'm not involved with. Those were basic needs that people in prison were more interested in than some bullshit campaign slogans or any other kind of promise. But I also told them some bullshit about Yogi looking out for their interests. This would come in handy for them if they ever had a beef with another ethnic gang. And finally, the vote for Yogi was sweetened with a pack of cigarettes or some other kind of zoo zoos or wham whams. The vote was held two weeks from the beginning of the campaign, and Big Yogi won hands down. In addition, he had major support from the BGF, Crips, Bloods, Vanguard, and some of the other black cliques on the yard. I thought I had made a good decision in backing Yogi, which established me on the yard as a brother who could be trusted and who could get things hooked up. It also meant I could roam the yard and not trip about watching my back because the word was out that I had engineered Yogi's campaign, which drew support from most of the significant players on the yard.

41

REGARDLESS OF THESE DISTRACTIONS—because although they were necessary for my survival, they were still distractions—I kept my eyes on the prize and pursued in earnest my college education via the San Jose State University program at Soledad.

My life at Soledad was structured around two activities that cut my sentence in half: one week I worked and the next week I went to school. My job as a tutor was fulfilling in that I was trying to help inmates develop their skills in an attempt to reduce their dependency on crime, so that maybe when they were released, they could find a job. The school was located just off the main yard in one of the many sealed-off enclaves at Soledad. The programs ranged from Adult Basic Education to GED classes. The classes I taught were for inmates who read from level one through level four. Most of them were black and tough and couldn't read or could barely write a coherent sentence. The curriculum consisted of flash cards with a word on one side and a picture depicting the word's definition on the other. In addition, there was a ten-step life skills module that was supposed to teach inmates the skills they needed to survive on the outside. I was paid fifteen cents an hour. When the college week came around, I had a new, fresh outlook: it was my opportunity to prepare myself for my future.

The college program at Soledad was held in Soledad Central, the maximum-security facility. The group that went over with me for classes from Soledad North was strip-searched each time, both departing and returning. But as far as I was concerned, I had had so many strip searches, one more just didn't matter at the end of the day because the humiliation was part of the prison program.

The college program was designed and taught by a great group of professors. Most of them had some political consciousness and many had been involved in either the civil rights movement or the black liberation struggle. If you graduated from the program, you would receive a BA in the interdisciplinary studies of the social sciences. I was having a ball, and without this college program, I might have possibly gotten bogged down in prison politics and caught a case and wound up doing life behind some bullshit. But that was not to happen. The courses covered the breadth of the social sciences and introduced me to a new world and a lot of great literature. I got a chance to read dozens of books like *Invisible Man* by Ralph Ellison, *Moby Dick* and *Benito Cereno* by Melville, *The Great Gatsby*, and tons of stuff by the giants of the social sciences: Freud, Weber, and Marx. I think for a time I was reading at least two or three books every two weeks, including personal selections, like the adventures of Harry Flashman by George MacDonald Fraser, from the prison library, which was where I spent a great deal of my leisure time.

My plan, should it hold up, was to finish my last two semesters here and graduate before I was released in August 1985. The college program was undoubtedly one of the only ways I could escape the boredom, the isolation, and the constant reminder that I was in prison. I had to stay focused, because with all of the shit going `own, I could still possibly not make it out to fulfill my goals.

42

I WAS CONSTANTLY REMINDED that prison was a place that without any warning could turn into a battleground. And when these battles erupted in Soledad, we would be locked down for weeks until the investigation was resolved. I would be sitting on my bunk reading a book, talking to my cellmate, or smoking a joint when the regular prison noise of bells, loudspeakers, and the collective voices of inmates were drowned out by the individual shotgun blasts from the guard towers and the even more frightening staccato of an automatic Mini-14. This would be followed by the lockdown, which meant you would be confined to your cell until each cell was individually searched, which could take weeks.

The problem with really doing time in one of the several CDC facilities was that they were nothing but "gladiator schools" for the prison gangs and the gangs that originated on the streets. There was always something going down, and whatever its cause, the solution was always violent. People were being stabbed, or "shanked," because they owed people money or for some gang-related incident in prison or from the street. Or sometimes an inmate committed suicide because his woman left him or the pressure just became too unbearable from the predator who constantly took liberties with weak and defenseless inmates. On certain occasions the gunshots were fired at inmates escaping, jumping like jackrabbits through the Salinas fields surrounding Soledad.

During the summer, after one of the many lockdowns had just been cleared, this young Crip named Ford approached me and asked if I could help him and his "roadies" out with a problem. Ford was one of the young guys I ran with when I got tired of hanging around the college guys, Yogi, or Charlie Boo. He was one of the weed dealers on the yard, and I think he liked getting high with me so I would talk about some old Black Panther war stories. He had begun his time at San Quentin, where he was befriended by Geronimo Pratt. Ford, who was young, black, and arrogant as hell, told me this was a beef behind some street shit that they could settle when they both got out. The biggest issue with them was that they didn't have the luxury of a gun while in prison, and they refused to put themselves in the position of catching a beef in the joint that they would never recover from.

I went to Yogi and also touched base with the BGF regarding this problem. I told all of them what the problem was so that no one could be recruited to counter what I came up with. It took a couple of days, but I convinced Ford and his adversary to have a fair one in a neutral cell block. On the day of the fight, I met Ford, his second, and the other brother and his second in the middle of the yard. I told them that the cell was clean and that no one should have any weapons on them. They were to enter the cell block at approximately twelve noon, the beginning of the open half hour, when we could move freely in and out of the cell block. We would close the door, and they were to get down until there was a clear winner. We would then let them out and it would be over, at least until they hit the streets. We set out for the cell block gate and walked past the female guard at the cell block station. We made it to the designated cell, opened the door, and put Ford and his combatant in the cell. Charlie Boo turned around, facing the rows of cells across from us, and pressed his back against the door so no one could leave or enter. There were a couple of loud thuds, several fists hitting skin, and then they got deep into it full speed for a few minutes.

And then the alarm went off and a lockdown was announced for the entire facility. Shit! Inmates were running everywhere, ducking into their cells, running up the stairs to the second tier. There was mass confusion. Charlie Boo sprang from in front of the door and headed down the tier. Ford and the other brother broke out of the cell and started to separate, but before they could, I grabbed both of them and asked, "Is it over?"

"Yeah, Forbes, yeah, man, it's cool," they both replied.

I let go and they broke full speed toward the guard station to exit the cell block, but it was too late. The gates were locked when we arrived, and if you were caught in another cell block during whatever was going down, that was not good for your jacket, especially mine. I looked at the black female guard who regularly took us across the perimeter for college and said, "Officer, would you please let us out?"

She just looked at me and replied, "It's too late; you and your friends are busted, buddy."

I waited a few seconds and asked her again and she just looked at me and my little group. And then something must have moved her and she popped the gates and we stormed through, and she hollered out to me as I ran past, "You owe me big-time, Panther." I saw her several times after the incident and the sister never said a word.

43

I FELT I WAS HAVING A GOOD RUN at Soledad as my sentence was winding down. I was finishing my college degree and I had a plan based on a strategy created by the self-improvement guru Napoleon Hill. This was my way of helping myself to assimilate back into society after being involved with the Party for the majority of my adult life. My confidence was high. I believed that I was going to make it.

I was up for what the CDC called an annual evaluation, which meant they were reviewing the amount of points I had either lost for good behavior or gained through write-ups and other negative infractions. These infractions would not increase your time but could get you transferred to a more hazardous institution like Folsom or behind the wall at San Quentin. If your points went down significantly, you could be transferred to a minimum joint, which is what I was pulling for at this hearing. The CDC officer in charge of the evaluation hearing told me my points were down and that I was being transferred to a minimum-security location at San Quentin. I was crushed when he said San Quentin. I naïvely asked if they could change the transfer to the country club–type joint just down the road here at Soledad.

He said, "Why?"

I responded, "Well, because I'm in the college program here, and I'm on track to graduate before I'm released."

He looked at me for a while and then looked at the other officers present and said, "This is final, Forbes. Besides, you're in prison, not college."

So that was that. My little plan was out the window and I was on the next thing smoking to San Quentin.

What upset me about the transfer to San Quentin was the penology system there, which was based on punishing a motherfucker and making your ass work. There were no education programs, just a job working for twenty-five cents an hour in the upholstery factory behind the wall. What intrigued me about San Quentin was the deep connection to my past. As I was being led across the courtyard one day not long after my arrival, I felt this almost numbing sensation in my legs. But I kept walking because my mind was racing with the knowledge that George Jackson was killed while trying to gain his freedom through these very same gates and in this courtyard. I could feel the difference in this place as opposed to any other prison. San Quentin was hallowed ground for a black man, a revolutionary battlefield where George Jackson was murdered by a CDC sharpshooter. On this site brave black men killed and died to change a system that was uncontrollably and with impunity murderous and brutal toward their kind. But the chilling aspect of this site and prison was that the war was still going on. A guard had been killed just days ago by a projectile fired from a blowgun in the cell block that housed most of the top leaders of the organization George created, the Black Guerrilla Family. All of the gangs in here were segregated together, housed in separate cell blocks.

Nevertheless, as part of my job in the upholstery factory, I was trained to make seats, backs, and armrests for these large comfortable chairs that the CDC Industries sold for a hefty profit to state-owned institutions. We were actually replacement, or scab, workers because the regular cons behind the wall who used to work here were on a permanent lockdown because of the recent guard murder. We were serious cheap labor. I remember my boss telling me how much labor and material went into making a chair and then being appalled at the price the CDC sold it to the state for. This was slave labor. But that didn't matter as much, because I was getting short and wanted to get out and get on with my life. And before I knew it, my next six-month evaluation was due. This CDC officer was going through my file, just like the guy at Soledad, and he came up with a completely different evaluation than his fellow officer in Salinas.

He said, "You had a Pell Grant going to college down there, isn't that right?"

"Yes, that's right, I was going to San Jose State," I said with some curiosity. I wondered what he was trying to get at.

"Did you really read all of these books that they have listed as expenses for the grant?"

Again, I was a little unsettled because this guy didn't sound like most of the CDC officers in these meetings. I said yes again.

"Then what in the fuck are you doing here in a place like this?" he asked in amazement.

I started to tell him what I was in for, but he cut me off, saying, "I know who you are and why you're in prison. What I'm asking you is why you aren't in a joint that has educational programs."

I said, "Look, I was at Soledad going to college and my points went down—"

He cut me off. "Do you want to go back to Soledad to finish your time?"

"Yes," I said.

He replied, "Fine, you'll be on the next bus out." Two weeks later I was back at Soledad.

• • • Back at Soledad things really started coming together for me. I could see the light at the end of the tunnel for the first time since I ripped that glove off my shattered hand in October 1977. It was January 1985. I was in the minimum-security joint at Soledad, which was the closet thing the CDC had to a country club–type joint. It looked more like a village than a prison camp. Shit. There were very few fights and almost no stabbings or warning shots fired from the guard towers. In fact, I could have sworn that there were times when I didn't see any guards in the towers. The college counselor told me that she could roll my Pell Grant over since I hadn't started the last semester and it would be easy to enroll me in the spring semester.

I took a work assignment that placed me in a most unusual situation during the evening hours. I was the janitor working in the main administration building in Soledad Central. This meant I was the con who cleaned the warden's office. The guard supervising me and the other cons on this detail was this brother who saw his job as a job and didn't get caught up in the con-versus-guard syndrome that affected most guards. In fact, this brother was so cool that when the NBA finals came on TV, he let us watch them in the warden's office. He didn't give a fuck, so I propped myself up behind the warden's big wooden desk, settled into his big leather chair, and enjoyed the game for the first time since I used to watch it in black and white with my dad.

I was working my way through Napoleon Hill's book. He wrote about an individual's planning his or her life as if it were a business. I wrote out a guide for future actions and probable successes in his suggested format. I was very specific about where I wanted to go in life and how I could possibly get there. There was some doubt because I still believed that despite my good intentions, anything could happen. I especially believed this because in my case I had eighteen years of experience that went undocumented and could not be placed on a résumé. My game plan was this: first, I would get out of prison. Second, I would get my BA at San Francisco State University. I had been accepted and I planned on enrolling in the fall of 1985. Third, I would get a job commensurate with my experience and education. I knew this would be hard, but I would try. I planned to go to graduate school sometime in the future.

All in all, the first stage of my plan came together without a hitch. I walked out of Soledad State Prison on August 9, 1985. The first day for a second chance at life.

Epilogue

ON AUGUST 22, 1989, I received a phone call from an NYU classmate named Earl Simons. "Flores, did you hear the news?" he asked with excitement in his voice.

"No, what news?" I replied.

He shouted into the phone, "I just heard it on the radio: Huey P. Newton was shot and killed in Oakland this morning."

"Thanks," I shouted back, and promptly hung up.

I checked my watch to see what time it was so that I could catch the nightly national news. I got up from my chair and walked around the small apartment I shared with my girlfriend, Lisa. I paced and paced, shaking my head. I was beside myself, because up until I heard Earl shout that Huey was dead, I was one of those people who believed that Huey couldn't be killed. I had a few hot and cold flashes and got dizzy. I went to the store to get a drink so that I could calm myself down, and then Peter Jennings broke the news. It was the lead story with a big picture and a short film segment. The Servant was really dead.

I tried to ignore him when I got out of prison and returned to the Bay Area. The last time I saw him was in 1977 at a central committee meeting at his house. While I was in prison I read about his frequent arrests for possession of drugs and drug paraphernalia. I also heard the rumors from guys in the joint that Huey was strung out and speedballing with coke and heroin. He had helped me with a lawyer when I needed one, but I was determined to keep my distance after I was released from prison. I never thought about why until this day.

Four years after my prison term ended in 1989, I was working and living in New York City. I had completed my undergraduate education at San Francisco State University and in the spring of 1987 was accepted into the graduate urban planning program at New York University with a full ride as a Patricia Roberts Harris Fellow. I completed my graduate work at NYU in 1989 and received two offers of employment. This was to be my first paying job as an adult. I was thirty-seven years old.

I was born in 1985 at the age of thirty-three, five years removed from my life as a fugitive. There was still the shadow that my past casts over my life. Since moving to New York City, I had told no one my real and complete story. I had mentioned only in passing to people while having a drink or smoking weed that I knew those guys in Oakland. Most people thought I was jiving them or just crazy. Eventually, I stopped talking about Huey or any of them. It's not that I was ashamed of my past, I just hadn't figured out how my past fit with my present circumstances. I was in the closet, and that's where I would remain for another five years.

I was acutely paranoid and probably suffering from some type of post-traumatic stress disorder. I surmised after hearing of Huey's death that the source of my distress wasn't Huey after all, but my past life coming back to haunt me.

I was dumbfounded and couldn't see my way out of the fix I was in. Inexplicably, I was in the same state of mind as when I was a fugitive. I dissembled about my past and where I had come from and told most people falsehoods. My live-in girlfriend didn't even know who I really was. In fact, only a few people from school had half my story, and even it was twisted. I wasn't afraid of just my past. I was afraid of the system I had fought to overthrow and that if they knew where I was, they would beat me down to the ground because I was one of those growling Black Panthers trying to pass himself off as a normal law-abiding citizen. I thought the system and its representatives would punish me if I came out and declared my past allegiances.

Upon close reflection, I realized that the passing of Huey P. Newton meant more than just the passing of a mentor or leader. It also meant that one less person was alive who actually knew what my past deeds were, and with each passing, that number would get smaller. But as I reflected more on my past and Huey, I realized that my state of mind was a learned behavior. I could lie and make people believe me. That was something I was taught in the BPP just in case I became a fugitive. I understood more about how this country worked than most people, another bit of information I gleaned from the BPP. Or as Mao would say, "Know your enemy, know yourself." I was a lover of books and I knew clearly that I picked that up from my interaction with Huey. For the short period I knew him, he had more influence on how I thought than any person in my life. As a young person in the BPP, I could not have known that, because he evoked not just praise and respect but a great deal of fear—much like the fear Machiavelli wrote about in *The Prince*. It had taken all of this time and his death to wash away this recurring belief I had about Huey: that he could read my mind. I tried not to think around him because he would focus those eyes on me, and I thought for sure he knew what I was thinking. He was dead now and I was free of his gaze.

Occasionally, I would find relief from rare gatherings of ex-Panthers. I could act normal and talk shit about old times. But then it happened. One evening this mix of ex-Panthers was integrated with some of my new friends and the chemical reaction bubbled to the top. I hooked up with Elaine Brown and my girlfriend, and at the close of the evening my girlfriend was looking at me in a very strange way. This happened several more times and my girlfriend started asking questions like "Flores, your friends treat you with a great deal of respect, as if you were once important or something. What's up with that?" I would blow her and my other friends off, but I eventually got up the courage to level with her and with some of my other new friends. Gradually, I spoke about who I was and what I used to do. They all took it well. Anyway, I had to come out of the closet, at least for professional reasons. My past was cramping my professional advancement. I had eighteen years of experience that I didn't know I could use.

By the mid-1990s my career as an urban planner was taking off but wouldn't fly because my past still tethered me to the ground. For the past ten or so years of my new life, I had lied about all my felony convictions. But as I moved through this new profession of urban planning, I learned I had a knack for it that was grounded in my past.

Everything, and I mean almost everything, about urban planning could be linked with what I had experienced and learned in the BPP. As a planner, one studied the structure of local governments and the process for moving deals through a pipeline. Well, we did that in the BPP while attempting to take over the city of Oakland and its port. Planners study demographic trends and then apply them to a plan of action. In the BPP we studied the demographic makeup of Oakland and determined a strategy that would elect Lionel Wilson as its mayor. The BPP used maps to depict our target areas, collected data on business locations and their sales trends, and devised strategies to manipulate their effectiveness. The methods we used are the same tactics used by corporations, nonprofits, and government entities today. When I trained as an urban planner, I developed skills and theory in the areas of economics, advanced statistics, geographical information systems (GIS), public administration and public policy, architecture, real estate development and finance, and land use analysis and regulation. It made me think of Masai and the master-class method he used to train the Buddha Samurai. Only this time, instead of mastering a gun and the theory and practice that would help me shoot straight, I mastered a computer and its various applications to urban planning.

• • • In 1998 I got my first break and hope for surviving the goddamn demon that was choking me and my new life almost to death. One of my new friends, Earl Simons, was a senior staff person in the office of C. Virginia Fields, then Manhattan borough president. At the same time I was a senior business adviser at the Small Business Development

Center at Baruch College, which is part of the City University of New York.

Earl called me one day and said he had an interesting offer to put forth. He was the director of the borough president's northern Manhattan office and had been charged with a major planning effort to revitalize Frederick Douglass Boulevard in central Harlem. He thought I was perfect for the job as project manager and wanted to put my name into the mix. It sounded great, except for one thing: there was a background check. I had avoided jobs that required real background checks, which meant they took fingerprints. Shit, there was no fucking way my prints would pass muster. I conveyed this to Earl and he told me that the borough president's general counsel had said that it would probably go through just as long as I didn't lie. I think the language she used was "providing a full disclosure of your past." Hmm!

I accepted the offer, went to the Department of Investigation, got fingerprinted, and waited for the boom to come down. I had been on the job for about three or four months when I received a phone call from one of the investigators at the DOI. He said, "Mr. Forbes, we have received your fingerprinting information from the Federal Bureau of Investigation and I would like to ask you a few questions."

I braced myself and said, "Fire away."

He said, "I see that you have had about eight major felony arrests, two felony convictions that involve the use of a firearm, with one resulting in a felony murder conviction and one prison term. Well, what were you doing to compile such a record?"

"I was a member of the Black Panther Party in California for ten years."

"Oh! Okay, that answers that. Now let's move on to your taxes."

Chronology of Events

1961

Huey P. Newton and Bobby Seale meet while attending Merritt College in Oakland, California.

1965

The Lowndes County Freedom Organization, an independent political party in rural Alabama, adopts the symbol of the black panther for its organization.

1966

Huey P. Newton and Bobby Seale develop the outline and framework for an organization to be named the Black Panther Party for Self-Defense. They also finalize a draft of the BPPSD Ten Point Platform and Program and founding of the Black Panther Party of Self-Defense.

In December Eldridge Cleaver is released from Folsom Prison.

Sixteen-year-old Bobby Hutton is the first male recruit of the Black Panther Party.

1967

Race-related rebellions break out in forty-three U.S. cities, including Washington, D.C.; Baltimore; Atlanta; and Detroit; more than 3,500 arrested and scores killed.

The Black Panther Party opens its first official headquarters in a storefront at Fifty-sixth and Grove streets in Oakland, California.

The Black Panther Party institutes armed patrols of Oakland police to curb overt acts of police brutality, thus creating the first programmatic response to the BPP Ten Point Platform and Program.

Eldridge Cleaver joins the Black Panther Party.

Publication of the first issue of *The Black Panther: Black Community News Service,* the Party's official news organ.

Bobby Seale leads twenty-six armed Panthers on a lobbying trip to Sacramento to protest the state legislature hearing on gun control.

The California State Legislature passes an antigun law (the Milford Act), prohibiting the carrying of firearms in any public place or street. Panther armed patrols are subsequently illegal.

Huey P. Newton is critically wounded in a predawn gun battle with two Oakland police officers. Officer John Frey is killed and Officer Herbert Heanes is wounded.

In Oakland, the Alameda County grand jury indicts Huey P. Newton on charges of first-degree murder, attempted murder, and kidnapping.

1968

The Southern California chapter of the Black Panther Party is founded by Alprentice "Bunchy" Carter. Many of the original members of this chapter, including Ray "Masai" Hewitt, were members of Carter's five-thousand-strong street gang, the Slausons.

Eldridge Cleaver, now minister of information, publishes *Soul on Ice.*

The Black Panther Party opens an office in New York City.

Martin Luther King, Jr., is assassinated in Memphis. As a result, riots break out in dozens of U.S. cities.

Bobby Hutton, seventeen, the first member of the Black Panther Party and its national treasurer, is killed by Oakland police following a shoot-out. Eldridge Cleaver is wounded and returns to prison for parole violation. Seven other Panthers, including chief of staff David Hilliard, are arrested.

The San Diego branch of the Black Panther Party is founded by Kenny Denman, an ex-convict who served time with Eldridge Cleaver.

Eldridge Cleaver is released from prison.

Huey P. Newton's trial opens in Oakland with more than six thousand protesters in support at the Alameda County courthouse.

Three Panthers—Tommy Lewis, Steve Bartholomew, and Robert Lawrence—are killed in a gun battle with Los Angeles police at a South Central service station.

Huey P. Newton is sentenced to two to fifteen years on a manslaughter conviction.

The Black Panther Party adopts a "Serve the People" programmatic focus, which includes initiation of a free breakfast program for children.

Eldridge and Kathleen Cleaver disappear three days before Eldridge is scheduled to turn himself in to serve the remainder of a thirteen-year sentence for a 1958 rape conviction. They eventually settle in Algeria.

The Black Panther Party has established thirty-eight chapters and branches with more than five thousand members.

1969

The first BPP Free Breakfast for Children Program is initiated at St. Augustine's Church in Oakland.

The Black Panther newspaper distribution reaches 100,000 sold weekly.

Alprentice "Bunchy" Carter and John Huggins, leaders of the Southern California chapter, are murdered by members of the cultural nationalist group United Slaves (US). Following this incident, a *Wall Street Journal* story links US leader Ron Karenga to the FBI.

Black Panthers John Savage and Sylvester Bell are murdered in San Diego in separate incidents by members of Ron Karenga's US Organization.

Bobby Seale is indicted and charged with planning riots at the 1968 Democratic National Convention.

In New York City, twenty-one Panthers are arrested and charged with conspiring to kill policemen and bomb police stations.

J. Edgar Hoover declares that "the Black Panther Party, without question, represents the greatest threat to internal security of the country." The FBI also pledges that 1969 will be the last year of the Party's existence.

Black Panther Bill Brent hijacks a plane to Cuba.

After three years in prison, Huey P. Newton wins an appeal and is scheduled to be released on appeal bond.

A New Haven grand jury indicts Bobby Seale on a first-degree murder charge; he is charged with ordering the murder of Black Panther Alex Rackley.

The Black Panther Party opens an international section in Algeria under the command of Eldridge Cleaver.

David Hilliard goes to trial in Oakland in connection with charges stemming from an April 6, 1968, shoot-out.

Ray "Masai" Hewitt is appointed BPP minister of education.

Black Panther Walter "Toure" Pope is killed by the Los Angeles Metro Squad as he drops off BPP newspapers at a store.

Bobby Seale is chained, bound, and gagged at the Chicago 8 trial.

Illinois state chapter BPP leaders Fred Hampton and Mark Clark are murdered by police in a predawn raid orchestrated by the FBI and the state attorney's office.

Members of the LAPD's newly created SWAT team and members of the Black Panther Party fight a six-hour gun battle following a predawn raid on Panther headquarters in search of illegal weapons. Several police and Panthers are wounded.

California state senator Mervyn M. Dymally charges that the December 8 raid is part of a national plan of repression against the Black Panther Party.

By the end of 1969, twenty-eight Panthers have been killed in confrontations with police and other agents provocateurs.

1970

California governor Ronald Reagan grants a request to extradite Bobby Seale to Connecticut to stand trial on murder and kidnapping charges related to the Alex Rackley slaying.

The Soledad Brothers—George Jackson, Fleeta Drumgo, and John Clutchette—are charged with the murder of a white prison guard at Soledad Prison in California.

Bobby Seale's *Seize the Time* is published.

The San Diego branch of the Black Panther Party is closed down. Panthers are transferred to the Riverside branch.

The Riverside police raid the BPP office. The Riverside branch is closed down and Panthers are transferred to Southern California headquarters in Los Angeles.

Huey P. Newton's manslaughter conviction is reversed by the California appeals court.

At Kent State University in Ohio, National Guardsmen kill four unarmed white students during campus antiwar protest. California governor Reagan calls the action justifiable.

The FBI annual report calls the Black Panther Party the nation's "most dangerous and violence-prone of all extremist groups."

Huey P. Newton is set free on $50,000 bail bond but still faces another trial in the shooting of Officer John Frey.

Jonathan Jackson, the brother of George Jackson, is killed in an attempt to free William Christmas (who was also killed), Ruchell Magee, and James McClain (who was also killed) from the Marin County courthouse. Several hostages were taken, including the judge, district attorney, and three jurors.

The Black Panther Party creates the Ideological Institute in Oakland for advanced training of a leadership cadre.

Angela Davis is linked to the Marin County courthouse incident and becomes a fugitive. She is placed on the FBI's list of Ten Most Wanted fugitives.

Angela Davis is captured in New York City.

1971

A dispute that had been private spills out into the public, signaling a schism in the Black Panther Party over philosophical differences and the types of actions Panthers should be involved in at this time. Newton expels Cleaver and the entire international section from the Party.

Geronimo Pratt and a dozen Panthers involved with the December 8 shoot-out in LA go underground.

Sam Napier, the national distribution manager of *The Black Panther* newspaper, is murdered by renegade ex-Panthers in New York City.

Robert Webb, a renegade Panther, is gunned down on a New York City street after accosting a female Panther while selling *The Black Panther* newspapers.

James Thomas Johnson, aka the Black Dog, and Gwen Goodloe are appointed as co-coordinators of the Southern California chapter.

David Hilliard is sentenced to a one- to ten-year prison term in connection with the April 6, 1968, shoot-out with Oakland police.

The Black Guerrilla Family (BGF) is organized in San Quentin.

Twelve Panthers in New Orleans are found not guilty of attempted murder of five policemen following a New Orleans gun battle in the Desire Projects.

Black Panther Party field marshal George Jackson is killed in San Quentin Prison by a California Department of Corrections sharpshooter. Also killed are three other prisoners and three guards. Panther Johnny Spain, along with five others, is charged in the aftermath with murder and attempting to break out of prison.

A four-day revolt at the Attica Correctional Facility, near Buffalo, New York, ends when more than a thousand state police and National Guardsmen attacks the prison. Forty-three people are killed and more than eighty injured.

Huey P. Newton, Elaine Brown, and Robert Bay visit China, meeting Chinese premier Chou En-lai.

Huey P. Newton wins dismissal of charges that he killed Oakland policeman John Frey.

1972

Huey P. Newton's book *To Die for the People* is published.

The political arm of the Southern California chapter of the Black Panther Party is closed down. Half of the Party's contingent in LA is transferred to Oakland while the balance, under the command of the Black Dog, stay behind to establish the Party's underground operations.

The Black Panther Party initiates its plan to create a base of operations in the San Francisco–Oakland Bay Area and begins closing down dozens of chapters and branches across the country and recalling the Panthers in these cities to Oakland.

The Black Panther Party initiates a five-year plan to take over the city of Oakland. The Party announces that Bobby Seale will run for mayor and

Elaine Brown will run for a city council seat, along with others on the BPP slate.

Under the tutelage of minister of education Ray "Masai" Hewitt, the Party creates a security cadre, aka the Buddha Samurai.

Minister of Education Ray "Masai" Hewitt resigns from the Black Panther Party and returns to LA.

Flores Forbes is appointed head of the BPP security cadre.

1973

Huey P. Newton's autobiography *Revolutionary Suicide* is published.

The Black Panther Party holds several large conferences/rallies promoting voter registration and African liberation. Tens of thousands of bags of groceries, clothing, and shoes are given away. Thousands are registered to vote and thousands are tested for sickle-cell anemia.

Elaine Brown runs for a city council seat unsuccessfully, and Bobby Seale runs for mayor, forcing a runoff that ends in defeat.

1974

During the Fox Lounge incident, Huey P. Newton and eight other Panthers are arrested and charged with assault on police officers by a joint Oakland police taskforce and ATF agents.

The Black Panther Party makes major leadership changes with the expulsion of Bobby Seale, David Hilliard, June Hilliard, John Seale, and Robert Bay; dozens of other Seale loyalists desert.

Elaine Brown succeeds Bobby Seale as chairman.

Huey P. Newton goes into exile in Cuba to avoid prosecution for pistol-whipping his tailor and for the shooting death of female prostitute Kathleen Smith.

Flores Forbes is appointed assistant chief of staff and armorer.

1975

Elaine Brown runs unsuccessfully for a city council seat.

1976

Lionel Wilson is elected the first black mayor of the city of Oakland.

1977

Huey P. Newton returns from exile.

Elaine Brown leaves the Black Panther Party and returns to LA.

In the Richmond incident, three Panthers are involved in a botched attempt to kill Newton witness Crystal Gray. One Panther is killed and BPP assistant chief of staff Flores Forbes is wounded and becomes a fugitive. Huey P. Newton says that the attempt to kill the witness was an act by overzealous renegades.

1978

Huey P. Newton is acquitted of charges of assaulting his tailor, Preston Callins, but is convicted on two gun charges.

1979

Huey P. Newton is acquitted of murdering Kathleen Smith.

1980

Flores Forbes surrenders to police in Martinez County, California.

Index

Los Angeles:
    BPP chapters in, 43, 46–47, 58–61,
        137–38, 142
    BPP evacuation from, 62, 64, 141
    BPP security in, 42–43
    December 8, 1969, shoot-out in, 40,
        42, 46, 54, 55, 57, 59, 63
    gangs in, 49–51, 142
    LAPD hostility, 40, 42, 44–49, 57–61,
        62, 69
    LAPD SWAT team, 40, 42, 46
    Red Zone in, 2, 44, 46, 62
    safe houses in, 47
    Sheriff's Department, 45, 46
    tunneling under BPP office in, 57,
        58–59, 73
    Watts BPP office in, 46–47, 48, 50–51
    Watts rebellion in, 14
Lucky, Andrew, 16

Machiavelli, Niccolò, 277
Malcolm X, 19, 76
Manson, Charles, 253
Mao Tse-tung:
    BPP ideology modeled after, 23, 66,
        75–76
    Little Red Book of, 22, 25, 32
    Long March of, 6, 66
    Military Writings of, 56
    quotations from, 4, 44, 277
Marighella, Carlos, 56, 146
Martinez County, California, jail, 225,
        229–32
Marx, Karl, 75, 266
Masai, see Hewitt, Ray
Matthews, Tony, 260
Meese, Edwin, 26
Merrill, Judge, 250
Mexican Mafia (prison gang), 257
Milford, Donald, 26
Milford Act (1967), 26
Minimanual of the Urban Guerrilla, The
        (Marighella), 56, 146
Mitchell, Felix, 151, 155, 240
Mitchell, Henry "Mitch," 168
Moby Dick (Melville), 266
"Mojo," see Powell, Maurice

Moore, Frances "Pearl," 3, 155–57, 234,
    239
Mount Erie Baptist Church, Southeast
    San Diego, 16, 20

Napier, Sam, 56
Naval Training Center (NTC), San
    Diego, 13, 23, 31
Neal, Father Earl, 24
Nelson (EMT):
    ambulance program run by, 217
    author's fears for safety of, 183, 187
    author's gunshot wound treated by,
        172–78, 179, 181–82
    found in the desert, 192, 206, 214,
        215, 216
    and Party networks, 179–80, 183,
        192, 216
Newberry, J. J., 114, 119, 121, 123
New Day in Babylon (Van Deburg), 50
Newton, Huey P.:
    and armed police patrols, 26
    and author as fugitive, 174, 180, 183,
        185, 197, 200, 214, 215, 216–17
    and author as prisoner, 230–32, 234,
        253, 275
    and author's legal defense, 216–17,
        231–32, 234, 275–76
    on being true to the game, 108
    as BPP founder, 4, 108
    BPP reports to, 86–87, 155
    BPP shaped by, 1–2, 6, 23, 25, 55, 65,
        70, 77, 81, 107–9, 115, 117, 134,
        157, 161, 277
    changing style of, 153–54, 161–62
    Cuban exile of, 6, 106, 141, 146, 159
    death of, 275, 276, 277
    death threats against, 81, 82, 87,
        89–90, 217, 252
    declaring war on drug dealers, 153
    disappearance of, 120, 198
    disintegration of, 214, 275
    in Fox Lounge incident, 113–14
    "Free Huey" movement, 5, 23, 24, 27
    and his tailor, 118
    housing complex of, 87–88, 93, 118
    and ideological split, 56–57, 78–79

Teart, Eniweta, 18
"Texas," *see* Johnson, Louis Talbert
Toussaint, Skipper, 260
Traun, Julie, 232, 244, 245, 248–49, 250
Tribble, Carl (alias), 203
Turner, Ike, 133
Turner, Tina, 133, 208
Tyson, Ronnie, 260

United Slaves (US Organization), 49–50

Vacaville, California, prison, 251–53
Van Deburg, William L., 50
Vanguard (Soledad clique), 264
Vietnam War, 19–20
Vukasin, Judge, 244

Wade, Wendell, 24
Wallace, Walter, 21, 23
Ward brothers, 85
War with Hannibal, The (Livy), 3
Washington, Barry, 260
Washington, Bruce "Deacon," 129, 131, 198
Washington, Harold "Rip Saw," 242
Washington, Melford, 260
Watts rebellion, 14
weapons:
    acquisition of, 39, 123, 243
    armorers and, 94–95, 121–26
    inventory list, 3, 124–26, 183
    Marine source of, 39, 43, 123, 141, 243
    open brandishment of, 135
    in police raids, 60, 100–103, 113–14
    in stern stuff, 98, 124, 136, 168
    theory and safety for, 77, 124
    three-man squads with, 124
    training in use of, 52, 55, 57, 76–77, 114
    transporting, 126, 141
    types of, 52, 76, 125, 126
Weaver Stance, 76–77
Webb, Alfie, 260
Webb, Robert, 56
Webb, Spider, 259–60
Webb, Steve, 260
Weber, Max, 266
White, Ellis, 136, 160, 161
Williams, Craig, 46–47, 51, 54, 64
Williams, Landon, 24, 25, 63
Williams, Randy "Cold Steel," 24, 63
Williams, Sharon, 63
Williams, Tommye, 54
Will to Power, The (Nietzsche), 3
Wilson, Lionel, 6, 131, 137, 141–42, 154, 158, 278
Wonder, Stevie, 194
Wretched of the Earth, The (Fanon), 19, 32, 146

Yates, Titus, 242
Younger, Ruth, 256–57, 263